# The New Nation

# The New Nation

## Anita Vickers

American Popular Culture Through History
*Ray B. Browne, Series Editor*

**GREENWOOD PRESS**
**Westport, Connecticut · London**

**Library of Congress Cataloging-in-Publication Data**

Vickers, Anita, 1952–
      The new nation / Anita Vickers.
          p. cm.—(American popular culture through history)
      Includes bibliographical references and index.
      ISBN 0–313–31264–8 (alk. paper)
      1. United States—Civilization—1783–1865.   2. Popular culture—United
   States—History—18th century.   3. Popular culture—United States—History—19th
   century.   I. Title.   II. Series.
   E164.V53   2002
   973—dc21         2001054701

British Library Cataloguing in Publication Data is available.

Library of Congress Catalog Card Number: 2001054701
ISBN: 0–313–31264–8

First published in 2002

Greenwood Press, 88 Post Road West, Westport, CT 06881
An imprint of Greenwood Publishing Group, Inc.
www.greenwood.com

Printed in the United States of America

The paper used in this book complies with the
Permanent Paper Standard issued by the National
Information Standards Organization (Z39.48–1984).

10 9 8 7 6 5 4 3 2 1

# Contents

# Contents

# Series Foreword

Popular culture is the system of attitudes, behavior, beliefs, customs, and tastes that defines the people of any society. It is the entertainments, diversions, icons, rituals, and actions that shape the everyday world. It is what we do while we are awake and what we dream about while we are asleep. It is the way of life we inherit, practice, change, and then pass on to our descendants.

Popular culture is an extension of folk culture, the culture of the people. With the rise of electronic media and the increase in communication in American culture, folk culture expanded into popular culture—the daily way of life as shaped by the *popular majority* of society. Especially in a democracy like the United States, popular culture has become both the voice of the people and the force that shapes the nation. In 1782, the French commentator Hector St. Jean de Crèvecoeur asked in his *Letters from an American Farmer*, "What is an American?" He answered that such a person is the creation of America and is in turn the creator of the country's culture. Indeed, notions of the American Dream have been long grounded in the dream of democracy—that is, government by the people, or popular rule. Thus, popular culture is tied fundamentally to America and the dreams of its people.

Historically, culture analysts have tried to fine-tune culture into two categories: "elite"—the elements of culture (fine art, literature, classical music, gourmet food, etc.) that supposedly define the best of society—and "popular"—the elements of culture (comic strips, best-sellers, pop music, fast food, etc.) that appeal to society's lowest common denominator. The so-called educated person approved of elite culture and scoffed at popular culture. This schism first began to develop in western

Europe in the fifteenth century when the privileged classes tried to discover and develop differences in societies based on class, money, privi-
lege, and lifestyles. Like many aspects of European society, the debate
between elite and popular cultures came to the United States. The upper
class in America, for example, supported museums and galleries that
would exhibit the finer things in life, that would elevate people. As the
twenty-first century emerges, however, the distinctions between popular
culture and elitist culture have blurred. The blues songs (once denigrated
as "race music") of Robert Johnson are now revered by musicologists;
architectural students study buildings in Las Vegas, Nevada, as examples
of what Robert Venturi called the "kitsch of high capitalism"; sports-
writer Gay Talese and heavyweight boxing champ Floyd Patterson were
co-panelists at a 1992 State University of New York–New Paltz sympo-
sium on literature and sport. The examples go on and on, but the one
commonality that emerges is the role of popular culture as a model for
the American Dream, the dream to pursue happiness and a better, more
interesting life.

To trace the numerous ways in which popular culture has evolved
throughout American history, we have divided the volumes in this series
into chronological periods—historical eras until the twentieth century,
the decades between 1900 and 2000. In each volume, the author explores
the specific details of popular culture that reflect and inform the general
undercurrents of the time. Our purpose, then, is to present historical and
analytical panoramas that reach both backward into America's past and
forward to her collective future. In viewing these panoramas, we can
trace a very fundamental part of American society. The "American Popular Culture Through History" series presents the multifaceted parts of
a popular culture in a nation that is both grown and still growing.

Ray B. Browne
Secretary-Treasurer
Popular Culture Association
American Culture Association

# Introduction

The era commonly referred to as the "early republic" or the "early nationalist period" was, unequivocally, the most unstable and tumultuous in American history. Victorious in the American War of Independence, the citizenry of the new nation weathered numerous social and political upheavals, among them diplomatic intrigues (the XYZ Affair, 1797–1798), controversial wartime security measures (Alien and Sedition Acts, 1798), wars (the Tripolitan War, 1801–1805, and the War of 1812), and domestic uprisings (Shays's Rebellion, 1786–1787, and the Whiskey Rebellion, 1794). Furthermore, the government was regarded by many as a grand experiment, one which the world had never seen before.

Historians differ on the dates of the early nationalist period, some preferring to include the years of the American Revolution itself (1776–1783), some citing the ratification of the Constitution (1789) as the beginnings of this era. This volume, however, covers the years concluding the Revolutionary War (1783), including the War of 1812 (sometimes known as the Second War for Independence), and leading up to the Western Expansionism movement (approximately 1816), thus encompassing a period of Anglo-American hostility. The signing of the Treaty of Ghent (December 24, 1814) ended this era of mutual mistrust between England and the United States. Only after reestablishing cordial relations with the parent country could Americans focus on westward expansion, an era characterized by a growing nationalism and its corollary goal of "enlarging the empire for liberty."

Thus, this book surveys specific cultural forms of American life during this unique age of Anglo-American hostility. Although tense relationships with European powers might have predominated the temper of the early nationalist period (and thereby had a profound effect on the culture), a political phenomenon had transpired. Within a 23-year time span, the new nation encountered a momentous exigency: the framing of two important political documents—the Articles of Confederation (1781) and the Constitution (1788)—signifying a radical transfer in political ideology. Under the Constitution, power would emanate from the people. No one branch of the government could ever predominate; a skillfully wrought checks-and-balance system eliminated such a possibility.

As the Preamble of the Constitution resolutely declares, the *people* intended to form a "more perfect union" than any in world history. Moreover, this union would be a republic of virtue. The expectation of the people as a whole was easily summed up by Dr. Benjamin Rush (1745–1813), patriot, author, educator, and signer of the Declaration of Independence: "Virtue, virtue alone . . . is the basis of a republic." Furthermore, republican virtue would be evidenced by a citizen's public contribution to the commonwealth and private adherence to the work ethic. Such virtue would not only discourage self-interest and avarice but also foster independence for all the citizenry.

This idea of American republican virtue had its roots in earlier Puritan philosophy. Just as the Puritan Fathers saw themselves on an errand into the wilderness, that special obligation of the "new Israel" to begin the world anew and to conceive a society that would serve as a beacon to the Old World, the Founding Fathers regarded the new republican order as their mandate to institute a new government that would secure the "certain inalienable Rights, that among these are Life, Liberty, and the pursuit of Happiness." This government would also serve as a beacon to the Old World, creating a nation that need not fear tyranny or be fettered by an artificial social stratum based on a blood aristocracy.

Literate new republican society concurred with the framers' mandate. Nonetheless, there was a great and ongoing debate regarding what form this new government should take. Roughly, there were three broadly based ideologies debated at this time: populist, mercantilist, and aristocratic. The populist view, based on the writings of Thomas Paine (1737–1809), called for active participation of the largest number of the citizenry. This participation would be manifested in general elections, town meetings, and referendums. The lower (and illiterate and marginally literate) classes generally distrusted the gentry's ability to speak for the majority of the people. Republican government, as defined by the populist view, would be as close as possible to the etymology of the word democracy (from the Greek *demos kratos*, meaning "people rule"). This form of government, sometimes referred to as "direct democracy," is founded on the idea that political decision making is the right of all, usually espousing the concept of majority rule.

Those of the middle class, primarily small business owners, proprietors, and artisans, held a more mercantile view of what direction the new republic should take. Here republican virtue (thus the strength of the nation overall) came from instillating the Puritan work ethic in all citizens. Wealth empowered a nation—and would fortify democracy without the continual need to give in to the notion of the common good. This mercantilist sentiment underscored the inherent Puritan belief that the accumulation of wealth, due to hard work and industry, was evidence of God's approval. Thus, a virtuous nation should be an industrious one. Through industry, the republic would grow.

The educated elite, on the other hand, formulated their view of what the republic should be based on the democracy of classical antiquity. Thinkers such as the Republican Thomas Jefferson (1743–1826) unilaterally envisioned a state governed by what he termed a "natural aristocracy," that is, an elite class based on native ability, intelligence, and common sense as opposed to the corrupt European concept of aristocracy based on inheritance and lineage. Jefferson posited that educational opportunity and the state's guarantee of freedom of speech would facilitate the rise in class and power of those of modest origins but great talent. The integral nature of this new aristocracy—and its willingness to participate in the government—would require them to selflessly place the interests of the nation before their own. Ironically, the elitist view of democracy and republican virtue precluded women's participation in government and sanctioned slave owning.

Culturally, these three broadly defined classes together forged an identity that drew from diverse heritages, European forms, historically unprecedented experiences in the new world, and, of course, the Revolutionary War. Many times cultural values transcended these arbitrary class lines and political alliances. The result was a national culture that emphasized the republican values of virtue, benevolence, rationality, and perseverance. Once freed from the tentacle-like hold of European cultural values, Americans brought forth indigenous arts (architecture, visual arts, literature, music, and performance) that revolutionized the world. They also proved their remarkable adaptability to terrain in devising innovative means of travel. American interest and avid participation in all forms of recreation evinced their unwavering belief in a festive culture. In culinary and sartorial pursuits, Americans once more demonstrated their adaptability, resourcefulness, and inventiveness. The early nationalist employment of innovative advertising—as well as the products and services advertised—reveals not only the early citizenry's commitment to commerce but also their great creative and entrepreneurial spirit. This was probably the most dynamic period in American history, and the cultural outgrowth from the period evidences that republican America was a fledgling nation that was energetic, adaptable, and far-reaching. In essence, the culture of the new nation reflected the values and impulse of the people.

# Timeline of Popular Culture Events

## 1783

Treaty of Paris (formal end of the American Revolution)
Thomas Jefferson completes *Notes on the State of Virginia*
Noah Webster, *The American Spelling Book* ("The Blue Back Speller")
Congress begins discussion of new capital for the nation

## 1784

Congress adopts the Land Ordinance (creation of new states)
Iroquois cede all lands west of the Niagara River to the United States
Charles Willson Peale, *Washington at the Battle of Princeton, January 3, 1777*
John Durang makes dancing debut with Lewis Hallam's theatrical troupe
Barnabas Bidwell, *The Mercenary Match*
American ship arrives in Canton, China, to trade ginseng
Death of Mother Ann Lee (founder of the Shakers)
Olaudah Equiano, *The Interesting Narrative of the Life of Olaudah Equiano; or, Gustavus Vassa, The African*

## 1785

Thomas Jefferson begins plans for Virginia state capitol building (completed 1799)
Congress relocates to New York City (temporary national capital)

# 1786

Johnson Green, *The Life and Confession of Johnson Green*

Construction of the Charles River Bridge (links Boston and Charlestown—world's longest bridge at this time)

Johann Friedrich Peter establishes the Collegium Musicum in Salem (Winston-Salem), North Carolina

Postwar economic depression

Congress adopts monetary system based on the Spanish peso (known by English speakers as the "dollar")

The great thoroughbred sire Messenger imported to the United States

# 1786–1787

Shays's Rebellion

# 1787

Constitutional Convention

Congress adopts Northwest Ordinances

Prohibitions against theatrical activity are lifted

Royall Tyler, *The Contrast*

Charles Willson Peale expands his Peale Museum to include the study of natural history

John Trumbull (painter) begins *The Declaration of Independence, 4 July 1776* (completed 1820)

Charles Willson Peale, *Franklin*

First steamboat in America launched (John Fitch)

Urania Academy concert (Philadelphia) in honor of the convening of the Constitutional Convention

Federalist Party adopts tune of "Yankee Doodle" for "A Yankee Federal Song"

Philadelphia Young Ladies Academy founded

# 1787–1788

Alexander Hamilton, James Madison, and John Jay, *The Federalist*

# 1787–1790

*Columbia* (captained by Robert Gray) circumnavigates the world

# 1788

Jean-Antoine Houdon, *General Washington*

Francis Hopkinson, *Seven Songs for the Harpsichord or Forte Piano*

Nicholas Pike, *Arithmetic*

Massachusetts declares slave trade illegal

# 1789

Washington elected first president of the United States

"The President's March" performed at Washington's inauguration

Robert Treat Paine, "Washington Presidential Theme Song"

William Hill Brown, *The Power of Sympathy; or, The Triumph of Nature. Founded in Truth* (first American novel)

Jefferson begins remodeling of Monticello (completed 1809)

New government begins under the Constitution

Congress establishes the U.S. Army

Day of Thanksgiving established by Congressional Resolution

William and Thomas Birch, *Bank of the United States, Philadelphia*

French Revolutionaries use "Yankee Doodle" as a marching song

Paper shortage forces newspapers to adopt six-point font size

Peter and George Lorillard advertise tobacco products in the *New York Daily Advertiser*

*Children's Magazine* established

# 1790

Census Act passed by Congress. First census: population 3,929,214

Total newspapers in United States: 106

Benjamin Franklin dies; over 20,000 mourners attend funeral

# 1790–1791

Ann Eliza Bleecker, *The History of Maria Kittle*

# 1791

First Bank of the United States chartered

Bill of Rights adopted

Washington, DC, established

Federal government imposes excise tax on whiskey

Susanna Haswell Rowson's *Charlotte Temple* published in England; republished in the United States in 1794

John Singleton Copley, *Repulse of the Floating Batteries at Gibraltar*

# 1792

Washington elected to second term

Congress establishes decimal system of coinage

American Benjamin West succeeds Sir Joshua Reynolds as President of the Royal Academy

Gilbert Stuart returns to the United States

Post Office Act establishes postage rate for newspapers at one cent

# 1793

Eli Whitney invents the cotton gin

Susanna Haswell Rowson begins American stage career

Mason Locke Weems, *Sure Certain Methods of Attaining a Long and Healthy Life*

*The History of King Pippin* published in Boston

English circus rider John Bill Ricketts opens first American circuses in New York and Philadelphia

Citizen Genêt arrives in the United States

# 1793–1795

Construction of the Pennsylvania and Lancaster Turnpike

# 1794

Whiskey Rebellion

Jay Treaty

Post Office Act of 1794

Mason Locke "Parson" Weems begins association with Mathew Carey

Thomas Wignell forms theatrical troupe

Boston has first theater season; Federal Street Theater opens

Susanna Haswell Rowson's comic opera *Slaves in Algiers; or, A Struggle for Freedom. A Play Interspersed with Songs* opens in Philadelphia

John Daly Burk, *Bunker-Hill* (produced 1797)

James Hewitt, *Tammany, or The Indian Chief*

# 1795

Charles Bulfinch, Massachusetts State House (completed 1798)

Judith Sargent Murray's *Virtue Triumphant* (*The Medium; or Happy Tea Party*) produced in Boston

Susanna Haswell Rowson, *The Female Patriot*

Susanna Haswell Rowson, *The Volunteers*

Charles Willson Peale, *The Staircase Group*

Hasty Pudding Club (Harvard) established

Rembrandt Peale, *Porthole Portrait*

Benjamin Carr, "Federal Overture"

Daniel Fenning, *America's Youth Instructor*

# 1794–1796

Thomas Paine, *The Age of Reason*

# 1796

Washington, "Farewell Address"

John Adams elected president

Pinckney's Treaty

Judith Sargent Murray, *The Traveller Returned* performed at Boston's Haymarket Theater

Benjamin West, *Death on a Pale Horse*

Gilbert Stuart, *Athenaeum Head*

*The Apotheosis of Franklin; or, His Reception in the Elysian Fields* (spectacle performance)

First suspension bridge built in the United States (Jacob's Creek, Pennsylvania)

Benjamin Carr, *The Archers*

Advertisement in *Providence Gazette* criticizes laziness and rudeness of domestic servants

# 1797

Hannah Webster Foster, *The Coquette; or, The History of Eliza Wharton*

Susanna Haswell Rowson's *Americans in England* (*The Columbian Daughter*) produced in Boston

Susanna Haswell Rowson advertises her female academy in Boston

William Dunlap, *History of the American Theatre and Anecdotes of the Principal Actors*

William Dunlap, *Fontainville Abbey*

U.S.S. *Constitution* (Old Ironsides) launched

## 1797–1798

XYZ Affair

## 1798

Charles Brockden Brown, *Wieland; or, The Transformation. An American Tale*

Charles Brockden Brown, *Alcuin*

William Dunlap, *André*

Alien and Sedition Acts

Alois Senefelder of Munich invents lithography

Edward Savage engraves *The Washington Family*

*The Death of Major André, and Arnold's Treachery; or, West Point Preserved* (spectacle performance)

"New Yankee Doodle"

Joseph Hopkinson, "Hail, Columbia"

Robert Treat Paine, "Adams and Liberty"

"Pig of Knowledge" advertised in *Salem Gazette*

Nicolas-Louis Robert (France) invents first mechanized paper machine

Virginia and Kentucky Resolutions

Boston school advertises instruction in boxing

## 1799

Death of Washington

Charles Brockden Brown, *Ormond; or, the Secret Witness*; *Edgar Huntly*; and *Arthur Mervyn, First Part*

Mason Locke Weems begins series of moralistic tracts

Benjamin Henry Latrobe, Bank of Pennsylvania (completed 1801)

*American True Blue; or, The Naval Processions* (spectacle performance)

*The Constellation; or, A Wreath for American Tars* (spectacle performance)

## 1799–1800

*Monthly Magazine and American Review* established by Charles Brockden Brown

# 1800

Thomas Jefferson elected president

National census: population 5,308,483

S.K. Wood, *Julia, and the Illuminated Baron*

Mason Locke Weems, *A History of the Life and Death, Virtues and Exploits of General George Washington*

Charles Brockden Brown, *Arthur Mervyn, Second Part*

William and Thomas Birch, *Congress Hall and New Theatre*

Susanna Haswell Rowson, *The Columbian Daughter; or, Americans in England*

First melodrama produced in France

Library of Congress established

Farmers begin to use wagons as modes of travel

Total newspapers in the United States: 260

# 1801

Tabitha Gilman Tenney, *Female Quixotism: Exhibited in the Romantic Opinions and Extravagant Adventures of Dorcasina Sheldon*

Benjamin West, *Angel of the Resurrection*

Benjamin Carr, "A Negro Song"

Crane & Company advertise plans to establish a paper mill in Dalton, Massachusetts

Joseph Dennie establishes *Port Folio* in Philadelphia

John Adams appoints the "midnight judges"

Yale president Timothy Dwight asks graduating class to take an oath never to vote for Jefferson

# 1802

*Americana; or, A New Tale of the Genii* (spectacle published)

*The Franklin Primer*

# 1803

Louisiana Purchase ($15m)

Jefferson appoints Benjamin Henry Latrobe as Surveyor of Buildings of the United States

William Dunlap, *The Glory of Columbia—Her Yeomanry*

First American piano built

David Zeisberger, *Collection of Hymns for the Use of the Christian Indians of the Mission of the United Brethren in North America*

*Literary Magazine and American Register* established by Charles Brockden Brown

New York State outlaws horseracing

# 1804

Adelio [pseud.], *A Journey to Philadelphia*

Catskill Turnpike

12th Amendment passed; vice presidency is determined by party ticket, not runner-up in presidential vote count

Aaron Burr kills Alexander Hamilton in a duel

# 1804–1806

Lewis and Clark Expedition

# 1805

Benjamin Henry Latrobe, Basilica of the Assumption of the Blessed Virgin Mary in Baltimore (completed 1818)

Rembrandt Peale, *Thomas Jefferson*

*Lady's Weekly Miscellany* established

William Rush founds Pennsylvania Academy of Fine Arts

*Orukter Amphibolos* (steam dredge) launched (first road locomotive in America)

# 1806

Charles Willson Peale, *The Exhumation of the Mastodon*

Noah Webster, *Compendious Dictionary of the English Language*

# 1807

Embargo Act

Tramway constructed in Boston

Robert Fulton launches the *Clermont* on the Hudson River

Percussion ignition system (in firearms) makes first appearance

Article 1, section 9 of the Constitution outlaws the importation of slaves into the United States

Fourdrinier Brothers (England) improve mechanized paper machine

Students riot at Princeton

# 1808

William Rush, *Comedy and Tragedy* (originally *Nymph of the Schuylkill*)

James Nelson Barker, *The Indian Princess; or, The Belle Sauvage*

Slave trade abolished in the United States

Famed American thoroughbred Diomed dies

# 1809

Washington Irving, *A History of New York*

*Laura* written by "A Lady of Philadelphia"

Congress repeals Embargo Act of 1807

First patent nostrum ad ("Dr. Robertson") appears in print

Georgia man sets mile-walking record at seven minutes, 30 seconds

James Madison sworn in as fourth President of the United States

# 1810

George Watterson, *Glencarn; or, The Disappointments of Youth*

*Theophiloanthropist* established by the Society of Theophilanthropy

Cribb-Molyneux boxing match

First veterinarian immigrates to the United States

# 1811

Isaac Mitchell, *The Asylum; or, Alonzo and Melissa*

Construction of the Cumberland Road (national turnpike) begins

*Juvenile Monitor, or Educational Magazine*

Boat race (between Long Island and New York) featuring boats made by rival manufacturers: Chambers of London and Baptiste of New York

# 1812

James Madison elected president (second term)

Samuel F.B. Morse, *Dying Hercules*, awarded Gold Medal by the Adelphi Society in London

# 1812–1815

War of 1812 (Second War of Independence)

# 1813

*Analectic Magazine* established with Washington Irving as editor

# 1814

Francis Scott Key, "The Star-Spangled Banner"

Capitol burned by British troops in Washington, DC

William Rush, *George Washington*

Hartford Convention

Treaty of Ghent (December 24, 1814)

# 1815

Professional theater company established in Frankfort, Kentucky

William Dunlap, *The Life of Charles Brockden Brown*

Samuel Worcester, *Christian Psalmody, in four parts; Comprising Dr. Watts' Psalms abridged: Select Hymns from other sources; and select Harmonies*

American inmates at Dartmoor Prison perform "Yankee Doodle" as an act of defiance

Battle of New Orleans

# 1816

James Monroe elected president

Gas lighting installed in the Chestnut Street Theater, Philadelphia

# Part One

# Life and Youth During the New Nation

# The New Nation

# 1

# Everyday America

Life in the United States during the early nationalist period could be characterized as contradictory. A government based on democratic principles constitutionally excluded more than half its population (women and those enslaved) from having a voice in that governance.[1] A country having unequivocally rejected a monarchy and the inflexible social strata that it imposed had an upper class that regarded the common people with distrust and contempt.[2] A nation united by nationalistic pride was constantly embroiled in state and party discord. A people who revered science and technology were subjected to medical treatment that had evolved little from that of the Middle Ages. A vast land of plenty, rich in vegetation and abundant in stock and poultry, was also one typified by poor diets. New cities, engineered by the latest technology, were subject to deadly disease and substandard sanitation.

The United States was largely an agricultural society during this period. Urban centers were beginning to grow substantially, but the majority of the population lived far apart. But this was also an era of a huge growth in both population and area. From 1790 to 1810, the population had nearly doubled with a net gain of 3,310,667 inhabitants.[3] Land area, which began with the original thirteen colonies, also nearly doubled (mainly due to the Louisiana Purchase).[4] Subsequently, from 1790 to 1810 the population per square mile went down two-tenths of one percent. But this large land mass did not remain unsettled for long. From the years 1787 to 1816, the country grew from the original thirteen colonies to nineteen states.

| State | Date Ratified the Constitution | Date Entered the Union |
|---|---|---|
| Delaware | December 7, 1787 | |
| Pennsylvania | December 12, 1787 | |
| New Jersey | December 18, 1787 | |
| Georgia | January 2, 1788 | |
| Connecticut | January 9, 1788 | |
| Massachusetts | February 6, 1788 | |
| Maryland | April 28, 1788 | |
| South Carolina | May 23, 1788 | |
| New Hampshire | June 21, 1788 | |
| Virginia | June 25, 1788 | |
| New York | July 26, 1788 | |
| North Carolina | November 21, 1789 | |
| Rhode Island | May 29, 1790 | |
| Vermont | | March 4, 1791 |
| Kentucky | | June 1, 1792 |
| Tennessee | | June 1, 1796 |
| Ohio | | March 1, 1803 |
| Louisiana | | April 30, 1812 |
| Indiana | | December 11, 1816 |

Regardless of region, urban life was uniform in the new nation with the exception of Philadelphia. Philadelphia, deemed the cleanest, most beautiful, and healthful of American cities, had benefited from the urban planning of William Penn's (1644–1718) gridiron system. (The streets in other American cities were, at best, disorganized.) Unlike other American cities that suffered from badly maintained cobblestone streets, often pitted with potholes, substandard sanitation, and no running water, Philadelphia could boast that a majority of its streets were paved and had gutters and curbs to aid drainage, that its streets were cleaned regularly, and that its water supply was furnished by steam pump. But even Philadelphia suffered from sewage problems. All American urban streets were filled with garbage, and sewage freely spilled into the gutters. Household slops (refuse) were thrown out in the middle of the streets. In cities, foraging pigs would then eat the slops, serving as four-legged street cleaners. (New York even had an ordinance designating that the slops be dumped in the middle of the streets, rather than the gutters, so that the pigs running down the middle of the street could easily find the slops.) The exception was Charleston, South Carolina, where buzzards were used instead of roaming pigs.

Overall, Americans, regardless of class or means, disposed of their trash in irresponsible ways. In smaller towns and rural areas, trash was thrown outside the door and left there to either rot or blow away. Urban dwellers designated an area in the yard as the trash pit (the same yard inhabited by an owner's animals—livestock, chickens, horses, etc.). Everything possible was thrown into the trash pit, even human waste. In low-lying areas such as the Philadelphia waterfront, Long Island, and the Chesapeake area, the trash pits often seeped into the drinking wells, polluting the water (Wolf, 58).

Such filthy conditions led to outbreaks of devastating diseases in both town and country. Medical science was in a state of flux, and Americans suffered, sometimes needlessly, from the lack of skill, knowledge, or availability of medical personnel. Although Philadelphia was the national center of medical and scientific study, as well as the home of the eminent physician, educator, writer, and leading patriot Dr. Benjamin Rush, the rest of the country was not as fortunate when it came to medical care and advances. Many times the care a patient received depended on the experience and firsthand knowledge of the caregiver. Medical doctors were men who may or may not have received adequate formal training. Most physicians received their training by working alongside an established practitioner, although by 1817 there were nine medical schools in the United States that granted medical degrees (Appleby, 110–111). Men accorded the title "Doctor" were those who had joined medical societies. For many doctors, medicine was a sideline, although the practice of medicine was becoming more and more professionalized. But often families were forced to rely on books, such as *Every Man His Own Doctor*, to diagnosis and treat their ailments themselves (Wolf, 200). The emphasis, though, was on the "man" in the title because no books dealt with female complaints or anatomy.

Medical doctors and female practitioners (which included midwives) ministered to patients. All prescribed and dispensed medicines and advice since there were no laws that precluded those without medical degrees from practicing medicine. Both male and female practitioners delivered babies now that obstetrics was regarded as a viable medical field. (Prior to this time, physicians were only called to the childbed when a fetus needed to be surgically removed. Childbirth then was the sole province of midwifery.) Although women had knowledge of the more "advanced" treatments such as bloodletting and calomel (a mercury compound) dosing used as a purgative, they were more likely to treat ailments and diseases with medicines made from herbs, roots, or barks (though more "traditional" doctors—those who were not practitioners of the "modern" practice of bloodletting—used the same types of treatment as these medical laywomen). Painkillers such as opium and laudanum (a tincture of opium) were also liberally prescribed, with little or no concern for their addictive properties. Tobacco was also viewed as a cure-all for a variety of ills: "It helps digestion, the Gout, and Toothach, . . . feedeth the hungry, . . . purgeth the stomach, killeth nits and lice" (qtd. in ibid., 202). Doctors prescribed alcohol just as freely. Each drink was prescribed for a specific condition or ailment: for nursing mothers, beer; for pain, brandy; for consumption (tuberculosis) and digestive problems, wine (ibid., 92).

Physicians and medical laity alike were constrained by the limited medical knowledge of the time. The standard treatment was humoral therapy. Humoral therapy was based on the theory that the human body was made up of four types of body fluids or "humors": blood, phlegm, choler (yellow bile), and melancholy (black bile). To maintain good health, a person's bodily fluids had to be in balance. Ill health was caused by an imbalance of the humors. The medical practitioner then, to restore balance, would expel the excess humor. The standard means of expulsion included bloodletting, lancing of abscesses, festering or blistering, and purging or puking (the eighteenth century term for vomiting).

Sometimes practitioners were extreme in employing humoral therapy (particularly bloodletting), resulting in the worsening of the patient's condition, even hastening death. A prime example of overzealous humoral treatment is the death of George Washington. Suffering from quinsy (inflammation of the tonsils) Washington had been bled repeatedly; Spanish fly (a topical skin irritant made from European blister beetle secretions) had been applied to his throat to promote blistering, and he had been liberally dosed with calomel. Weakened and virtually tortured by his medical treatment, Washington died an excruciatingly painful death.

Some medical practitioners (usually physicians) chose to apply solidistic medical treatment, either alone or in combination with humoral therapy. Solidistic medicine was based on Newtonian physics and attempted to regulate the "solids" (blood vessels and nerves) of the body. Rather than expelling fluids, solidistic therapy called for use of drugs, herbs, and tonics to stimulate or relax bodily functions. Solidistic treatment could also be risky if the medical practitioner did not carefully monitor dosages.

By and large, late eighteenth-century medicine was hampered by the lack of technology. There was no accurate way of determining body temperature except by touch (clinical thermometers had not yet been invented). Listening to a patient's heart and lungs had to be done by pressing an ear to the chest. (Stethoscopes did not exist.) Taking a patient's pulse was done by trial and error because few people owned watches with second hands. Medical scientists had yet to discover that by tapping a patient's chest or abdomen, a practitioner or physician could discover excess fluid or tumors. Even the most highly skilled sur-

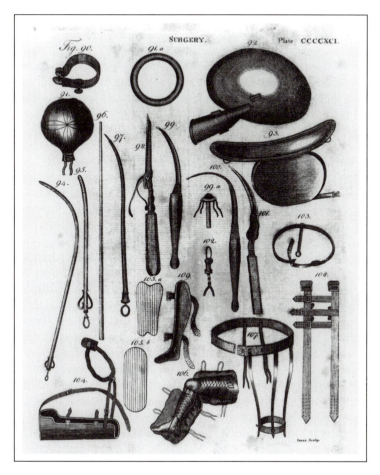

Surgical instruments of the eighteenth century.
Courtesy of the Library of Congress.

geons used instruments more reminiscent of medieval torture than science: trephines (instruments with circular sawlike edges) for boring into the skull, tooth extractors, tourniquets, forceps, and surgical saw blades. Poor or misguided medical care was decidedly a cause for concern and caution.

Personal hygiene was also a problem for Americans. Because running water was a luxury in any American home, keeping clean took great effort. In most locations water had to be brought in from a well or cistern. Often men would strip to the waist and bathe at the public trough. For those who preferred indoor facilities, bathing was an arduous task since bathtubs did not exist. Rich and poor alike bathed either at an outside pump or at the kitchen sink. (Proper Boston, however, had ordinances dating back to the 1750s prohibiting any resident over the age of 12 from bathing outside before sundown.) To remove dirt, bathers would vigorously rub themselves with a rough towel. (Soap was reserved for the laundry.) Daily bathing was considered peculiar behavior. Not until the mid-nineteenth century was daily bathing viewed as an acceptable and healthful practice.

Dental hygiene was also a challenge because the bristled toothbrush was not available until the nineteenth century. Wrapping a finger in a soft cloth and rubbing each tooth with the cloth was the common way to clean teeth. Fortunately, there were practicing dentists who had been trained in medicine and surgery. Unfortunately, dental charlatans proliferated. Poor diet, inadequate hygiene, and rudimentary dentistry resulted in a population that suffered from rampant tooth decay, oral pain, and tooth loss. All levels of society were affected. Numbered among the "dentally challenged" were Presidents Washington and Adams. (Washington's problems with his false teeth are legendary. As for Adams, during the 1800 presidential election, he refused to give public speeches because he was embarrassed by his toothless state.)

In general, Americans were not an overly clean people (J. Larkin, 129). Bedding was often infested with fleas and bedbugs. Homes were often overrun with ants, roaches, flies, and mosquitoes because floors were inadequately swept and no screens barred flying insects from entering the home. (Wealthy southerners draped gauze curtains around their bedsteads, curtailing the invasion of flies and mosquitoes, but this was a very costly measure.) Innovative homeowners would hang wasp nests from the ceiling, reasoning that the wasps would attack winged invaders rather than human inhabitants (Wolf, 67). Mothers constantly checked their children for head lice infestations. Foul stenches were everywhere. The smells from the "necessary house" (outhouse) and unemptied chamber pots were all too evident in town and country, especially on warm or windy days (J. Larkin, 126). Even the cleaning solution used in print shops and households reeked. Called "chamber lye," the solution was made of highly concentrated urine and was used to clean type and to degrease wool.

The American love of tobacco added to the filthy conditions in the home and in public places. In addition to their belief in tobacco's so-called curative powers, citizens indulged in tobacco for non-medicinal reasons: to smoke it, chew it, and expectorate it. Men and women smoked long-stemmed clay pipes and took snuff. Wealthy men particularly enjoyed the latest Caribbean import (1790s), the cigar or "segar," which was relatively expensive at three cents apiece. Chewing tobacco, on the other hand, was indulged in at every social level. It was inexpensive and could be chewed while working. (Smoking while working was difficult.) More genteel chewers would expectorate into spittoons—or at least the spittoon was provided in better establishments. Most male chewers, however, chose to spit frequently and indiscriminately. Public floors were often covered in blackened saliva.

Health and hygiene were not the only problems Americans faced. Protection (or lack thereof) from the criminal element was great cause for alarm among Americans, though police protection did not appear to be a concern of the municipal government. In city and country alike the hiring of capable night watchmen, jail keepers, officers of the law, and even hangmen was difficult, especially since seven out of ten attacks on constables or police officers were perpetrated by the "law-abiding" citizenry (Wolf, 252). Patrolling streets at night was a challenge. In rural areas and small towns moonlight provided the only illumination. In the larger cities, streets were only slightly better lit. Oil lamps, but only when it was not raining or when the moonlight was dim, provided much needed light for city streets. Many times citizens had to resort to organizing watch patrols within their neighborhoods to ward off attackers and the criminal element. Sometimes the city did hire night watchmen equipped with handheld lanterns to patrol the streets. Sensible night travelers carried personal weapons in case of attack. During daylight hours constables were available, but the real danger was at night—either from crime or from fires.

Fire was the most pressing urban danger, but as with watch patrols, municipal governments did not view fire protection as its responsibility. Fire protection in cities was left to one of two options: volunteer fire companies or mutual companies (the company would only put out the fires of property belonging to its members). Some unscrupulous firefighters showed up at fires not to battle the blaze, but to loot the burning property. Even the fire engines were sent out at a price since they were usually privately owned. Property owners were, in many cases, at the mercy of the unprincipled or those who wanted a return for their efforts.

## REGIONAL LIFE

In the latter part of the eighteenth century, only the far eastern regions (from the coast to approximately one hundred miles inland) of the United States had been settled for a long period of time. This included cities, towns, and established farming communities in both the northern and southern states. Any land west of this small strip was considered to be part of the frontier. Thus, the quality and type of everyday life in the United States was contingent on where one lived and how long that area had been settled. Lifestyles varied in the North and the South and in well established settlement areas to the frontier.

The northern population tended to cluster in villages, towns, and cities with outlying farm communities within a reasonable traveling distance. New England alone had over one thousand towns. In fact, over half of urban communities (those defined as having populations in excess of three thousand) were in New England (Wolf, 217). From colonial times the New England impulse was to sustain a cultural, social, and spiritual center for residents. Drawing on their Puritan tradition, New Englanders relied on one another for spiritual sustenance and support. Having a church for the community to come together to worship was of prime importance. Those who had moved outside of a city, town, or village in hopes of cultivating outlying land eventually would set up their own centers for meeting (beginning with establishing a church), thereby creating a new village. First and foremost, New Englanders believed in having neighbors.

The Mid-Atlantic states did not have the clusters of small communities as did New England, but they had a respectable number of large towns and villages. Farms were farther apart, but the Mid-Atlantic states solved communication and networking problems by establishing county systems of government. The larger towns and villages were often county seats, serving a wide radius of inhabitants. Unlike New England, the Mid-Atlantic states did not have small population centers of those who shared the same religion and thus required a central church. Because the Mid-Atlantic states had originally been settled by a wide variety of peoples who held differing religious beliefs, a single church could not provide the communal center. Instead, the need for a central marketplace united residents in the Mid-Atlantic communities. The county seat, as the center of government, naturally became the locus for the buying and selling of agricultural goods.

In New England and the Mid-Atlantic region, residents were more apt to follow the English code of culture. That is, northern domestic standards emulated that of England: homes were no longer the ramshackle structures of the colonial period, but dwellings of permanence. Northerners remodeled—or sometimes tore down—existing structures so that they could have the latest type of roof, windows, chimney, and other outward manifestations of affluence. Also, like their English counterparts, northerners assessed the quality of living by what was in the house, not necessarily what the living conditions in the house were. For example, the less prosperous might not have been able to afford a home with more than one sleeping chamber (whole families often slept in one room), but they made sure they had a more-than-adequate supply of serviceable linen. Gracious living in Philadelphia (one of the earlier national capitals) might be measured by the type and number of place settings one might have for dinner, rather than the fact that livestock was prominently tethered on the front lawn of the city's most fashionable street.

Southern living reflected its agricultural society. Unlike what was found in the North, widely dispersed populations, most of which were small farms, characterized southern demographics. Only a very few owned or managed large plantations and estates. The northern need for having neighbors or establishing a nearby communal center was missing in the South. Southerners held fast to their idea of personal autonomy. Distance enhanced the southern sense of being master of all one could see. Also, prominent southern planters relied on a slave-driven economy. Even small farmers owned a few slaves—or at least aspired to own them. (The ownership of slaves, and the number owned, often determined one's place in the rigid southern social hierarchy.) By virtue of land ownership and wealth, the planter elite became the social and political leaders of the South.

Even though four of the first five presidents of the United States came from the South—all four, in fact, were Virginians—southerners would eventually become more sectionalistic than nationalistic in their policies. As the North became more concerned with progress, industrialization, and economic opportunity, the South became more indifferent—even hostile—to northern ideas of moral reform and enterprise. They particularly took exception to the northern stance toward slave owning. Southerners began to characterize the northern lifestyle as crass and prided themselves on the refined and courtly values of southern culture. The outcome was that the small, moneyed elite spent vast sums on beautifying their estates and indulged in outward displays of wealth and power. The gaps between the levels of the southern social stratum became more and more pronounced. At the top, the planters wielded power and exerted profound influence on southern culture as a whole. In between were the small planters who lived simply but embraced the ideals of the planters. Small planters owned less land, had fewer slaves (approximately 5–20), and lived in wooden frame houses (Nye, *Cultural Life*, 116). Yeoman farmers, who made up 75 percent of the white southern population, owned no slaves and farmed small plots of land of middling to poor quality. At the bottom were the illiterate dirt farmers (referred to as "crackers") and the enslaved. The former lived in substandard housing and barely were able to feed themselves and their families. The treatment of the latter varied from situation to situation, some humanely, others subjected to horrific acts of mental and physical cruelty.

The frontier made up the largest landmass of the United States during the early nationalist period, especially after the purchase of the Louisiana Territory from France in 1803.[5] Setting out for the frontier was particularly appealing to the young people of New England, who found little opportunity to establish new farms in well settled New England. But living on the frontier was exceptionally rigorous. Only the most hardy and resilient succeeded. Pioneer farmers were faced with uncertain climate and soil conditions, the threat of Native American hostilities, limited resources (supplies, extra labor), and sometimes failing crops. Life was lonely. Settlements were far apart and often difficult to reach. Roads—if there were roads—were poor. Transporting goods and produce back East was extremely problematic. Westerners often faced crossing the mountainous terrain that separated them from the eastern marketplace. More often than not, those on the frontier had to forgo the amenities that were considered necessary for "civilized" living on the eastern seaboard. Worse, the frontier was plagued by lawlessness and, notably, two well-known uprisings against the government: Shays's Rebellion in Massachusetts and the Whiskey Rebellion in western Pennsylvania. Both uprisings caused immediate and acute concern throughout the United States.

Independence had not alleviated the economic problems of the country, especially those of the common people. In the case of Shays's Rebellion, Massachusetts farmers, burdened by heavy taxes, high debt ratios, and low farm prices, rebelled after the state legislature repealed paper money and tender laws. The legislature also refused to legalize the offering of goods as a means of satisfying debts. (This was a crucial part of frontier economy.) Reacting bitterly, the people demanded an amendment to the state constitution to reduce the costs of government as well as a plan for economic relief. When nonviolent means produced no governmental response, the farmers took up arms. Angry mobs of frontier farmers carrying guns and clubs prevented the county courts and the Springfield session of the state supreme court from conducting business. The several armed skirmishes between the militia and the insurgents, captained by former Revolutionary War officer Daniel Shays (hence the name of the rebellion), fomented public furor in neighboring states. Organized into regiments that comprised roughly one-fifth of the population in a five-county area, the Shaysites attempted to seize the arsenal at Springfield. Subsequently, the rebellion was successfully put down when the militia stopped Shays's forces in February 1787. (Shays himself escaped into Vermont.)

The rebellion did have a positive outcome for the overburdened Massachusetts farmers: the legislature consequently passed laws designed to alleviate the dire economic straits of debtors. Even though the Shaysites' agenda had never included destruction or redistribution of land, for many years afterward Americans believed otherwise. Some, in fact, feared that the national government, already weakened under the Articles of Confederation (1781–1789), would be vulnerable to further acts of insurgency.[6] The prolonged conflict in Massachusetts, considered to be one of the most powerful and influential states in the Confederation, demonstrated to many Americans the vulnerability of the individual states in the loosely knit union (Szatmary, 123). The year the rebellion was suppressed (1787) delegates from 12 states (Rhode Island refused to send representatives) met in Philadelphia to frame the Constitution and establish a strong federal government.

The Whiskey Rebellion (sometimes referred to as the Whiskey Insurrection) was an armed response to a federally imposed tax on distilled liquors. The tax, proposed by Treasury Secretary Alexander Hamilton (1755?–1804) and enacted by Congress in 1791, was intended to ease the national debt. Once again frontierspeople, already disgruntled with what they perceived as the federal government's ignominious failure to defend them against marauding Native Americans, vehemently questioned the logistics of the hated tax. Whiskey was the most important frontier trade commodity, both as product and as barter. (Western farmers would convert their grain into whiskey for sale back East because whiskey was far easier to transport than grain.) Accordingly, frontierspeople viewed the whiskey tax as economically and politically repugnant, especially in light of the government's impotence and negligence in protecting these citizens who felt that they were being unfairly burdened with an excise tax (Slaughter, 95). In other words, frontier citizenry believed that they were being ordered to support financially a government that had failed to support them militarily. As a result, excise agents were met with violence.

Proclaiming themselves ideological descendents of the Sons of Liberty, frontier insurgents talked of secession and independence. Frontier hostilities toward the federal government escalated. There were numerous effigy burnings and physical intimidation of federal agents. By the autumn of 1794, President Washington was compelled to call out a militia of 12,950 men from Pennsylvania, New Jersey, Maryland, and Virginia to quell the insurgency. The insurrection quickly collapsed, its leaders fleeing deeper into the wilderness to escape military retribution. Like Shays's Rebellion seven years earlier, the Whiskey Rebellion was successfully extinguished but was not lightly dismissed by the public or the government.

The aftereffects were pervasive and politically disruptive. Overall, the Federalist Washington administration (and the Adams administration that followed) viewed both Shays's Rebellion and the Whiskey Rebellion as dangerous threats to the government and society as a whole. The general public, too, found the rebellions frightening. They associated insurrection with savagery. Because the Whiskey Insurrectionists had chosen to emulate the Boston patriots of the 1773 Tea Party (who had dressed as Native Americans, complete with war paint and other accoutrements), memories of the Whiskey Rebellion in particular evoked the belief in and the fears of Native American atrocities in the public's mind. (Whiskey Insurrectionists also instigated mock Native American peace treaties at their mass meetings, sustaining in the minds of many Americans the image of the savage and of savagery.)

Consequently, easterners (both in the North and the South) regarded the frontier as a region typified by violence, anarchy, and primitive existence. Frontier citizenry regarded the federal government warily, often choosing to disregard it entirely, because they felt that the government served eastern interests only. Distrust between the United States proper and its outlying western territories grew throughout the period. But frontier hostility and lawlessness, which had emanated from regionalism, were not the only problems facing the nation.

## SLAVERY AND RACISM IN THE NEW REPUBLIC

A fundamental difference between the North, the South, and the frontier was the attitude toward slavery. Although northerners had slaves at the time of the ratification of the Constitution (1789), by 1804 most northern states had abolished slavery.[7] In the late eighteenth century, northerners who still owned slaves trained them for specific duties and regarded them as members of an extended family (Wolf, 37). But the spirit of the Declaration of Independence had resonated with northerners who, having never depended on the institution of slavery for economic reasons, began to rethink the moral implications of perpetuating slavery in the North (Appleby, 155). This new moral conscience, coupled with the Quakers' ongoing efforts to abolish slavery, persuaded state governments from Maryland northward to abolish slavery in the years between 1777 and 1804.

Though slavery may have been abolished in the North, racism was very much a part of northern life. No longer dehumanized in the North as "property" (the inventory of slaves was analogous to keeping inventory of one's livestock), ex-slaves in the North had an existence that was in direct contrast to the Declaration's statement "that all men are created equal, that they are endowed by their Creator with certain unalienable Rights, that among these are Life, Liberty, and the pursuit of Happiness."

Northern free blacks did not have voting rights, only a few owned property, and most professions were closed to them. Instead, African Americans in the North were relegated to the most menial jobs: servants (such as butlers or maids), chimney sweeps, or fruit sellers. Because most African Americans resided in the homes of their employers, they had virtually no private home space. Accordingly, they often met (in large numbers) in public places to socialize and network. In Philadelphia, they conducted social affairs and celebrated holidays on the city's "Negro Burial Ground." In other cities, African Americans congregated on the courthouse square or in the street. The high visibility of African American gatherings made the White population uneasy. (They feared the

African Americans were meeting to plot insurrection.) For this reason, communities began to pass laws restricting such meetings.

Intra-racial bias was also present in the northern African American community. In their desire to be respected by the predominantly White community, established African Americans concertedly distanced themselves from ex-slaves from the South and the Caribbean who had migrated to the now-free North. Black and White leaders of the American Convention of Antislavery Societies warned their African American members to abstain from speaking "southern dialect," from flaunting a "sauntering gait, unrestrained singing and laughing, exuberant dancing," and wearing flamboyant clothing (qtd. in Wolf, 249). Categorically, this response stemmed from the White community's fear and antipathy of a growing ex-slave population, but it also was a result of the well established African American community's desire to become part of the middle class. With their desire for upward mobility came a repudiation of their collective backgrounds and cultures.

By 1804 slavery had become solely associated with the South—both states and frontier. Southerners felt compelled to defend their "peculiar institution," especially in the wake of northern self-righteousness. Southern proponents of slavery argued that slavery was, in many ways, an act of benevolence, reasoning that by enslaving pagan Africans, White Christian society had, in effect, saved the souls of these captive people. Many slave owners were quick to point out that the "average" southern slave had a higher standard of living than poor Whites in all other areas of the United States. The issue of personhood and autonomy did not figure into this "benevolent" depiction. The North/South tensions caused by the slavery issue would continue to escalate in the nineteenth century, ultimately becoming a major cause of the Civil War.

## CENTERS OF EVERYDAY LIFE: THE CHURCH AND THE TAVERN

Regardless of where Americans chose to live—town or country, city or frontier, the North or the South—every community had two establishments that were considered to be the center of American life: the church and the tavern. Obviously, the larger cities became hubs of culture and commerce—and thus provided myriads of houses of worship and eating, drinking, and lodging establishments. But even the smallest New England town (technically rural villages), the smallest Pennsylvania burg, or the most sparsely populated and geographically dispersed southern or frontier community was certain to have a church (or its equivalent) and a tavern that also provided food and lodging accommodations. Church and tavern coexisted within the community, each supplying services vital to the needs of the people.

The United States was a predominantly Protestant country from the era of colonization and continued to be so throughout the early nationalist period. (Catholics and Jews were barely tolerated, if at all.) Ironically, only half of the population aligned itself with a church or religion. Some were unbelievers (atheists) or skeptics (agnostics), but many were believers who did not see the need to worship or belong to a particular church. But for those who did align themselves with a specific religion or sect, the early nationalist period was a time of immense change and energy that had been ushered in by the religious phenomenon known as the Second Great Awakening (1795–1835), which was less emotional, but equally as influential, as the Great Awakening that had preceded it by a half century.[8]

The Second Great Awakening invigorated those who were believers and provided the impetus for moral reform (notably, the temperance movement, the establishment of foreign missions, women's rights, and the abolitionist movement in the North). Church membership greatly increased in all denominations. As a result, churches were a fundamental part of all communities, no matter if it was the local Congregational Church in New England, a plain Quaker meetinghouse in Pennsylvania, or a church at a crossroads in the South. Those aligned with a church or sect made sure that one of the first buildings erected in the community was a church or, if that was not possible, they arranged for a place where services could be held.

Urban areas throughout the country and rural New England had well established churches and congregations. But in the more thinly populated areas of the United States, the appearance of churches depended on the ethnic mix of the local population and the cooperation between sects. For instance, the rural citizenry in parts of New York erected numerous churches to accommodate the various ethnic groups. At the time of the Revolution, Newtown, New York (located at what is now LaGuardia Airport), population approximately one thousand, could boast of Presbyterian, Anglican, Quaker, and Dutch Reform congregations (Wolf, 218). Pennsylvania, fundamentally a rural state (with the exception of Philadelphia), had a large proportion of German immigrants who had come to America to farm. No matter how small the German settlement, it undoubtedly would have both Lutheran and German Reform Church congregations (ibid.).

Sometimes (and this occurred more often in the rural Mid-Atlantic states, the South, and on the frontier) the community could not support more than one church building, even though the population was made up of more than one denomination. In those cases, the community would build a "united" church, which was shared—often not amiably—by the various congregations. Some sects (such as the Quakers and the Mennonites) had no building designated as their church. Instead, they preferred to hold services in the homes of their congregants on a rotation basis. In southern rural communities churches were frequently built at crossroads or on the top of a hill. These rural churches rarely had a bell to call the congregants to service because they did not live close enough to the church to hear the ringing (ibid., 221).

In particularly remote parts of the frontier where settlements were rare (and a building for worship did not exist), camp meetings (outdoor revival meetings) replaced the freestanding church and traditional theology. (Frontier worshipers often picked and chose what theological points they wished to obey.) Usually led by a traveling evangelist, camp meetings went on for days. Frontier followers would travel great distances to take part in a camp meeting, bringing tents or erecting makeshift shelters to stay in. Whole families took an active part in the meetings, which went on way into the night. Struck by religious emotionalism, the revivalist followers reacted strongly. Accounts of the period report that men and women climbed trees, barked like dogs, rolled on the ground, passed out, and jerked and roared in a frenzy (Nye, *Cultural Life*, 218).

Though the behaviors at camp meetings were the most extreme type of worship, the meeting itself fulfilled the same ecclesiastical, spiritual, and communal needs as the church did in other communities. Both camp meetings and churches served not only as a place to worship, but also as a common meeting place. (Camp meetings, however, were more of a special event than a part of everyday living.) In the case of rural churchgoers, Sunday worship allowed them to take advantage of meeting outside the church to catch up on the latest news, national and local. (Their workweek did not allow much, if any, time to socialize. Sundays were often the only days in which busy rural families had a little spare time.) In the case of communities where the courthouse was miles away or infrequently in session, those who had minor legal disputes often would arbitrate them among themselves in the churchyard. (If there was a courthouse in the vicinity, it usually had another building attached to it, such as a jail, a store, or a tavern.)

Like the church, the tavern afforded a central meeting place for the community. Being a nation of drinkers of spirits for all occasions, the United States was, as one would expect, heavily populated with taverns. (With a few exceptions, Americans drank much and frequently.) But taverns served other essential purposes besides providing drinks, such as furnishing lodging for weary travelers. In rural and frontier areas, taverns were often located at the crossroads and subsequently served a dual purpose as tavern and general merchandise store. These "crossroad" stores were an intriguing combination of bar, store, and various other establishments that were needed by the community. For example, at a crossroad store a patron could have a drink (often brewed or distilled by the proprietor), have a hearty meal, shop for dry goods, post a letter (in the absence of an official post office, crossroad store owners would function as postmasters), and even conduct personal banking business. (Crossroad stores handled deposits, extended credit, and loaned money.) Some proprietors functioned as brokers for farmers who needed to sell their crops or buy crops when theirs had not yielded the expected harvest (Wolf, 222).

Taverns naturally became centers for political discussions, which often escalated into heated debates. From the earliest times in American history, taverns were often places where men met to argue the hotly disputed issues of the day. Americans continued this tradition after they won independence. In special circumstances, the village tavern served as a meeting place for the community to deal with the latest urgent concern. Basically, the tavern became the community mainstay for drinking, lodging, bargaining, gambling, game playing, and debating. Its importance in the community cannot be overemphasized.

Because of this very importance, local governments heavily regulated taverns. The local authorities were almost universally adamant that a tavern's location be close to major thoroughfares and provide adequate lodging and bedding for travelers, as well as stable accommodations for horses. Many communities also specified what type of liquor could be sold, who it could be sold to (generally, Native Americans, African Americans, apprentices, and servants could not be served alcohol), who could sell it (local authorities wished to ensure that the proprietor was someone of good moral character), and how it could be charged. Local governments were not above levying "sin taxes" (license and excise taxes) on alcoholic drinks—with the stipulation that sin tax revenue went for public improvement (such as maintenance of municipal buildings and salaries for officials).

## EMPLOYMENT AND THE WORKPLACE

The United States was fundamentally a nation of farmers. At the time of the Revolution, demographics show that nine out of every ten Americans farmed for a living. This statistic did not change throughout the rest of the eighteenth century (Wolf, 140). Yet there were those citizens who earned their living through plying their craft, engaging in commerce, or entering the professions. Small farmers (who were in the majority) by necessity had become masters of sundry crafts. They were often adept coopers, blacksmiths, farriers, carpenters, bakers, and brewers, in addition to their farming duties that included plowing, planting, harvesting, and animal husbandry. But on large plantations, in small villages, and in urban centers, specialized craftsmen were in demand. As communal centers began to expand, inhabitants looked to the master artisan or craftsman to produce products and aid in erecting much needed buildings. Citizens desired well wrought goods for their every-day needs and valued the expertise of carpenters and woodworkers when constructing their homes and other essential buildings. Even the smallest rural communities needed a woodworker (to serve as carpenter, joiner, or cooper), an expert in cloth and clothing production (weaver and tailor), a skilled leather worker (tanner and shoemaker), and a competent metalworker (blacksmith) (ibid., 178). Most worked for either cash or exchange of goods (for instance, a craftsman might work for produce rather than receive a monetary payment).

As cities grew, so did the urban dwellers' (particularly those who were more affluent) desire for manufactured goods and luxuries not readily available. Shops flourished, catering to consumer interest. Shopkeepers stocked such luxuries as chocolates, paper, clocks, fine clothing, earthenware and china, silver and gold ware, and guns. Some merchandise obviously had to be imported from Europe, but skilled American artisans and craftsmen produced many of the goods sold in shops. Bakeries flourished as well as confectionary shops. City dwellers had neither the space to store flour in bulk nor the large ovens to bake breads and pastries. Thus they needed to buy baked goods on a daily basis. Wealthy consumers had acquired a taste for sugary treats that had been imported from Europe. Enterprising Americans quickly learned the fine art of candy making to gratify the sweet tooth of the rich.

Besides legitimate (that is, "respectable") merchants (dealers in international trade) and shopkeepers (the local retailers), others swept up in the entrepreneurial spirit of the nation became vendors of assorted goods. In the city "hucksters" traveled the streets, their carts laden with various goods. Their rural counterparts, "peddlers," sold rural and frontier families household necessities that ranged from straight pins to utensils to pots. "Mountebanks" (hawkers of quack medicines and the like) were very successful in selling their sham goods to a credulous audience at county fairs. Regardless of goods or credibility, a seller could always find a buyer in a nation that had growing mercantile interests.

Those involved in the business of providing goods, by either making or selling them, became an integral part of the workplace. But the fortunes of these workers and shopkeepers were volatile. Depending on the market and the fluctuating economy, a merchant or craftsman might have extremely high profits one year and face bankruptcy the next. For instance, the unpopular Embargo Act of 1807, which prohibited the exportation of goods, severely hurt farmer, artisan, and shopkeeper alike.[9]

Because of the risk an entrepreneur was taking, workshops and workplaces were generally small, employing no more than ten people. The less prosperous owners worked alongside their apprentices and employees. The truly successful owners or masters spent less time with their workers and more time engaged in social and political ventures. An intense communal spirit characterized the working environment itself. Master, employees, and apprentices enjoyed a cordial relationship. The workday may have been long, but it was pleasant, so much so that it was not uncommon to hear employees singing loudly and lustily as they worked. Drinking alcoholic beverages on the job was not only tolerated, but also expected. Workers normally began drinking in the late morning and continued into the afternoon. (The drinking was often accompanied by meals or snacks throughout the day.) Workers many times stopped work to engage in card playing, joke telling, gentle repartee, and more drinking. When they did work, an apprentice was assigned to read aloud the newspaper. This often led to animated discussions of the latest political events or local scandals. By quitting time, workers were typically sated with food, drink, and discussion.

Regrettably, large portions of workers were not fortunate to have full-time employment. Many workers were employed on a day-to-day basis. Even though wives and children worked to supplement the family income, many families were penniless. The elderly also had a difficult time eking out a living in a nation that valued youth, skill, and strength. Those who fell on hard times eventually became public charges, relegated to the community almshouse (poorhouse) along with petty criminals, the mentally ill, the physically disabled, vagrants, and the abandoned. In the mind of the community, almshouses had two main functions: They furnished the means to support the public charges (farming was the mainstay of the almshouse) and they provided moral reform for the homeless and the undesirable. Some inmates were able to return to the community, but many lived out their days in conditions that were, many times, substandard. (There was no differentiation in the treatment of the mentally ill, the physically disabled, the criminal, or those who just could not find employment.)

Not many careers were available to those who aspired to loftier ambitions than farming, shopkeeping, or skilled labor. Clerical and management positions were few because businesses, banks, and factories were small, and large shops were rare. An educated young man could opt to become a doctor, a lawyer, a teacher, or a clergyman. The training for the first three varied. Only doctors, lawyers, and teachers of the most privileged backgrounds completed a university education. Just as aspiring doctors trained under the tutelage of someone well established in the profession, lawyers-to-be "read the law" with experienced lawyers. None of the three professions required licensure, although lawyers did have to be admitted to the bar to argue cases before the court. The training and experience of those entering the ministry varied from one denomination to the next.

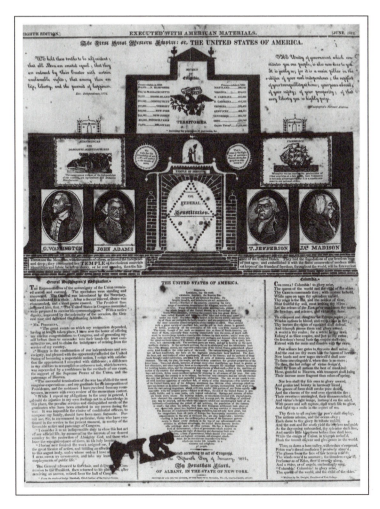

Patriotic broadside (1812). Courtesy of the Library of Congress.

## THE POST-REVOLUTIONARY TEMPER: GOVERNMENT AND POLITICS

Americans during this period were a highly politicized people. Of paramount interest to all citizenry was the formation of the federal government and a national identity. How to accomplish this consumed the interest of the American people and provided the topics of conversation of the coffeehouse and tavern, lectures and town meetings, and newspapers and broadsides. American citizens were vociferous in their criticism of their government and their political leaders. This was an era in which all citizens—not just those of the more privileged classes—felt they could raise their voices with impunity, whether it was by writing to the president directly, by publishing essays and editorials that persistently held leaders accountable, or, in extreme cases, by inciting armed conflicts. Even leaders who eventually were deified by the nation, such as Washington, were subject to intense scrutiny and even ridicule. Unpopular laws and policies were enacted and then revoked because of the resulting public furor. The early nationalist period was, generally speaking, a time when emotions ran high. But it was also a time distinguished by the framing of a dynamic Constitution (1788–1789) and a Bill of Rights (1791) that protected the intrinsic civil liberties of most of its citizenry by creating strong leadership on the national level.

## Political Figures

A list of the key political figures of the time reads like the cast list from the world stage of political history. Many of those who played important roles during the Revolutionary period exited the national stage either because their fierce brand of patriotism did not translate well into peacetime (Thomas Paine), or because they preferred involvement at the state and local level (Samuel Adams), or, sadly, through death (Benjamin Franklin). Taking center stage once more, thereby defining a nation, was George Washington (1732–1799), commander in chief of the Continental army and first president of the United States.

Washington's importance in the formation of the government cannot be overly emphasized. He, more than any other, defined the presidency. Washington had the people's respect and, more important, had earned their trust. He had proven that power would neither corrupt him nor would he be unable to relinquish it (a very real fear). When Washington resigned as commander of the Continental army with the intent of retiring to Mount Vernon, none other than George III marveled, "If he does that, he will be the greatest man in the world" (qtd. in J.J. Ellis, *Founding Brothers*, 130).

Washington's vice president and successor, John Adams (1735–1826), the critical, impulsive, learned, and outspoken patriot, had served the nation honorably and faithfully. Relegated in the last eight years to a job that he described as "the most insignificant office that ever the Invention of Man contrived or his Imagination conceived," the ambitious Adams was more than ready to ascend to the presidency (qtd. in ibid., 166). Unfortunately for Adams, his administration was encumbered by a vice president (Thomas Jefferson) from the opposing party, his choice to retain Washington's cabinet (whose collective loyalty resided with Wash-

George Washington, first president of the United
States (lithograph of portrait by Gilbert Stuart).
Courtesy of the Library of Congress.

ington, not Adams), ongoing tensions with France, and a tense
relationship with fellow Federalist Alexander Hamilton.

The third president of the United States, the contradictory Thomas
Jefferson, took the oath of office as his disgruntled predecessor rode out
of town back to Quincy, Massachusetts. Arguably, no other American
during the period exerted such wide-ranging influence on the culture of
the republic. Essayist, legal scholar, architect, advocate of human rights,
musician, art patron, wine connoisseur, Jefferson was truly a renaissance
man in every sense of the word. He was also a slave owner who, at the
end of his life, justified the perpetuation of the hated institution by concluding that to abolish it would be logistically and fiscally implausible.

John Adams, second president of the United States (lithograph of portrait by Gilbert Stuart). Courtesy of the Library of Congress.

(Jefferson believed that the races were incompatible. Therefore, the only solution he saw to emancipation would be a back-to-Africa migration.)

Many of the moneyed elite distrusted Jefferson, his followers, and his policies, considering him to be a dangerous visionary. On the other hand, the common people considered Jefferson to be their champion because he fully advocated the agricultural life (like so many of his fellow Virginians). In 1784 he wrote, "Those who labor in the earth are the chosen people of God if ever He had a chosen people, whose breasts He has made His peculiar deposit for substantial and genuine virtue" (qtd. in Elkins and McKitrick, 195). Because most Americans were farmers, an inordinate number of the common people embraced Jefferson and his policies on the basis of his advocacy of the farming life. They, like Jef-

Thomas Jefferson, third president of the United States (lithograph of portrait by Gilbert Stuart). Courtesy of the Library of Congress.

ferson, felt that city life, although it offered culture and learning, was corrupt, crowded, and disease-ridden.

But the notion that Jefferson was the champion of the common people is a myth. As much as Jefferson praised the virtues of yeomen farmers, he did not deem that they should have a substantial voice in the government. Instead, he felt that the government should be drawn from the natural aristocracy. Only those who had the highest interest, honor, and patriotism (and obviously had risen from obscurity to national prominence) would be eligible for public office (G.S. Wood, *Radicalism*, 180). Though he courted the favor of the common people, Jefferson did not identify with them.

Jefferson's friend and closest adviser, James Madison (1751–1836), be-

James Madison, fourth president of the United
States (Thomas Sully, artist; David Edwin,
engraver). Courtesy of the Library of Congress.

came the fourth president of the United States in 1809. Prior to assuming
the presidency, Madison had compiled one of the most distinguished
public careers in the United States at the time. As a delegate to the Constitutional Convention, Madison played a major role in the planning,
drafting, and ratification of the Constitution. With Hamilton and John
Jay (1745–1829) (who became the first chief justice of the Supreme Court),
he collaborated in the writing and publishing of the influential *The Federalist*.[10] Clearly a legal mind of the highest order, Madison is generally
considered to be the primary author and sponsor of the Bill of Rights.
After his political differences with Federalist ally Hamilton, Madison
aligned himself with Jefferson, under whom he served as secretary of
state.

**Political cartoon (1813) illustrating American-British relations during the War of 1812. Courtesy of the Library of Congress.**

Under Madison's administration, the United States took armed possession of what was then the Spanish province of west Florida. In his second term, the United States entered another war with Great Britain, the War of 1812 (Second War of Independence). Despite the Washington administration's successful establishment of a policy of international neutrality, the United States was constantly being brought into the ongoing conflict between its former mother country (Great Britain) and its Revolutionary ally (France). Great Britain vigorously blockaded French ports and forced neutral countries to call at British ports and pay duties. Worse yet, the British had continued to commit hostile acts of aggression, notably the halting of American ships and impressing of American seamen by falsely charging them as deserters of the Royal Navy.

Americans had also been distressed over British activities on the American continent. The British had openly been supplying the Shawnee nation with weapons, encouraging Shawnee attacks on American settlers in the Northwest Territory. After the American victory over the Shawnee at the Battle Tippecanoe (1811), Americans were more determined than ever to rid themselves of the British. (The Battle of Tippecanoe brought William Henry Harrison [1773–1841], later ninth president of the United States, into national prominence.) Finally, tensions reached a fevered pitch and the United States entered a second war with Great Britain.

Political cartoon showing British satire on Madison's handling of the War of 1812. Courtesy of the Library of Congress.

Still, the public largely blamed Madison for the war (in the press it was sometimes referred to as "Mr. Madison's War"). When the British came to burn Washington (1814), Madison and his wife Dolley (1768–1849) had to ignominiously flee the burning capital (although the resilient first lady saved priceless paintings from the executive mansion at great risk—the British troops were rapidly approaching). As the United States began to win significant naval battles and became more successful in restricting British commercial shipping, Madison's popularity rose significantly. General Andrew Jackson's (1767–1845) resounding defeat of the British in New Orleans was cause for national rejoicing. Although the Battle of New Orleans ended on January 8, 1815, three and a half weeks after the signing of the Treaty of Ghent (Belgium), news of the signing of the treaty and the victory at New Orleans arrived in Washington at about the same time. Having proven to be a formidable force on land and sea, the United States became less and less dependent on European aid in handling conflicts. They saw themselves as an American people, not as recently independent colonists or as merely citizens of a state or region. Nationalistic pride was evidenced in all areas of popular culture: in song, writing, and art.

Subsequently, by the time he left office Madison was regarded as a

Capture and burning of the U.S. Capitol by the British in 1814.
Courtesy of the Library of Congress.

national hero. He was succeeded by James Monroe (1758–1831) whose early career was distinguished by his strong opposition to Washington's Federalist policies. An ardent Jeffersonian, Monroe was appointed envoy extraordinaire and minister to France to assist in negotiations for the Louisiana Purchase. He later became secretary of state in the Madison administration, as well as secretary of war (1814–1815).

As America's elder statesman, Benjamin Franklin's (1706–1790) role in American history seemed to span the eighteenth century. Franklin was present at each defining moment in the formation of the new republic: the First Continental Congress, the signing of the Declaration of Independence, the negotiation of the Treaty of Paris, the Constitutional Convention, and finally, the signing of the Constitution. Once assured that the new national constitutional government was firmly in place, Franklin (despite declining health) turned his efforts to the abolition of slavery (J.J. Ellis, *Founding Brothers*, 111). It was his last public act. On April 17, 1790, Franklin died, leaving the country without its most witty sage.

Alexander Hamilton, who had served under Washington during the Revolutionary War, became one of the driving forces in the formation of the republic. The leading proponent of the "federal solution" (a strong federal government designed to promote and support a sound banking system that would result in fiscal stability and growth), Hamilton eloquently argued for the ratification of the Constitution. In the Washington administration, Hamilton served as the nation's first secretary of the treasury.

Hamilton was the arch-Federalist, eventually conflicting with Jefferson whose ideology and politics were in direct opposition to his. He was also the architect for a federal program that established a national bank, excises taxes, and a substantial domestic debt and subsidized manufacturers and a standing army (Elkins and McKitrick, 19). But Hamilton made many enemies, within his own party (notably John Adams) and with the Jeffersonian Republicans who despised the aristocratic Hamilton and his policies that favored commerce and industry. His mortal enemy was Aaron Burr.

Of all the prominent political leaders of the time, no one more than Aaron Burr (1756–1836) could boast such an impressive ancestry yet end a political career so ignominiously. (Burr's grandfather was none other than the great American theologian and philosopher Jonathan Edwards [1703–1758]. Burr's father, Aaron Burr Sr. [1716–1757], like Jonathan Edwards, was president of the College of New Jersey [renamed Princeton University in 1896].) Burr was a skillful but ruthlessly ambitious and unscrupulous politician. As a reward for his efforts on behalf of the Republicans in New York elections, Burr was placed on the 1800 national ticket as Jefferson's running mate. When Jefferson and Burr tied, Burr refused to accept the vice presidential spot for which he had been nominated—which did not endear him to Jefferson. (Until 1804, with the passage of the Twelfth Amendment, the winner in the presidential election—regardless of whether that person had been running for president or vice president—became president. The runner-up became vice president.) In 1804, the Republicans replaced Burr in the vice presidential spot with George Clinton (1739–1812). Burr then ran unsuccessfully for governor of New York.

Incensed by what he perceived as Hamilton's interference in the presidential election of 1800 and in the governor's race of 1804, Burr challenged Hamilton to a duel, killing him. The public response was one of outrage and deep sorrow. Hamilton was viewed as a martyr and Burr as a cold-blooded murderer. Hamilton's funeral in New York drew great crowds. His coffin was led through the streets, followed by his riderless gray horse, then by his family, political leaders, dignitaries, and the faculty and students of Columbia College (now Columbia University). Throngs of bereaved people brought up the rear of the procession. The nation was devastated.

Pro-Hamilton newspapers fed the public's voracious appetite for the details of Burr's treachery. Many of them concocted lurid stories of Burr drinking toasts with his cronies over Hamilton's death and tales of an ambush. The latter led to the creation of a wax replication of the duel, complete with Burr's alleged henchmen in the bushes. Below the replication was inscribed the following melodramatic verse:

> O Burr, O Burr, what has thou done?
> Thou has shooted dead great Hamilton.
> You hid behind a bunch of thistle,
> And shooted him dead with a great hoss pistol.
> (see J.J. Ellis, *Founding Brothers*, 27)

In the minds of the American people, Burr was essentially finished in politics. Yet within the year Burr disgraced himself even more, causing the public to equivocate his name with the arch-traitor Benedict Arnold (1741–1801). Believing that a war was imminent between the United States and Spain over the boundary between the United States and Mexico, Burr devised a plan to invade Mexico with the intent of setting up an independent government there with himself as its head. It was also rumored that he planned to instigate a secessionist movement in the southwestern territory and annex it to Mexico (which, if it went as planned, would be ruled by Burr). Betrayed by his co-conspirator, U.S. Army General James Wilkinson (1757–1825), Burr was apprehended, arrested, and tried (but acquitted) for treason.

## Political Decorum and Standard of Conduct

A pressing problem confronting the new government was the issue of decorum and conduct of its leadership, especially in a public forum. Americans were temporarily at a loss about how to conduct public affairs, such as a presidential inauguration, or even how to address the head of state, notably the president of the United States. After rejecting and successfully freeing themselves from a monarchy, citizens eschewed the pomp and majestic trappings associated with such, especially citizens in the western territories. Others felt that there should be some remnants of ceremony. Another great debate in a series of ongoing great debates had begun.

One of the most vocal advocates for using titles and incorporating pomp and ceremony in government proceedings was Vice President John Adams. At Adams's prodding, the Senate convened a special committee to resolve the issue of what the proper way to address the president was and to determine what procedures should be followed for the first inauguration. Adams charged this committee with answering such questions as (1) Should the Congress remain seated or should they stand while the president addressed them? (2) Should the Speaker of the House of Representatives be addressed as "Honorable"? and (3) How should

Philadelphia reception for the inauguration of George Washington, April 20, 1789. Courtesy of the Library of Congress.

the president be addressed? Their initial responses to these questions were (1) to remain standing, (2) no, and (3) "His Highness the President of the United States and Protector of their Liberties." The House, when asked to take up the same issues, agreed with the Senate's decision regarding issues one and two but balked at the elaborate formal address for the president. The Senate acquiesced. Therefore, the official address of the president was and is *The President of the United States.*

The resolution of how to address the president set the tone for republican decorum. Despite the objections of Adams and Revolutionary leader Richard Henry Lee (1732–1794), who both truly believed that the employment of titles was the hallmark of civilized behavior (Adams, in fact, petulantly observed that the term "president" made him think of the head of the local fire company), the country adopted a straightforward code of address and decorum echoing that of the ancient Republic of Rome. This is understandable considering how the study of Roman classicism had pervaded the ideology of the governing class (Elkins and McKitrick, 48).

The Roman republic was marked by simplicity in all areas: aesthetics, literature, decorum, and lifestyle. (Like many Americans—notably Jefferson—Romans espoused the agricultural life as promoting the greatest good.) Having thrown off a monarchy, many Americans were eager to discard the trappings associated with king and court. Emulating Roman custom thus suited Americans immensely, but they were concerned about maintaining a balance of virtuous simplicity and dignified decorum.

Martha Washington's reception. Courtesy of the Library of Congress.

President Washington set the standard, which was modified under the Jefferson administration. Very proper and austere in his personal demeanor, Washington struggled with questions of presidential etiquette. He finally decided to set aside time during the day to receive those calling on him with official business, and socially not to accept invitations or hold lavish entertainments. (Dinner parties during the Washington administration were staid, boring affairs.) The president also rejected the more modern greeting of shaking hands (Americans of all classes had avidly embraced this custom as a polite gesture of equality), choosing to greet callers with a small bow. In addition, presidential dress was rigidly prescribed. Washington was always in full dress: velvet suit, powdered hair, cocked hat with appropriate cockade, buckled shoes, and gleaming sword sheathed in a white leather scabbard (a covering for a sword or dagger), although for his inauguration Washington wore a good Republican suit of brown broadcloth, the material a gift from Hartford, Connecticut. John Adams continued the tradition, appearing at his inauguration in a suit of gray broadcloth devoid of knee buckles and elaborate buttons (McCullough, 468). The effect, though, missed the mark. Whereas Washington, with his impressive height (6'3½") and bearing, was a model of Republican simplicity and decorum, Adams, a shorter, portly man (5'7"), simply looked nondescript.

Jefferson broke with the pageantry of his predecessors. Gone was the courtliness and posh ceremony that had punctuated the Federalist administrations. Rather than arriving at his inauguration in an elaborate coach, Jefferson walked to the Capitol to take his oath of office. Not only did Jefferson refuse to strap on the ceremonial sword, he also greeted visitors in threadbare slippers (sans toes) and a well-worn coat. He eschewed riding out in an elaborate coach in the style of Washington and Adams; the third president preferred to ride out on horseback. Many times an appointment to see the president was not necessary. Jefferson was known to greet drop-in visitors as early as eight in the morning wearing the aforementioned tattered slippers. In fact, in a memorandum dated November 1803, Jefferson sparingly outlined the rules of etiquette for the government, stressing "when brought together in society, all are perfectly equal, whether foreign or domestic, titled or untitled, in or out of office" ("Memorandum," 705). The president also encouraged citizens to write to him with comments, complaints, or suggestions. In fact, Jefferson paid the postage upon receipt (thus costing the writer only the pen and ink required to write the letter) and read all letters. Many were supportive. Some blatantly asked for political favors or money. Others were less than laudatory: "Thomas Jefferson, you infernal villun," "The retributive SWORD is suspended over your Head by a slender Thread—BEWARE!" and "Thomas Jefferson you are the damnedest fool that God put life into, God dam you" (qtd. in Johnson, 249).

Jefferson's administration harkened back to the impulse for a more stringent republican simplicity. His successor, James Madison, restored to the presidency more of the form and ceremony that had marked the Washington and Adams administrations. Cannon salutes and a militia escort proclaimed the onset of Madison's inauguration. The fourth president and his remarkable wife Dolley entertained lavishly, but in the grace and style of Virginian hospitality. Fashion and decorum thus had resurged in the later years of the new republic.

## Partisan Politics

At first the United States did not advocate a party system. Indeed, the political impulse was to create a nonpartisan form of government. Political platforms were not considered when determining candidates for the presidency. The sole qualification for president was whether the candidate played a significant role during the Revolution and particularly if it was done at great risk (J.J. Ellis, "First Democrats," 34).

But by the 1790s two political parties had evolved, the Federalists and the Republicans. These were not the same as political parties today. They certainly did not view themselves as having any permanency or that the opposition had any legitimacy (G.S. Wood, *Radicalism*, 298). The Feder-

Political cartoon depicting two forces attempting to pull down the pillars of "federalism" and "democracy." Courtesy of the Library of Congress.

alists viewed themselves as a select group who, because of education and social status, were naturally favored to govern. The Republicans perceived their role as challengers to a group that presented a threat to the republican government. Thus their role was to be transitory. Once the Federalist threat was vanquished, the Republican opposition would no longer be needed. Despite such altruistic intents, both political parties resorted to less than gentlemanly behavior when it came to campaigning for candidates (in the 1800 election, neither Jefferson nor Adams actively campaigned for office—party regulars did the mudslinging). Partisan politics rapidly deteriorated to engaging in gross innuendo and slander of the opposition. Sometimes the political squabbling went beyond a war of words. Sometimes it turned deadly.

## Dueling: The Ultimate "Solution" to Partisan Politics

One of the less than admirable customs that Americans adopted from Europeans was the aristocratic practice of code duello (dueling). Those who had insulted (or what was perceived as having insulted) a gentleman were challenged to a duel on "the field of honor." In the American colonies, dueling was a fairly recent phenomenon. During the war, Europeans who had enlisted in the Continental army brought the practice with them, and afterward Americans quickly embraced the deadly custom. But the impetus for American duels was very different from that for Europeans. In Europe, gentlemen settled quarrels over women and gambling by dueling. Americans, on the other hand, felt that meeting on the field of honor was the most appropriate means for resolving political conflicts. Numerous men needlessly lost their lives by defending partisan politics with pistols. Dueling became so preeminent a solution for political conflict that the dueling ground in Bladensburg, Maryland, was commonly referred to as "The Congressional Dueling Ground."

The most notorious of all duels was the one between Vice President Aaron Burr and Alexander Hamilton on the dueling grounds of Weehawken, New Jersey, in 1804. Although Hamilton found the practice of dueling repugnant, as a man of honor he accepted Burr's challenge. Hamilton, firing first, deliberately missed Burr. By the rules of code duello, Hamilton could not fire again and had to await Burr's shot. Burr carefully aimed and shot the helpless Hamilton in the side, wounding him mortally.

Burr and Hamilton, however, were not the only high-ranking government officials who unwisely chose to settle their political differences by code duello. Andrew Jackson, hero of the Battle of New Orleans (1815) and seventh president of the United States (1829–1837), had the infamous reputation of being a particularly fierce duelist. In 1806, in response to Nashville, Tennessee, lawyer Charles Dickinson's published insult in the *Nashville Review* that Jackson was a "worthless scoundrel," a "poltroon" (a base coward), and "a coward," Jackson met Dickinson on the dueling field, killing his opponent outright. Philip Hamilton, son of Alexander Hamilton, preceded his father in death when three years earlier at Weehawken he lost his life in a duel with a Jeffersonian opponent. Two congressmen, G.W. Campbell of Tennessee and Barent Gardenier of New York, took to dueling pistols to settle their differences (begun on the House floor) over Jefferson's Embargo Act.

Duels over political issues were not limited to politicians. Newspaper editors were frequently challenged to duels (and answered those challenges with pistols cocked and ready). Eleazar Oswald, editor of the *New York Advertiser*, wounded famed Philadelphia publisher Mathew Carey in a duel. New York, in fact, held the dubious distinction of holding the largest number of duels between newspapermen. The most infamous of the journalistic duels occurred in 1808 when John Daly Burk (1776?–1808), a New York editor known for his frank and forceful writings, lost his life on the field of honor, shot through the heart by a duelist known only as Monsieur Coquebert.

Even though many prominent citizens objected to dueling, the custom still persisted into the nineteenth century. In 1802 a congressman from

Virginia proposed the formation of a committee to investigate whether duelists should be disqualified from holding Federal office. The House refused his proposal. The government thus tacitly sanctioned the abhorrent practice despite its moral and ethical ramifications.

## DEFINING A PEOPLE AND A CULTURE

The early nationalist period was indeed a turbulent one, rife with political and social conflicts. The slavery issue was beginning to divide the people who were trying to "create a more perfect Union." The East Coast and the frontier struggled to coexist for the good of the whole. The nation aspired to a higher standard of living even though it was a largely undeveloped society. As the new nation struggled to define itself, it was subjected to uprisings, perceived abuses of power, and international conflicts. The nation also endeavored to create and sustain a government that would "establish Justice, insure domestic Tranquility . . . and promote the general Welfare."

But at the end of the period, the United States was now truly a nation and no longer a political and social experiment. Americans had a national identity and, with it, a sense that theirs was a mission to establish a uniquely American culture. The people of the United States had begun to excel, or already had, in the arts, sciences, recreation, and government—endeavors that are integral parts of a national culture.

# The New Nation

# 2

# World of Youth

From the Revolutionary period onward, America was a land where youth was an integral part of the formation of the republic. With a few exceptions, by today's standards the Founding Fathers were a youthful lot. Jefferson was 33 at the writing of the Declaration of Independence. Hamilton was a mere 22 when he served as Washington's aide-de-camp in the Continental army and 30 when he served at the Constitutional Convention (and authored most of the *Federalist Papers*). The brilliant Madison, primary author of the Bill of Rights, was 36 at the time of the Constitutional Convention. Even Washington, who was affectionately referred to by his troops as "The Old Man," was only 44 when he was appointed commander in chief of the Continental army. The average age of a Constitutional Convention delegate was 43, a significantly young age when one considers that Franklin, at 87, raised the average considerably (Bowen, 4).

But the life expectancy of most Americans was short (except in the New England states where people lived to be quite old). In that context, the Founding Fathers, despite their youthful ages by today's standards, were middle aged. (Many did live much longer than the average, partly because as members of the more privileged classes they had healthier diets and could afford better medical care.) The average life expectancy for Euro-American men and women who lived to be 20 was 45; for African Americans the age dropped to 35 (Appleby, 63).

In the late eighteenth century the death rate had soared owing to the influx of new potentially fatal diseases: yellow fever, cholera, and tuberculosis.[1] All age groups were affected, but these diseases, especially invasive, spread quickly through communities, decimating whole families.

Small children under the age of two were particularly vulnerable to disease and often succumbed, despite the efforts of desperate parents and conscientious physicians. Numerous babies were stillborn or died soon after birth. The highest death rates for the period were for those newborn to two years (ibid., 189).

The high infant mortality rate, due to disease and poor birthing conditions, perceptibly influenced the American attitude toward their children and the country's youth in general. Children were treasured. Letters from the period often express a parent's love and devotion (and, in the case of premature death, desolation). Children played an integral role in the family, first as beloved babies carefully nurtured, then as helpers and companions. As they entered adulthood, this first generation of American citizens significantly contributed to and impacted the national scene.[2]

## CHILDREN AND THE FAMILY

Unequivocally, Americans cherished and protected their children. Families were quite large, out of necessity. Because of high infant mortality rates and the need for labor on the family farm or in the family business, American families needed to reproduce frequently and regularly to maintain the status quo. Within a year after marriage, most wives gave birth to the first of many children, after which they had a subsequent child every two to three years. This pattern continued throughout the marriage. (A family did not stop having children at some predetermined requisite number.) Thus, an eighteenth-century American woman often had dependent children with her up until her death (Norton, 71).[3]

The naming of children was a particularly important decision within the family. Early republican families followed the earlier practice of naming children after parents, grandparents, and other extended family members. Naming established a linear continuity within the family, as a way of perpetuating familial identity (ibid., 86). Even when a child died, often the baby born afterward was given the same name as the deceased. (In some cases a third child would be given the same name as the two siblings whose deaths had preceded its birth.) This did not negate the deceased child's identity within the family unit. Rather the second naming was an attempt to reestablish the name continuity and to assuage the family's feelings of loss.

Although parents knew the chances were high that a child would be stillborn or die within a few weeks of its birth, the loss was still difficult to bear. Even more devastating was the death of an older child. Letters and journal entries of the period record the palpable sorrow and anguish of both republican mothers and fathers over the loss of a child. In 1799 New York lawyer James Kent, reflecting on the death of his eighteen-month-old daughter six years earlier, confessed that "no Event in my

Life had ever before taught me the genuine agonies of Grief. My whole Soul seemed to be buried in my child. . . . I think of the lovely Babe to this Day" (qtd. in ibid., 89). Republican parents' heartache and desolation over the death of a child was lifelong.

A number of children did survive, resulting in families with large numbers of children whose ages spanned from infancy to twenty years and up. But despite being one of many, a child's individuality was not lost within the family unit. From a child's birth, a mother closely bonded with her baby, partly because American mothers had rejected the English practice of hiring wet nurses. The American mother, regardless of class, was committed to nursing her own child.[4] Babies were weaned at the year mark, sometimes gradually, sometimes abruptly.

Weaning did not lessen the emotional ties between mother and child. Mothers continued to forge strong ties with their young. Although the day-to-day responsibilities of child rearing more or less belonged to women, men took an active interest in their children's upbringing and education. Extant correspondence of fathers, whose businesses took them away from the family for lengthy periods, is fraught with paternal pleas to hear every detail of their children's development. Fathers also did not hold back in expressing their longing to see their children. Their letters were emotive when it came to discussing the children (this in an era where husbands addressed letters to their wives as "Dear Mrs.---" and wives to their husbands as "Dear Mr.---").

As toddlers, American children were indulged, sometimes with calamitous results. Children were allowed to explore with little or no intervention by a parent. There are many recorded instances of children falling down wells or cisterns, burning or cutting themselves (the scalding of children who had pulled pots off the fire was quite common), and breaking bones in falls (ibid., 94). Yet parents continued to permit their children to wander and explore on their own. Correspondence between Abigail Adams and Harriet Pinckney Horry reveals that reining in a child's adventurous spirit was not an option, even among the educated classes. Adams and Horry were mothers of spirited toddlers whose antics often resulted in falls. Instead of restraining their children, both mothers devised helmets for their young daughters to protect their heads (ibid., 93).

But the moral training of a child was another matter entirely. Fathers and mothers provided a united front when it came to instilling a sense of duty in their children. Young citizens were not only raised to be virtuous and benevolent, but also dutiful. Children were compliant and respectful; rare was the occasion that a well raised child would act rebelliously. Moreover, a child's obligation to parents and country extended well into adulthood. Elderly or infirm parents were cared for by their children, financially and physically. To do less was considered dishonorable.

American youth also took on more responsibility at an earlier age than their European counterparts. As soon as she was able, a young girl became a valuable helpmeet to her mother and subsequently strong ties were forged between mother and daughter. Elder daughters were actively engaged in raising younger siblings. Accordingly, young girls were considered to be young women by their early teens and were afforded the appellation "Miss" as a courteous form of address. Soon they were expected to marry and have families of their own. Boys entered apprenticeships, became active members of the family business, or labored on the family farm at about the same age. To prepare themselves for their roles as future political, financial, legal, or religious leaders, upper-class young men enrolled at the university. By the time a young man was in his late teens, no matter what his station in life, he had left the confines of his family through marriage, by embarking upon a career, or leaving his birthplace altogether.

The abundance of land lured the young into the territories. Land was cheap and credit easily available. Many saw the new land as a means of making a fortune—especially those whose family holdings were small or nonexistent. Youth who remained in the urban centers also saw opportunity, leaving their families early to pursue jobs in factories and other industries. For the most part, American youth matured early and took on immense responsibilities as they began to enter adulthood. Many had, however, prepared for their journey into the world by acquiring an adequate to excellent education.

## EDUCATION

American schools during the early nationalist period demonstrated the same decided class bias as they had under colonial rule (Nye, *Cultural Life*, 152). American educators also adhered to the same educational philosophy of their colonial forebears; that is, they did not recognize the unique needs of childhood. Instead, children were regarded as undisciplined and undeveloped adults and were treated as such. The purpose then of an American education was to inculcate adult ideas into a child's mind (ibid., 165).

Lower-class children (boys and girls) attended schools that centered on the rudiments of literacy; middle-class boys attended schools that included trade, crafts, and literacy; and upper-class boys attended institutions that provided the education and training of a well-bred English gentleman. In the United States seventeenth-century interest in learning escalated in the eighteenth century, although the educational emphasis of the mid- and upper-classes shifted. As the United States expanded trade and grew industrially, the need was less for a scholarly gentility (reflecting the classical curricula of the seventeenth and early eighteenth centuries) and more for an educated class whose background reflected more utilitarian pursuits.

During the early years of the republic, the "Latin" or "grammar" school (a holdover from a colonial America that emulated the British educational system) was gradually being replaced by the academy as the mainstay for secondary education. Even though they had shortened their plans of study by several years, Latin schools were hopelessly preoccupied with teaching Latin and Greek, subjects that might have met the needs of the university-bound wealthy but not the requirements of an upwardly mobile middle-class young man. Academies prepared both the college-bound and those going into business for success. By 1800 the typical academy provided a well-balanced curriculum: mathematics (algebra, geometry, trigonometry), English, logic, public speaking, surveying, commercial studies, and at least one course in science, either in biology, botany, physics, or geology (ibid., 162). They also offered curricula based on the student's future plans: a four-year, more classically based plan for those headed to the university, a three-year English course of study (as opposed to classical training) for future businessmen and entrepreneurs, and a teacher training course for much needed quality instructors in lower division schools (ibid., 162). In addition, republican America saw the need for formal education for girls and young women as well as boys and young men.[5]

For families who wanted their daughters to receive the advantages of a well-rounded education, female academies (also known as female seminaries) provided a means for the daughters of the wealthy to improve their minds. The preeminent Philadelphia Young Ladies Academy (founded in 1787) offered a curriculum on par with that of male academies, with the exception of not offering classes in the sciences and the classics (both still considered to be the province of men). By 1800 other female academies had sprung up, often founded and administered by women.

There was also a movement for educating all citizens, regardless of class, gender, or economic means. Public figures such as Dr. Benjamin Rush spoke out frequently for the need of a literate and informed electorate. Jefferson, Madison, Noah Webster, Franklin, Jay, and other leaders lent their voices in support of an educated nation. Washington, in his "Farewell Address" to the nation, posed the rhetorical question that

" 'Tis substantially true that virtue or morality is a necessary spring of popular government. . . . Who, that is a sincere friend to it, can look with indifference upon attempts to shake the foundation of the fabric?" and immediately answers that the nation should "[p]romote, then, as an object of primary importance, institutions for the general diffusion of knowledge. In proportion as the structure of a government gives force to public opinion, *it is essential that public opinion be enlightened.*" (425, emphasis added)

This was a tall order for the new republic. The quality of the American educational system was, at best, uneven, usually based on an individual community's means to attract quality teachers and oversee the curriculum. But finding qualified teachers was difficult. The training of teachers was nonexistent. Communities hired whoever was available. Often these were itinerant tutors with little more education than their students. "Dame" schools (schools for younger children taught by impoverished widows or spinsters as a way of eking out a living), another option for educating children, were still in existence. Sometimes the community was fortunate enough to hire a college student or a clergyman. But a community had to be diligent in overseeing the quality of teaching. Unfortunately, school records from the period document that many teachers were alcoholics, sadists, thieves, or virtually unlettered themselves (Nye, *Cultural Life*, 163).

Good teachers were hard to find, but they did exist. Part of the problem was that teaching was an ill-paying and grueling profession, one that offered little degree of respect within the community. As late as 1798, a Connecticut teacher received pay of 67 cents per week, and others did not fare much better. Classes were large and students ranged in age from six to 30 (ibid., 164). Order was difficult to maintain and often a teacher had to resort to corporal punishment. Beatings were inflicted, sometimes with a three-foot club, sometimes with a cat-o'-nine-tails, and in the case of one Massachusetts school, beatings were meted out at the schoolyard whipping post (ibid.).

Luckily, some of the more forward-thinking communities insisted that competent, well educated men teach their young. (Except in dame schools, women did not teach the equivalent of a preparatory school—that is, the eighteenth-century equivalent of high school—until the establishment of the female academy.) In communities where education was considered very important (thus the pay scale was significantly higher than the average), the quality of instruction was quite high. Well educated men (sometimes university men, often young men who had completed the teacher training course at the secondary level) were entrusted with the education of the young in these communities. Educators who did take their profession seriously became involved in a second revolution—a revolution of the American educational system.

At the forefront of the educational revolution was lexicographer Noah Webster (1758–1843). As a young teacher in New York, Webster was frustrated with British-derivative texts. Believing that American children should be taught their own history and culture, he developed distinctly

American educational texts, notably *The American Spelling Book* (1783), an American grammar (1784), a reader (1785), and the *Compendious Dictionary of the English Language* (1806), the preparation for his American dictionary.[6] Webster's efforts promoted the virtues of what he termed "Federal English" (American English) over that of the overly staid and complex British English. (Webster was an early proponent of spelling reform.)

Others, mindful of the American desire for a useful American education, devised new textbooks for the new republic. Although the British Hodder's *Arithmetick* (1719) predominated the market, three uniquely American arithmetic texts were increasingly used. Both Daniel Fenning's *America's Youth Instructor* (1795) and Benjamin Franklin's *American Instructor, or Young Man's Best Companion* (1748) provided more utilitarian advice than the common sum book. Not surprisingly, Franklin's book, in addition to providing chapters on navigation, reading, writing, bookkeeping, surveying, wills, contracts, and medical advice, gave "Prudent Advice to Young Tradesmen and Dealers" (Nye, *Cultural Life*, 158). The most popular of the American arithmetic texts was Nicholas Pike's *Arithmetic* (1788), which, although it offered no explanations for the problems it presented, did include such useful formula as the calculation of measures for beer and ale.

History and geography texts were now included in a single text, the reader. The reader now became a multiple-use text, rather than just a tool to teach reading.[7] *The Franklin Primer* (1802), a commonly used reader, included history geography, hymns, and catechism, as well as readings and spelling lists. Webster also entered the reader market with texts for older children: *Grammatical Institute, American Reader*, and *Reader's Assistant*. But American history was normally not part of the history taught from and read in readers. Not until after the War of 1812 did the citizenry of the Unites States, now imbued with nationalistic spirit, see a need for American history to be part of the American curricula.

Indeed, the new nation was cognizant of the need to educate its citizenry at all levels and to provide an American education, not one derivative of the traditional British system. In particular, higher education responded to the needs of the new nation. The old system that heretofore had excluded all but the upper classes underwent a revolution of its own. Hence, of prime importance during this period was the changing and shaping of the American university system.

## ROLE OF THE UNIVERSITY

Paramount to the formation of leadership (and thus the perpetuation of the republic) was the education and training of the talented elite at the collegiate level. Prior to the Revolutionary War, American colleges and universities were modeled after those of Oxford and Cambridge, with the exception of William and Mary (1643) and the University of Pennsylvania (1755), which followed the Scottish system. American universities soon discovered that the British plan, composed of separate colleges, did not lend itself to distinctly American needs. Thus they were promptly modified into freestanding institutions. British curricula also did not lend itself to American needs. Colonial college students were, by and large, less prepared for a college course of study than British students. Consequently, the American curriculum was radically altered to accommodate the scholastic deficiencies of the American student. By the Revolutionary War, the American university greatly differed in organization and purpose. After the Revolution, universities would undergo an even more thorough transformation.[8]

Post-Revolutionary universities began to move toward secularization. In the past religious denominations that were determined to produce if not clergy at least well educated Christians founded many pre-Revolutionary universities—notably Harvard (founded 1636). But higher education had not kept pace with the temper or the wishes of the new republic. The newly formed United States, unlike the American colonies in the seventeenth century, did not have an urgent need to educate and train clergy. Instead, the United States needed men (women were precluded from higher education) who could assume leadership roles. Furthermore, the republic discovered that it must draw on all of its citizenry, not just the wealthy, and educate them accordingly. As Robert Coram wrote in *Political Inquiries* (1791), the education of young Americans should "not be left to the caprice, or negligence of parents, to chance, or confined to the children of wealthy citizens; it is a shame, a scandal to civilized society, that part only of the citizens should be sent to colleges and universities" (qtd. in Nye, *Cultural Life*, 175).

States began to charter secular universities that were devised to educate those with promise, not just money. Within a 17-year period, 14 universities had been chartered with the purpose of preparing capable citizens for leadership: Transylvania (Kentucky), 1783; Dickinson (Pennsylvania), 1783; St. John's (Maryland), 1784; Charleston (South Carolina), 1785; Georgia, 1785; Franklin (Pennsylvania), 1787; North Carolina, 1789; Vermont, 1791; Williams (Massachusetts), 1793; Bowdoin (Massachusetts, now Maine), 1794; Greenville (Tennessee), 1794; Blount (Tennessee), 1794; Union (New York), 1795; and Middlebury (Vermont), 1800. Even though American universities suffered great financial hardship (many were on the brink of bankruptcy, others did go under), they grew at an accelerated rate to meet the needs of the citizenry.

Collegiate life was rigorous and strict. Students were held to a stringent regimen of classes, study, some recreation, prayers and services (depending on the university), and rising and retiring times. University administrators deemed that higher education should discipline the mind, provide moral guidance, and focus less on scholarship and more on ethical or religious learning (ibid., 185). The behavior of students was closely watched, and punishment for transgressions against the rules was assiduously carried out. Faculty carried the additional burden of checking up on students after classes had been dismissed for the day. Young collegians were expected to conduct themselves as gentlemen. This meant that dancing, drinking, fighting, gambling, fornicating, and general rowdiness was forbidden. Malefactors were fined according to the severity of their transgression. For instance, at Union College, missing chapel was assessed three cents and drunkenness three dollars while at Harvard (in puritanical Massachusetts) theatergoers were assessed a three-dollar fine (ibid., 186).

Still, undergraduates engaged in unseemly mischief as a way of relieving the tension of an austere lifestyle and a demanding curriculum. Usually the penalty was a fine, but in the case of more egregious transgressions the offender could be subject to suspension or even expulsion. For the most part, transgressions were minor. Unfortunately, on a few occasions mischief escalated into violent behavior: rioting (Princeton, 1807), shooting guns out of windows (North Carolina), and horsewhipping of faculty (Virginia).

These incidents and their perpetrators were in the minority. Young men at the university generally worked hard and long at their studies. Young Americans, like their parents, were driven by the belief in upward mobility based on effort and a desire to make a substantial contribution to American society. Scholastic success often ensured the collegian success in his chosen life's work.

Education was, however, not the only concern of American youth. Most young men and women were concerned with matters of the heart. Courtship and marriage were of utmost importance, since "making a good marriage" could be advantageous to one's social status (particularly in the case of women) and personal happiness. In a republic founded on virtue, premarital behavior was highly scrutinized by society in general.

## COURTSHIP AND MARRIAGE

### Courtship and the Moral Code

Citizens of the new nation were greatly concerned with issues of sex (especially premarital). Courtship practices throughout the country varied from region to region, partly owing to divergent historical attitudes regarding sexual mores. Despite divergent practice, republican parents

unilaterally agreed that their children—especially their daughters—
should remain chaste until married. Young women who engaged in dalliances or allowed young men to take "untoward" liberties soon developed reputations as "bad girls," thus severely limiting their chances of
making a good marriage. Young men who engaged in premarital sex
were not subject to societal sanctions, unless their behavior became egre-
giously unacceptable. The eighteenth-century rake (so fashionable in Europe) was not admired in American society.

Daughters of the gentility went to great pains to keep the ardor of
their suitors in check, probably because they, more than young women
of any other class, knew that reputation was everything, that not to maintain an unsullied reputation was to risk one's future. This does not mean
that young gentlemen of the period refrained from making untoward
advances. (They did.) The duty of restraint was, however, placed on the
woman, not the man (Norton, 53).

Lower-class women were held to the same strict moral code as their
more genteel sisters, but their suitors were often more persistent than
their aristocratic counterparts (since the moral code—that is, as it per-
tained to gentlemanly behavior—was not instilled as often in the upbringing of lower-class men and boys). Proper young women fended off
advances, remaining pure and thus marriageable. Unfortunately, there
are documented cases of young women who were not successful, suc-
cumbing to passion and thus finding themselves in jeopardy. Women
abandoned by deceitful suitors were left with the stigma of bearing a
child out of wedlock, incurring the harsh moral judgment of society no
matter what their social class.

Women who bore children out of wedlock not only ruined their own
reputations and chances of marriage, but also those of their female relatives. Sisters and cousins of "fallen women" found their chances of making an honorable marriage severely diminished. Americans, on the
whole, were a morally unforgiving people. Only the luckiest of women
in this situation were able to find a spouse willing to disregard her
youthful indiscretions and accept her child into the family. But more
often than not, family and community rejected women who found themselves in such circumstances.

This is not to say that premarital conceptions were low. Immediate
marriage often was the solution to the predicament. Men of the middle
to upper classes were more likely than men of lower social standing to
marry their sweethearts if a child was on the way. Although these "premature births" raised some eyebrows, eventually the community accepted the couple as a respectable addition to the community. (The
family had, in any event, been legally sanctioned.) Moreover, the New
England practice of "bundling," a remarkable practice born out of Yankee frugality and utility, transcended societal disapproval and censure

because there was a tacit understanding that a bundling couple might engage in premarital relations, hastening the marriage date.

## Bundling

Bundling had been a long-established practice in the North by the lower classes. New Englanders, being by nature a people who prided themselves on their hospitality, were hesitant to send a visitor out into the cold on a winter night. Since most households had limited beds (sometimes only one), the visitor would be offered what bed space was available, often sharing a bed with the host or hostess. Because courtship time was at a premium (evening was short because often fires were doused and candles were snuffed early as an economic measure), the suitor was allowed to share a bed—fully clothed—with the object of his affection. And because of this the suitor was apt to call on a young woman more often if he knew that he would not have to return home, after a short visit, through the harsh New England winter at night. Thus the couple was bundled together, sometimes under the watchful eye of the young woman's parents—and sometimes not.

By the late eighteenth century, bundling was, in theory, abolished along the East Coast, but in reality was still practiced as "tarrying" (Calhoun, vol. 1, 130). Never was it collectively condoned, but poor families did tolerate it. (Clergy often decried the practice, but New Englanders persisted in bundling despite ecclesiastical opposition.) This is not to say that all young New Englanders resisted the temptation that bundling offered. Recent historical research has revealed that not only were there New England cases of premarital sex and births occurring in less than nine months after marriage, but that in some villages one-third of brides were pregnant at the time of their marriage (Norton, 55). Such high numbers of premarital pregnancies (which undoubtedly caused some societal concern) did not stop the practice. After the war in many parts of New England it was still accepted as customary, and the practice was well-known throughout the country.

In fact, the custom of bundling was even broached in popular entertainment. Royall Tyler's (1757–1826) play *The Contrast* (1787), the first successful play written by an American and performed for American audiences, references bundling as a preferable courtship ritual to the European archness and coquetry that was beginning to creep into American society. (One of the themes of *The Contrast* is the distinction between the artificiality of European conventions with the more sensible, honest—yet less fashionable—American practices.) The rustic character Jonathan, who simultaneously serves as comic relief and the voice of loyalty and morality in the play, is befuddled by the continual romantic game playing of New York society. He longs for "twenty acres of rock, the Bible, the cow, and Tabitha [his New England sweetheart], and a little peaceable bundling" (*The Contrast*, 38). In *The Contrast* bundling is presented as a far more honorable American custom than the games of seduction played by Jonathan's British foil (whose antics revealed an exploitive and disrespectful regard of American women). Jonathan's plaintive musing resonates with a truthful simplicity that conveys the practical intimacy bundling afforded a young couple with little time and means to get to know each other before the ultimate step: marriage.

## Marriage

The Colonial American custom of marrying young persisted into and throughout the early nationalist period. In a land of opportunity and promise of expansion, young people were less likely to be concerned with establishing a place in society before marriage. Therefore, Americans married at a significantly younger age than their European counterparts. Franklin observed, as early as 1773, that "new Settlers in America, finding plenty of Subsistence, and Land easily acquired whereon to seat their Children, seldom postpone Marriage thro' fear of Poverty" ("Proposed Act," 708). Men and women usually married before the age of 22, and, in some areas, even younger. For instance, daughters of wealthy Charleston, South Carolina, families married between 16 and 18, Kentucky frontiersmen between 18 and 20, their brides at 14 to 16 (Calhoun, vol. 2, 14).

Those on the frontier had a particularly relaxed attitude toward the bonds of matrimony. Many frontier couples opted to live together before marriage—mainly because clergy was scarce. Couples had to either wait months for a circuit-rider clergyman to arrive, live without the benefit of clergy altogether, or enter a "left-handed marriage" (one officiated by dubious justices of the peace, army officers, or even the bride's father) (Nye, *Cultural Life*, 139). In the more densely populated areas, people rigidly adhered to convention. Clergy or legitimate public officials conducted marriages. Left-handed marriages were rare in these areas.

Overall, young couples in late eighteenth-century America exercised more free will when it came to choosing a mate than their parents and grandparents had. Younger sons and daughters could now enter into marriage without waiting until all older siblings had married. More than ever, young people married whom they wanted when they wanted. Parents no longer arranged their daughters' marriages. (Even before the Revolution, young women could and did decline their parents' choices. Arranged marriages were never popular with British Colonial America, attesting to an independent spirit that was intrinsically American from the beginning.) Though women did not actively choose their mates (decorum dictated that the man proffer marriage), they ultimately did reject or accept marriage offers on their own. Of course, daughters were still, in some cases, influenced by parental opinion. John Adams's daughter Abigail ("Nabby"), though ardently courted by aspiring lawyer (and dramatist) Royall Tyler, yielded to her father's tacit disapproval. (Adams regarded Tyler—wrongly—as a rake and a libertine.) Sensitive to her father's disapproval, Nabby discouraged Tyler and eventually chose her father's secretary, William Stephen Smith.[9]

The attitudes of republican youth concerning marriage differed from those of earlier generations. Marriage was no longer viewed as hierarchical; that is, the husband served as the head of the family, the wife subordinate to his dictates. Instead, couples entered marriage believing that it should be companionate; that is, founded on friendship, mutual respect, affection, commitment, and sympathy (Woloch, 54). Thus a marriage was expected to reflect the more egalitarian principles of republican society. Although the companionate marriage paradigm was more prevalent among moneyed city dwellers, even in more remote areas the idea of a less authoritatively structured marriage found favor. Brides chose husbands not because they felt pressured into being married, but because a companionate marriage would provide them with a life of happiness.

Yet republican marriages, albeit based on mutual love, respect, and faith, were marked by deference to the husband. Parents raised daughters to be agreeable to male opinion. Even Jefferson, whose views toward the behavior and role of women were more open-minded than most, counseled his elder daughter Martha that "the happiness of your life depends now [referring to her upcoming marriage to her second cousin, Thomas Mann Randolph] on continuing to please a single person" (qtd. in ibid., 55). The success of the companionate marriage was based on accord that stemmed from female deference.

Although some young people chose to remain single, the majority chose marriage and family. Marriage offered emotional, social, and financial stability in an unsure and chaotic time. For women a companionate marriage assured her a respected place in the family. Unlike her mothers and grandmothers, a young wife was regarded as a partner whose loving efforts increased a marriage's felicity. For men marriage was an "indispensable Duty" to society (Norton, 43). But for young husbands and wives, marriage was the foundation on which to build a family and a place in society. There was, however, one significant group of persons denied legal marital status and thus protection under the law: slaves.

## Slave Marriages

Denied legal sanction, enslaved couples did, nonetheless, forge deep emotional bonds that culminated in marriage ceremonies of their own design. Like White couples, slave couples often sought approval to marry from members of their own population, especially those who were highly regarded within the group (Appleby, 177). But unlike White couples, betrothed slaves were prohibited from forming marriages on their own. Slaves had to receive the permission of the master to marry, even though the marriage would not be recognized under law. In cases in which the slaves had a more amiable relationship with the master, the master often participated in the slave wedding ceremony, thereby reinforcing the master's approval of the union.

While many slave marriages were intra-plantational, some were between couples from neighboring plantations. Less often (but still occurring), a slave might be united in marriage with a free Black, although these were certainly not met with the same approval as a marriage between two slaves would have been. In due course slave owners discouraged slave marriages between slaves of different plantations and between slaves and free persons. Shrewd slave owners preferred slave marriages within their plantation because children born from the match would automatically become their property. (In marriages in which the partners were from different plantations, the resulting children became the property of the owner of the mother.) The result was that the slave community on large plantations became a great and complex extended family of mothers, fathers, cousins, uncles, aunts, and so on (ibid., 178).

## YOUTH'S PLACE IN THE NEW NATION

From birth through young adulthood, the first generation of American citizens was determined to leave its mark on the American scene. Cherished from infancy, raised as forthright individuals, young Americans viewed their role as guardians and perpetuators of a new world order. American youth, for the first time in history, exercised more choices: in education, in profession and career, and in marriage. A new nation had begun to stretch across the North American continent, and youth embraced the opportunity that a republican government afforded and the promise that western expansion held.

# Part Two

# Popular Culture of the New Nation

# 3

# Advertising

In many ways advertising chronicles the development of a national culture. The type and amount of advertising employed within a community has a direct correlation to its cultural mindset, which is its bedrock beliefs and values system. By looking at how goods and services were advertised, to whom they were advertised, and what was being advertised, one can surmise what was important to the people and why it was important, especially when looking at the early republican era.

Advertising had been an integral part of American culture since the 1600s when enterprising shopkeepers had hung eye-catching signs above their shop doors. Post offices and courthouse walls had been bedecked with posters and broadsides (large handbills) as early as 1660 (Goodrum and Dalyrymple, 13). Colonists had been advertising their services and wares in newspapers since the early eighteenth century. Well designed signs for inns and taverns were prevalent in both town and country. Sometimes the best advertising was simply by word of mouth. All in all, Americans promoted their products and services regularly.

## ADVERTISING IN THE NEW REPUBLIC: HOW
## GOODS AND SERVICES WERE ADVERTISED

Advertising in the early years of the nation was limited to local, rather than national, coverage. Although a nation, communication among the states was difficult, largely due to the almost primitive system of transportation. Thus, what news (and thereby advertising) there was was conveyed only locally.[1] Because of this, advertisers had to target their goods and services to those in the immediate vicinity. In the late eighteenth and early nineteenth centuries, the means for advertising had changed little from those used one hundred years before: newspapers, magazines, broadsides and handbills, and signs.

## Newspapers

By the end of the Revolution, the United States could boast 43 weekly newspapers and one daily. By 1790 there were 106 newspapers; in 1800 there were 260. Obviously, newspapers thrived under the new republican government. Often they were the only means of conveying news and items of importance to the community, no matter how insignificant these events might have been perceived. Newspaper advertising had a decided advantage over other forms of advertising. Principally, newspapers had healthy subscription lists and reached a wide variety of people. Thus, by advertising, merchants and others could reach a fairly large, diverse audience on at least a weekly basis.

Newspaper advertising had flourished in the colonies. Consequently, the practice of promoting one's goods in newspapers had been firmly ensconced in American life. Moreover, the story of newspaper advertising in the United States can be traced back to Benjamin Franklin. Franklin was, without a doubt, a gifted and clever promoter, a skill he unabashedly employed when advertising others' and his own services and wares. When he took over the *Pennsylvania Gazette* in 1729, the masthead he used revealed his interest in advertising over journalism; it boldly proclaimed that the newspaper was published in "Philadelphia: Printed by B. Franklin and H. Meredith at the New Printing Office near the Market, *where Advertisements are taken in*, and all Persons may be supplied with this paper for Ten Shillings a Year" (qtd. in J.P. Wood, 46; emphasis added).

The *Pennsylvania Gazette* rapidly obtained the largest circulation and the largest volume of advertisers. The *Gazette*'s advertising columns revealed that Franklin advertised everything: notices about runaway servants and slaves, goods of all sorts (especially those for sale in his own shop), schedules of ship sailings, and other sundry items (ibid., 48–49). Furthermore, Franklin stressed not only the functional features of a product, but also what pleasure and ease it might give to the consumer (Williamson, 4–5).

Franklin and his imitators were able to compose and print wonderfully clear and powerful newspaper ads partly because of the quality of the paper available at the time. All paper in the eighteenth century was 100 percent rag content. Rag paper is extremely durable, strong, and, most important, takes ink excellently. The quality of rag paper allowed the publisher to print high contrast advertisements, almost guaranteed to attract the eye of the most obdurate potential customer. Publishers, such as Franklin, were able to produce ads that made use of the contrast between ample white space and the rich blackness of the print.

Unfortunately, owing to economic necessity, by the early nationalist period the arresting advertisements of Franklin's heyday had disappeared. Papermaking in the eighteenth century was an especially costly and time-consuming process. Until the early years of the nineteenth century, paper was produced one sheet at a time.[2] Normally, it would take three laborers an entire day to produce enough paper for one day's press run for the local newspaper.

Not only was papermaking a protracted process, but also the availability of material presented severe problems. In pre-Revolutionary America, the rags used in the making of paper were imported mainly from England. (The colonists, ever utilitarian, preferred to use their rags for making quilts and braiding into rugs.) By the time these items were no longer of use (that is, they had deteriorated) and would be sold to paper manufacturers, years had passed, thus delaying the papermaking process. After the war, the rag supply from England was acutely cut back. Paper, which was needed for books, documents, currency, writing material, and newspapers, was at a premium.

Franklin was concerned about the American paper shortage and successfully led a movement to organize mills for the express purpose of manufacturing paper. Once this was done, others launched extensive publicity campaigns to induce citizens to save rags (Train, 255). Enterprising door-to-door peddlers often traded hardware for rags, which they later resold by the pound to paper mills. These combined efforts helped to alleviate the paper shortage, but the availability of enough paper to serve American needs remained a problem throughout the early years of the nineteenth century.

Accordingly, when it came to advertising, newspaper publishers had to forgo the aesthetics established by Franklin and conserve space. Gone were the large blocks of white space, centered headlines, and large font sizes. Prior to 1789, newspapers had used twelve-point Caslon type. But because of the paper shortage, for the next 70 years they used a six-point font (Goodrum and Dalyrymple, 16). Consequently, copy was not easy to read. In addition, publishers considered it more impressive to run many short ads rather than fewer long ones. This made reading advertising copy even more of a challenge. Because there was little break between copy and any sort of distinguishing type style or size, the ads tended to blend together. Very few ads stood out at first glance. Readers were forced to read through most of the ads to find one of particular interest. For this reason the emphasis in newspaper advertising shifted from garnering attention to developing content.

Despite the paper shortage, American advertising in newspapers increased significantly during the last two decades of the eighteenth century (Mott, *American Journalism*, 157). Publishers' response to the demand for advertising (which, of course, was very much in their own financial self-interest) was to revert to single-column measure. The unit of space measurement at this time was twelve lines, called a "square." At three shillings per square at the first running (two for the second), advertising was quite lucrative for the publishing industry, despite the expense of paper. Some papers, such as the New York *Argus* and the Philadelphia *Aurora*, dedicated more than half their total space to advertising. Daily newspapers dedicated the entire front page—with the exception of one column for news items—to advertisements. Even when papers issued extra editions for important breaking stories, these were filled with advertising as well. In the early nineteenth century, mercantile papers (newspapers aimed at the merchant class) would sell from four-fifths to nine-tenths of their space to advertisers (ibid., 200).

## Magazines

Unlike the ads published in newspapers, advertising in the magazines of the day was discreet. Magazines during this period did not have a specific focus or content. They were a mixture of essays on a variety of subjects—such as agriculture, science, morality, and the arts—and venues for aspiring poets and writers of novels and fiction. Usually ads were placed on the front and back covers, occasionally on the text pages. On the whole, most magazine publishers felt that advertisements should be restricted to the covers (Mott, *History of American Magazines*, 34). In the 1790s the well respected *Massachusetts Magazine* began the trend of printing double covers. Double covers permitted the publisher to include up to seven pages of advertising without interrupting the flow of the text.

## Broadsides and Handbills

Another quick means of advertising was the use of broadsides and handbills. Broadsides were the width of a newspaper, but twice the length. (Newspapers were much smaller than they are today. For example, the *New York Sun* measured 9" × 12".) As a consequence, there was more space available for copy, copy that would not compete with other ads found in newspaper and magazine columns.

Broadsides had many advantages over newspaper and magazine ads. First, they were easy to post. Advertisers would have a set run of broadsides, which allowed them to hang the broadsides almost everywhere in the public view. One particularly effective use of the posting of broadsides was the practice of hanging them in bunches by stagecoach doors and river packets. Bored travelers would pluck off the copies and use them as reading material on long, fatiguing journeys. Second, the size of the broadside presented the advertiser with a means to present wares and services in an aesthetically pleasing manner. Not limited by tiny columns and one small, standardized font size and type, broadsides employed a wide variety of type, borders, and graphics, a return to the style of advertising advocated by Franklin. Third, on a broadside a merchant, for example, could offer a detailed inventory of his store's stock. Many broadsides of the period are characterized by long lists of goods and services or carefully rendered woodcut illustrations, or both. Because of their portability and creative approaches, broadsides and handbills proved to be a most effective way of marketing.

A more specialized type of handbill was the "tradesman's card" or "trade card." The name is a misnomer because the trade card was not a card at all but a sheet of paper. Trade cards publicized the place of business, its owner's name, and the goods that were offered there. Most featured elaborate and impressive copper engravings or woodcuts (some reproduced the sign of the shop). Trade cards were more of an announcement than the type of advertisement found on broadsides and handbills. (For example, a broadside for a dry goods seller might list all the types of textiles available for purchase at the store. A trade card would announce the proprietor's name, address, a brief description of the business, and perhaps a woodcut illustration.) Such diverse professions as surgeons, tailors, dancing masters, booksellers, gunsmiths, wigmakers, chandlers, coopers, and dentists, as well as others, relied on trade cards as a means of advertising their existence. The advantage of trade cards (like broadsides) provided the advertisers with the means of advertising their establishments to a large clientele without having to compete with other advertisers on the same page or in the same column.

## Sign Painting

From colonial times, Americans had adopted the European custom of hanging distinctive wooden signs over their places of business. Especially important in European signs was the employment of graphics, a medieval holdover. (During the Middle Ages very few people could read. Hence, pictures were very important in signage.) Unlike medieval Europe, late eighteenth-century America was a highly literate country, but Americans held fast to the European tradition of using pictures in their signs.

Many times signs for inns and taverns were painted by prominent American artists of the day. Gilbert Stuart, renowned for his portraits of Washington, is known to have painted the sign for the King of Prussia Inn in Pennsylvania; and Matthew Pratt, a student of the famed artist and teacher Benjamin West, painted several signs as well (Lathrop, 168).

Less-gifted American portraitists supplemented their incomes substantially by painting signs for merchants, chandlers, and innkeepers. The end result was a colorful marketplace in town and country, artfully rendered and imaginatively presented.

American signs adhered to the medieval use of large graphics and little wordage. Particularly popular was the use of animals and birds (such as the federal eagle) in republican signs, a clever means of advertising one's wares and one's patriotism. Other signs used the medieval symbols associated with one's business, such as the bookbinder's Bible and a dove, the weaver's spinning wheel, or the pawnbroker's three golden balls.[3] Americans also loved to incorporate vivid color in their signs, so much so that Philadelphia, then the largest city, was awash in color, more than any European city. Subsequently, the American marketplace was one that was vibrant and dynamic.

## ADVERTISING IN THE NEW REPUBLIC: WHO WAS THE AUDIENCE?

A captive audience distinguished the advertising employed during the early republican era; that is, since there was a dearth of goods and materials, there was a ready-made market for whatever one would be selling. As a largely agrarian nation, most Americans made, grew, or traded for what they needed. What they could not make or grow was highly prized. Popular salable items included staples such as coffee, tea, and salt and other necessities such as tools and hardware.

The main problem facing the American marketplace was that those of modest means did not have the cash to purchase items. Farmers usually traded their surplus. Those who labored were paid in room and board, with a very small cash stipend. As a result, Americans did not earn a living; they made a living (Goodrum and Dalyrymple, 17). This presented a problem in the marketplace. Limited cash flow might have meant limited sales, but advertisers were adaptable. At the bottom of many newspaper ads and broadsides, the seller would make known, "We will sell low for cash or *country produce*" (ibid., emphasis added).

Shopkeepers (those selling fine wares) directed their ads at those of affluence and status because these people would be interested in purchasing more luxurious items. The focus of these ads, however, revealed the subtle shift in national attitude and the growing national pride. Prior to the Revolution, merchants would take out lengthy advertisements and compose elaborate broadsides that notified potential customers that the most fashionable imported items had just arrived from England, Holland, and the Far East (Williamson, 5). The key phrases here are "just arrived" and "imported." As colonists, Americans identified and valued the European over the domestic.

After the war, Americans, conscious of their new identity, began to choose American goods over European goods. It was considered unpatriotic to prefer foreign goods to American ones. Not only was buying imported goods construed as a lack of support of American industry, but it also perpetuated the assumption that anything European was superior to American. The country's leaders did what they could to aid this movement to buy American. George Washington, whose sartorial splendor was well-known, began to insist that his clothes be made from American-made materials. Other presidents followed his example. The strategy worked. Before long the key phrase in advertisements was "American-made," rather than "imported." A true patriot wore American-made clothes and purchased American-made goods.

## ADVERTISING IN THE NEW REPUBLIC: WHAT WAS BEING ADVERTISED

Despite the media employed, the state of advertising in the new republic was lackluster (ibid.). Most of the advertisements were for goods, services, lost items, western land holdings for sale, and slave auctions. A significant number of ads were rewards for runaways [indentured servants, slaves, wives, etc.] and real estate notices (Fowler, 31). Ship and stagecoach schedules were regularly advertised, as well as descriptions of cargoes arriving in port. Frequently, ads appeared that related to the growing publishing industry: pressmen, apprentices, and rags to be made into paper. The only types of ads conspicuously missing at this time were "personal" ads. These did not appear until the 1830s and were created by James Gordon Bennett, founder of *The New York Herald*. During the early nationalist period Americans were more concerned about making money or expressing political views than addressing affairs of the heart and other matters commonly found in the personal columns.

In the earlier years of the new nation, most ads were notices of what was available for purchase or what someone would like to purchase. Sometimes ads announced particular ceremonies or events that would be of interest to the public. Always included were ads offering rewards for lost or stolen goods, for the apprehension of thieves, and for runaway indentured servants, slaves, and family members. Reward ads were usually very detailed, especially in the case of runaway slaves.[4]

This was also the time when companies that would establish a long and prosperous advertising history began openly to market their wares. In 1789 Peter and George Lorillard advertised their tobacco wares in the *New York Daily Advertiser*.[5] Tobacco, like patent medicines, was often advertised for its curative properties. (Smoking was viewed as not only a pleasurable experience, but also one that extended one's life span.) In

1801, Crane & Company, which eventually produced the paper used for currency and treasury bonds by the United States Treasury, advertised plans for establishing a paper mill in Dalton, Massachusetts. In 1817 the William Colgate Company actively began to advertise their soaps and candles. (This is the same Colgate that today produces soaps and other sundry items.)

Occasionally an ad would appear directed at delinquent clients and patrons (a common problem). Some were caustic in tone; others reflected a more sensitive approach to dunning wayward clients. Americans were, from the start, forthright and plainspoken in their attitude toward business matters. But not all advertising was of mercantile or commercial concerns. From time to time an unusual announcement might appear, proclaiming the exhibition of a so-called natural marvel. Exotic animals such as lions, baboons, camels, moose, and cassowaries (large birds found in the East Indies) were exhibited for a price to a curious public. One of the most "miraculous" finds was advertised in the May 4, 1798, *Salem Gazette*: a "Pig of Knowledge." This porcine wonder was advertised as being able to read, spell, tell time and the date, distinguish colors, count, do arithmetic, and "any Lady or Gentleman may draw a card from a pack, and keep it concealed, and the PIG without hesitation will discover the card when drawn" (qtd. in J.P. Wood, 63). The price of admission was a quarter for adults, half of that for children. The Pig of Knowledge exhibition targeted a respectable audience, because the concert hall used was also advertised as having "strict attention paid to keep the place fit for the reception of Ladies."

A few newspaper ads were designed not to solicit business but to make a social statement. A rather lengthy (thus costly) ad in the *Providence Gazette* dated October 14, 1796, addressed the issue of the laxity in manners and effort of domestic servants of the community. Signed by "HOUSEHOLDERS," the ad offered a $500 reward for any person who could "restore . . . that degree of Honesty and Industry, which has been for some time missing" (qtd. in ibid., 65). Outlined in this very satiric ad were the improper behaviors Providence matrons had to contend with from their help: gossiping, "leering and hankering after persons of the other sex," stealing, constantly demanding higher wages, and having "an impudent appearance." The men of the new republic were no less shy about voicing their opinions than the women. Particularly in the New England and the Mid-Atlantic states, advertisements were a means for a citizen to proclaim his political and social beliefs. Regrettably, the advertising of political perspectives degenerated into a reprehensible advertising practice, that of "posting."

In the early years of the nation's capital, outraged politicos who perceived that they had been affronted by a political opponent's charges would "post" insulting notices in handbills and broadsides throughout the city. At first the insults were posted at taverns and other popular meeting places. Soon newspaper publishers saw the perverse advantage of selling advertising space for postings. (First, it was lucrative, and second, the postings themselves generated public interest.) Many postings resulted in deadly political duels—which was usually the poster's intent. The first recorded instance of a posting and its consequence was in 1804 when General James Wilkinson challenged Congressman John Randolph to a duel, which Randolph declined (Appleby, 42). Thwarted in his desire to meet Randolph on the field of honor, Wilkinson posted insults directed at Randolph all over Washington. Wilkinson's tactics soon became a favorite means of hurling invectives. Infuriated congressmen and newspaper editors alike engaged in postings, and many duels were the result.

Postings were essentially a nineteenth-century phenomenon and symptomatic of the devolution of advertising in the United States at that time. Aside from such incredible assertions as listed in the advertisement for the Pig of Knowledge, during the late eighteenth century advertisers were fairly responsible in their claims. But in the nineteenth century, the tone and content of American advertising had changed dramatically. In their zeal to sell at all costs, American advertisers (like their British counterparts) were less than truthful in their claims (Bauer and Greyser, 5). Like politicians, commercial advertisers began to attack their competitors ruthlessly, another reflection on the irresponsible journalistic practices that had invaded the news and editorial pages of the time.

Heretofore unheard of in the eighteenth century, in the nineteenth century, the latest "wonder drugs" and "miracle cures" made their appearance in advertisements. These types of spurious claims would later plague advertising throughout the nineteenth century when truth in advertising was merely an idealistic notion, not a legal mandate. In 1809 the ads of the ubiquitous "Dr. Robertson" (an early patent medicine man) began to overrun the advertising space of newspapers.[6] In the June 5, 1809, issue of the *Political and Commercial Register* (Philadelphia), the good doctor listed in a column the various ailments his nostrum had cured; among these were cures for colds, flux [diarrhea], asthma, consumption, stomach pain, influenza, worms, gout, rheumatism, stomach pain, and deep decline (J.P. Wood, 92). To validate his claims, Dr. Robertson included the names of those "cured" of these debilitating ills. (Not surprisingly, the names of the cured were rather mundane: "Mrs. Brown," "Captain Walker," "Mr. Oliver.") Other swindlers and charlatans followed Robertson's example. Advertising had now become big business, and a fertile ground for fleecing and mendacity.

Essentially, advertising in the new nation was born out of necessity but grew out of forces that were in direct contrast to the American republican ideals of virtue and rationality. Americans advertised to inform potential customers of the goods and services that were available to them, often offering accommodations for payment. Whether the subject of the advertisement was goods that were essentials that the average American could not make or grow or forms of entertainment that ranged from high cultural events (lectures, concerts, theatrical productions) to exhibitions of a Pig of Knowledge or an East Indian cassowary, the language and content of American ads were straightforward and resolute. Up until the early 1800s, American advertising (no matter how distressing the topic might be to twenty-first-century audiences) was characterized by an almost purity of content. With the appearance of the patent nostrums, however, advertising rapidly became reprehensible and absurd, demonstrating the shift in the ideals of early republican society to those of the era of western expansionism.

# 4

# Architecture

The end of the Revolutionary War furnished the new nation with more cultural opportunities than just the important formation of a new government. Political ideology would also dominate the question of what the nation would look like culturally, especially when we survey the architecture of the period. Americans could not agree on what type of republic the nation should be, or what architectural style would reflect the new republican culture.

The educated elite (such Constitutional framers as John Adams and Thomas Jefferson) felt that the American republic would be best based on the republics of ancient Greek and Rome. Rule was to be by the "best men" (Jefferson's "natural aristocracy"), those whose talent, knowledge, and intellect, rather than lineage, made them the most fit to govern. The rising mercantile class, on the other hand, believed that the strength of the republic would come from its accumulation of wealth, expanding on economist Adam Smith's idea of "enlightened self-interest." This notion particularly appealed to Americans who ascribed to the work ethic of Puritan America: the idea that wealth acquired by diligence and hard work was a sign of God's Providence. Finally, the more populist view of the followers of Thomas Paine held that the government should comprise the widest electorate, resulting in a general engagement especially at the local level.

Disparate as these three groups may seem, all converged on a single issue: that America should be a republic of virtue. Taking their ideological cue from the Enlightenment movement and their Puritan legacy, Americans saw themselves as creating a new society. Just as the Puritans had envisioned themselves as architects of a metaphoric "City on the

Hill," that is, as creators of a new, uncorrupted society that would serve as a beacon to Europe (a society that they regarded as immoral and base), Americans would become the architects of a society in which the ills of European society would not exist.

In order to create a new republican order, the new society required new buildings to house its citizens and its institutions. For that reason, a national architectural style quickly became of great concern. Americans from all three groups of thought presupposed that in architecture they could physically convey their belief in their new, virtuous republican society. Buildings, therefore, would reflect the republican order, signaling the beginnings of an American culture.

The existing state and local government buildings were quickly deemed inadequate. Moreover, buildings were now needed at the national governmental level. Hence, within the early nationalist period, the United States experienced a phenomenal growth in building—and the desire for an "American" style of architecture.

Colonial Americans had always been rapidly building, primarily because of a burgeoning population (and one that was also transitory). Early colonists required immediate shelter. Colonial shelters, though, were not intended to be permanent. As colonial fortunes grew, earlier buildings were razed and new, more elaborate ones were erected in their stead.

Colonists were able to build and rebuild because building supplies were plentiful—far more plentiful than they had been in England. Heavy forestation on the North American continent provided builders with more than adequate material. This plentiful wood supply allowed the colonists to build rapidly and frequently. And because of its lightness, wood offered more versatility in design and implementation than the traditional European materials of brick and stone. Such flexibility provided colonial builders with the opportunity to experiment with architectural style, allowing them to depart from the tradition of massiveness (a hallmark of European masonry), creating structures that were characterized by detail and spaciousness. Wood construction enabled craftsmen and carpenters to hone their respective skills.

During this time, there was no need for professional architects. Colonial builders followed the plans of earlier, established British architects, such as Inigo Jones, James Gibbs, and William Kent.[1] For the most part, American builders followed European guidebooks rather than creating their own designs. In addition, colonial builders emulated many styles beside British. Pre-Revolutionary buildings reflected the influence of the Dutch, the French, the Swiss, and the Germans. However cosmopolitan the architectural style might have been, there was never really an "American style" of architecture per se (Nye, *Cultural Life*, 268–269).

Colonial buildings inevitably demonstrated an expansiveness and attention to detail that differed greatly from the European style. Colonial aristocrats did, however, often opt to imitate the precision-cut masonry that distinguished English architecture through the use of painting and plastering wood, brick, and fieldstone exteriors (G.S. Wood, 113). Nonetheless, from the start, American architecture had its own distinctive style (Nye, *Cultural Life*, 268).

Unfortunately, the Revolutionary War had halted building. Scores of colonists turned patriots served in the Continental army, depleting the availability of skilled craftsmen. Materials were needed for subsistence rather than for erecting new edifices. Once the war was over, however, the necessity to resume building immediately arose. Structures destroyed and ravaged by war needed to be replaced, and the new central government required new buildings, as well as renovations and buildings for state and local governments.

This great demand for new buildings—especially new buildings that would reflect a more American vision—resulted in the emergence of a new profession on the North American continent: the professional architect. A new republican order required a more visionary approach to architectural design, one that would express and advance the principles and aspirations of the newly formed United States.

Although far-sighted in their approach, professional architects in these formative years, like their political contemporaries, did not share the same idea of what an American order was or what it should be. In brief, architecture in the new republic could be broken down into two main groups: those who chose to adapt English styles (often referred to as "late Georgian") and those who eschewed British architecture in favor of emulating the more romantic Greco-Roman (neoclassical) style. The two architectural schools of thought did share a few basic attributes. Both styles utilized a rectilinear plan (that is, a plan that moved in and was bounded by straight lines); each also included in its designs curved or elliptical projections. The composition of exteriors and the design of rooms evinced the architect's concerted focus on a central motif (for example, a complex entrance or a portico), thereby leaving more ample surfaces in contrast (Green, 109). Furthermore, both styles emphasized the convenient and the utilitarian, such as in the plan of corridors, stairways, and closets.

In addition, the late Georgian and the neoclassical styles accentuated detail, a definite movement away from the rococo style of the earlier part of the eighteenth century. (Rococo was characterized by its heavy use of curving—the "c" and "s" were the fundamental shapes—an asymmetrical design, and natural forms of ornamentation.) The archaeological discovery of Late Roman buildings, which were remarkable in their rejection of the more elaborate, earlier "classical" pattern, inspired late Georgian architects. Deviating sharply from the earlier, more rococo

Georgian style, which was characterized by a reliance on ponderous cornices, massive doorways, and pavilions, late Georgian refined detail so that it was graceful and delicate, setting it apart from previous architectural styles.

Simplicity of detail, as well, was an integral component of the neoclassical style. Surface ornamentation became unconventional—almost austere. Before long, the neoclassicists drew up plans that were imaginative rather than imitative of the classical form. Their sense of proportion and use of unadorned geometric decoration subsequently revolutionized architecture in England and America (ibid., 111).

Despite these similarities, late Georgian and neoclassical reflected two very distinct architectural schools of thought. Each style was prevalent in a specific region: late Georgian in New England, neoclassical in the South. In many ways, the two styles not only illustrated the American tendency toward regionalism, but also the polarization of republican thought in the new society. Late Georgian unmistakably was British in origin and inspiration. Neoclassical, on the other hand, rejected the English style, instead turning to an ancient republic as the stimulus for its vision. More important, each was advanced and promoted by a self-made architectural designer: Charles Bulfinch of Massachusetts and Thomas Jefferson of Virginia.

## LATE GEORGIAN: CHARLES BULFINCH

Charles Bulfinch (1763–1844) had a long and distinguished career as the first native-born professional architect in the United States. A Harvard graduate, Bulfinch toured Europe for two years where he studied many of the great architectural works of Italy and France. When in London, he first became acquainted with the works of the Adams brothers (Robert and James) and the architectural style that bore their name: Adamesque.

In short, the hallmark of Adamesque style was its control and elegance. Based on the recent archaeological discoveries of Herculaneum and Pompeii, the Adamesque style utilized the classical elements of architecture, often blending Ionic pilasters (rectangular columns with scrolling ornamentation) with Doric entablatures (the oldest, and plainest, Greek style). The Adamesque style synthesized various forms, resulting in a style that incorporated classical orders with a distinct sense of proportion.

After his return from Europe, Bulfinch decided to adapt the Adamesque style to reflect New England needs and tastes. He believed that Adamesque was well suited for New Englanders who, even though they were some of the fiercest proponents for independence, were still tied culturally to England. Independence from Britain had resulted in a marked rise in fortune for New England manufacturers and merchants. Federalist by nature, this suddenly affluent group became enamored with what they perceived as being aristocratic styles and tastes. Therefore, the buildings for this region would be British in design and origin.

Using his London notebooks as his source, Bulfinch adeptly appropriated the Adamesque style, creating an American version (Nye, *Cultural Life*, 270). This style (sometimes known as "Federalist") quickly swept New England. It was not, however, a slavish imitation of the British. Bulfinch transformed the Adamesque into a style that resonated with American sensibility. Albeit his original intent was to give New England architecture the appeal and distinction of that of London, Bulfinch's legacy was a style that was uniquely American. Simplicity of form and a versatility of design characterize his designs. Although his first attempts were not very inspiring, two of Bulfinch's earlier churches (no longer in existence), in Taunton and Pittsfield, Massachusetts, were delicately Adamesque in their translation of masonry into wood (Green, 114).

Government buildings became the mainstay of Bulfinch's architectural career. Especially notable are the state houses at Hartford, Connecticut, and Boston, Massachusetts. The Hartford building, the first major government building in New England to be erected in post-Revolutionary America, is distinguished by its well proportioned and congruous edifice (ibid., 115). The overall impression is one of delicacy and balance.

Of particular consequence was a competitive phenomenon among cities at this time. Cities, regardless of region, wanted "signature" buildings (R. Hughes, 120)—that is, the design of buildings would have cultural resonance. A prime example of this was Bulfinch's design of the Massachusetts State House (1795–1798). This new building was commissioned to replace the old state house erected in 1712. For Bostonians, the older state house harbored rancorous associations with former British rule (especially the despised taxes imposed by an oppressive mother country). Worse yet, the old state house overlooked the site of the 1770 Boston Massacre.

Bulfinch's state house expresses this fierce desire for signature buildings. It is reflective of the temper of the Commonwealth of Massachusetts, not necessarily that of the nation. For instance, Bulfinch chose not to imitate Jefferson's plan for the Virginia state capitol (1785–1799), which was modeled on the architecture of ancient Rome. Rather, he used as his prototype William Chambers's Somerset House in London (1776–1786).

The Somerset House had been specifically designed as a government building. Thus its design could easily be altered to fit the requirements for an American government building. From the Somerset House, Bulfinch copied the seven-arched entrance and the pillared loggia directly

State house, Boston, Massachusetts, by Charles Bulfinch. Courtesy of the Library of Congress.

above. A glistening dome crowned the state house. (In 1802, Paul Revere was commissioned to cover the dome in copper. By 1874, the dome was gold-leafed—which it still is today.)

The Massachusetts State House reaffirmed New England's close cultural ties with England, while liberating the seat of government from a mood of the historical animosity, one that the old state house, by its situation and design, had evoked. More important, the design of the state house resolutely underscored the citizenry's belief that Boston was extraordinarily distinct from Virginia (ibid., 121).

Bulfinch's American version of the Adamesque style influenced other young architects of the period. Samuel McIntire (a student of the works of Christopher Wren and Inigo Jones) almost single-handedly transformed Salem, Massachusetts, into a model of this new Federalist style (Nye, *Cultural Life*, 270). By 1815, every street in Salem reflected the vision of McIntire's interpretation of Bulfinch's Adamesque style (O.W. Larkin, 87). Other architects and city planners followed suit, transforming the New England commons and streets into the spare elegance of the Adamesque style (ibid., 88).

Another follower of Bulfinch, Asher Benjamin, produced numerous pattern books espousing Bulfinch's Federalist style. Among these were

*The Country Builder's Assistant* (1797), *The American Builder's Companion* (1806), and *The Rudiments of Architecture* (1814). *The American Builder's Companion* title page proclaimed that this was "a new system of architecture, particularly adapted to the present style of building in the United States" (qtd. in Green, 114). Followers of Bulfinch, such as Benjamin, regarded themselves as the purveyors of a uniquely American architectural style, one that reflected the temper and the needs of the new republic.

As the population moved westward into the Northwest Territory, enterprising New England carpenters and builders trailed after the new settlers into the untouched territory. Often these craftsmen took Benjamin's books with them, thus introducing Bulfinch's version of the Adamesque into the new territory. Even today, one may find numerous examples of the Federalist style in Illinois, Michigan, and Ohio—Benjamin's drawings were used for the construction plans (Nye, *Cultural Life*, 270). But as the Adamesque style moved westward, it became more an approach to form than a style used to replace colonial forms (O.W. Larkin, 89).

## NEOCLASSICISM: THOMAS JEFFERSON AND BENJAMIN HENRY LATROBE

Just as Charles Bulfinch became the leading proponent for what became known as the Federalist style, a style that acknowledged and even celebrated the English architectural tradition, Jefferson's efforts became synonymous with what is often termed "neoclassicism" (sometimes referred to as "romantic classicism"), a style that turned to the ancients for inspiration. Jefferson's role as an architect in the formation of the new governmental structure is obvious. But his role as an architect and advocate for a new, national architecture is also apparent. His political career often afforded him opportunities to study and appraise disparate European architectural forms. For instance, while serving as a minister to France, a younger Jefferson developed a decided preference for ancient Greco-Roman and Palladianism, an architectural style based on the theories of Renaissance architect and theorist Andrea Palladio (1508–1580).

Very early in his study of architecture, Jefferson had rejected late Georgian architecture, deeming it inadequate to express the vision of a new republic. Prior to the Revolution, Jefferson had made a concerted effort to eradicate the late Georgian style that he observed growing around him. At Williamsburg, he had drawn up plans to enhance the Governor's Palace with immense porticos on each side (Green, 125). Altogether he regarded late Georgian style as an architectural curse since English buildings, in his opinion, were even less refined than American (O.W. Larkin, 79). The contemporary practice of enlarging edifices and topping them with cupolas was abhorrent to Jefferson—obviously an insufficient approach to creating a national architecture that would reflect a new order (ibid.). Jefferson wished that building in the new nation be swift, but also appropriate in style (Nye, *Cultural Life*, 271).

Like many American architects during this period, Jefferson chose to study the structures of ancient Greece and Rome. Without reservation he judged the English-based Adamesque style unfit to be an architectural model for a nation founded on republican ideals. More in keeping with the national frame of mind, he felt the Greco-Roman style would be far more suitable to meet the needs of the republic. At this time Americans often compared themselves to valorous Romans and beneficent Greeks. Classical-designed national emblems, Greco-Roman mottoes, and an American version of the Roman eagle permeated American iconography (ibid.). Consequently, a movement to imitate the Greco-Roman style seemed to be the logical next step.

Government buildings, in particular, were perceived as singular representations of a nation's essence and ideology. Thus, classic antiquity logically would be a fitting source for architectural inspiration, especially since classical architectural principles mirrored philosophical principles— order, accord, and constancy—valued by the new republicans. Particularly appealing was that the classical style demonstrated that not only could buildings be glorious, but also that their design could be based on mathematics, thus foregrounding the rational and the logical. Architecture began to be considered an art form that was scientific, firmly established on mathematical principles and rationalism. Undeniably, this philosophy would appeal to the people of the Enlightenment period.

Classical antiquity, then, became the model for the national architecture. Like the rest of the world, the recent excavations in the Mediterranean entranced Americans. Thus, the initial form that the national architecture would take was not new. Instead, it would be one of derivation. A national architecture could be founded on models from antiquity that Jefferson said had "the approbation of thousands of years" (qtd. in ibid.).

Palladianism became a primary source for creating a new, national architectural movement. Palladianism focuses on harmonic proportions (clarity, symmetry, and order), as well as adapting ancient classical decorative motifs and forms. By the seventeenth century, Inigo Jones had introduced the Palladian style in England, where it became a prevalent and popular architectural style for two hundred years. Attention to detail was manifested in the use of elegant pilasters, engaged columns, doors with open sidelights, and blind arcades (Green, 111).

Early on, Palladio's work appealed to Jefferson's astute sense of balance and rationality, especially Palladio's theory that proportions in fine architecture were derived from natural laws. Many of Jefferson's plans reflect the influence of Palladio. (Monticello and the University of Virginia, two of Jefferson's preeminent achievements, are very Palladian in style.) Subsequently his own drawings were as scrupulously planned as Palladio's (O.W. Larkin, 80).

An ardent republican and early sympathizer to the French republic movement, Jefferson was also keenly influenced by French architecture, which also owed much of its vision to classical antiquity. The French were actively engaged in rebuilding Paris within a classical style. When he was invited to design the new Virginia state capitol in 1785, Jefferson used the Maison Carrée (a Roman ruin in southern France, the name means "square house") as his model. For Jefferson, this ancient temple was the consummate example of cubic style (ibid.). The plans for the capitol were a modification of the temple form with a Palladian emphasis. Jefferson streamlined his government temple, choosing to employ simpler Ionic columns in place of the more elaborate Corinthian order.[2] The result was the first significant example of American neoclassical architecture (Nye, *Cultural Life*, 272).

Two particular architectural projects exemplify Jefferson's vision of what American architecture should embody: his home, Monticello, and the University of Virginia. Both illustrate his indebtedness to Palladio, his affinity for the ancient Roman, and his interest in French architecture. The former represents Jefferson's spiritual center as well as his aesthetic ambition (R. Hughes, 114). The latter expresses his belief in education as a means of fostering a natural aristocracy (ibid., 116).

A brick and frame structure, Monticello ("little mountain") became a life's work for Jefferson. He began planning Monticello as early as 1767, but it was not completed until 1809. In his original design, Jefferson used an English pattern book as the basis of his floor plan and the drawings of Palladio for the facade. By 1784 when Jefferson left for France, Monticello in its initial form was complete.

When he returned from France five years later, he began to radically alter and enlarge Monticello so that his home would reflect his new ideas of what architecture should be. At this point, much of the original house was torn down to facilitate the dramatic modifications. While in Paris Jefferson had observed "all the new and good houses are of a single storey. That is of the height of 16 or 18 f. generally, and the whole of it given to rooms of entertainment, but in the parts where there are bedrooms they have two tiers of them from 8 to 10 f. high, with a small private staircase" (qtd. in ibid., 114).

Following Jefferson's belief in the superiority of the French one-storey structure, Monticello has the appearance of a single-storey building; in reality, it is three stories. Using as his model Pierre Rousseau's Hôtel de

Monticello, residence of Thomas Jefferson. Courtesy of the Library of Congress.

Salm (a building that was under construction during Jefferson's sojourn in France), Jefferson incorporated a dome over Monticello's centralized octagonal "sky room." The wings were subsequently dropped below grade, creating roofs that formed terraces. Filled with his various inventions and maps and relics, the 35-room Monticello reflects his numerous interests as well as his changing aesthetic.

After Jefferson left the presidency in 1809, he embarked on what has unequivocally been determined as his finest architectural design achievement: the University of Virginia (ibid., 116). Jefferson founded the University of Virginia with the intent that it would promote and educate the natural aristocracy of Virginia.[3] A Deist and a secular humanist, Jefferson rejected the religious tradition that had provided the foundation for the colonial universities.[4]

For that reason, he cast aside available European models for university design, such as Oxford and Cambridge, because of their church origins (ibid., 116). The model for Jefferson's plan (based, in part, on the advice of preeminent neoclassical architect Benjamin Latrobe) was, instead, the retreat of Louis XIV of France: the Marly-le-Roi, which had 12 pavilions (six on a side) that led to a rotunda that served as the king's quarters. The lawn at the opposite end was left open, leaving the view of the rotunda unobstructed.

Jefferson's plan differed from the Marly-le-Roi only in that ten pavilions (five on each side) instead of twelve were built. Each pavilion included classrooms on the ground level with faculty living quarters on the floor above. Between pavilions were the student dormitories. The spacing between the pavilions was determined by the size of the dormitories. The further a structure was from the central rotunda, the more the space was increased between neighboring buildings. The design concept was to extend the perspective of the lawn. The manipulation of space here symbolically suggested that the wisdom and knowledge associated with the university would radiate into the Virginia countryside (ibid., 117).

The centerpiece of Jefferson's design, however, is the rotunda, a scaled-down version of the Roman Pantheon (ibid.). The domed rotunda was elevated on a stepped base. By making the rotunda a spherical structure, Jefferson architecturally employed several extended metaphors: the rotunda's top half provided the configuration for the library (that is, the "brain" of the university); the light radiating through the skylight above represented the power of Nature; finally, the books within denoted the power of Reason (ibid.).

Jefferson's contribution to architecture was immense. His adaptation of classical architectural style provided brilliant visual metaphors for the purpose of perpetuating the ideas guaranteed in his Declaration of Independence and other writings. Probably more so than any other American architect during the early republican era, whether amateur or professional, Jefferson as an architect and as an advocate for a unique national architecture left a remarkable legacy. Even today what we perceive as a national style of architecture can be traced back to Jefferson's vision.

Jefferson was, however, not solely responsible for the creation of this neoclassical approach to a national architecture. His appointment in 1803 of Benjamin Henry Latrobe (1764–1820) as Surveyor of Public Buildings of the United States was instrumental in the creation and perpetuation of an official national architecture. Latrobe, who had emigrated from Britain in 1795, had been trained at Moravian College in Saxony and had extensively traveled throughout Italy and France. Afterward, he studied under the British neoclassical architect Samuel Pepys Cockerell. His knowledge of French and neoclassical architecture was incorporated into his drawings that were distinguished by classical detail and geometrically apportioned designs, as his design of the facade of the Second Bank of the United States (1818) attests.

Latrobe's authority and influence became far-reaching. Jefferson's appointment of Latrobe enabled the latter to exert his authority over other government architects. His greatest influence over American architecture was, however, due to his work on outside commissions. An early com-

The Second Bank of the United States by Benjamin Latrobe.
Courtesy of the Library of Congress.

mission in Philadelphia, the Bank of Pennsylvania (1799–1801), was extensively imitated for years. The exterior and interior were equally exquisite.[5] An edifice of outstanding grace and splendor, the Bank of Pennsylvania was especially noteworthy in the development of American architecture for several reasons: it was the first consequential building designed by a professional architect; it introduced Greek order to American architecture; and it won immediate acclaim for its beauty and expressiveness (Green, 131). Indeed, Latrobe asserted, "I have changed the taste of a whole city" (qtd. in Nye, *Cultural Life*, 272).

In many respects, Latrobe's grand pronouncement was true for he had been instrumental in altering the architectural preferences of Philadelphians. Post-Revolutionary Philadelphian architecture began to shy away from the Adamesque style in favor of the neoclassical. Essentially, Latrobe's austerely designed Bank of Pennsylvania was the impetus for this shift (R. Hughes, 118).

Unlike his sponsor, Greek, rather than Roman, architecture influenced Latrobe. For Latrobe, Roman architecture was a product of an empire that was not democratic (hence not in line with the American vision) and was too ornate and magisterial for American buildings (Nye, *Cultural Life*, 273). Latrobe pronounced Roman monuments as being unrefined, the Arch of Constantine "a crowded patchwork of parts" (qtd. in O.W. Larkin, 93). He felt that the architecture of ancient Greece was far more compatible to American democratic ideals since both Greece and the United States celebrated the freedom of the people. In a speech to the Society of Artists in Philadelphia, Latrobe explained that the purity of Greek art and architecture echoed the virtuousness of its democratic principles. Consequently, in ancient Greek architecture, art and ideology were in accord. When the new nation eventually realized that art is integral to the core of the republic, Latrobe avowed that "indeed the days of Greece may be revived in the woods of America, and Philadelphia [will] become the Athens of the western world" (qtd. in ibid.).

The Basilica of the Assumption of the Blessed Virgin Mary in Baltimore (1805–1818)—arguably, Latrobe's most impressive work, which is still in existence today—is elemental in plan. Arched windows and the curved apertures of the belfries alleviate its severe beauty. Aside from the onion-shaped domes (a later addition), the Basilica's facade is magnificent, a true expression of the simple forms used in the basic plans (Green, 132).

Latrobe was also a talented civil engineer. In his capacity as Superintendent of Water Supply in Philadelphia he reconstructed the old sidewalk pumps and gutters system of Philadelphia. Because of his innovative design, Philadelphia became the first American community to use steam pumps in its water system. From the reservoir, water flowed throughout the city in wooden pipes. The Center Square Pump House was designed as an amalgamation of engineering and neoclassical architecture (O.W. Larkin, 93). Offices flanked its sides; the tank was above with the pump chamber below, all within logically allotted proportions. Here function, form, and aesthetics truly came together.

Probably Latrobe's most famous contribution to American building was his redesigning of the Capitol in Washington, DC. Burned in 1814 by British troops during the War of 1812, it was only a smoldering shell when Latrobe set to work. It was his task to correct and rebuild the damaged wings, design the Hall of Representatives (known today as Statuary Hall), plan the great rotunda, and modify the earlier, less aesthetic plans for the eastern and western central fronts (ibid., 92). Today, Latrobe's mark can be seen in the western front of the Capitol, the gate lodges and fence posts on the Capitol grounds (his design), and the Library of Congress (ibid.). Essentially dismissed by President James Monroe in 1817 (Latrobe officially "resigned"), he was succeeded by Charles Bulfinch, who did use his predecessor's plans for the wings of the Capitol, but chose to complete the rotunda with plans of his own design. Even though Bulfinch ultimately completed the work on the Capitol (that is, in this time period),[6] Latrobe's work had far-reaching consequences on American architecture in general.

U.S. Capitol and Pennsylvania Avenue before 1814. Courtesy of the
Library of Congress.

## FROM CONEGOCHEAGUE TO A NATIONAL CAPITAL:
## THE DESIGN AND ARCHITECTURE OF
## WASHINGTON, DC.

The shifting of the nation's capital from New York to Philadelphia in
1789 did not solve the government's need for expansion (particularly,
the need to create new federal buildings in a set area). The issue of a
capital city was not a new one. In June 1783 Congress (while in session
at the Old City Hall in Philadelphia) had discussed seriously the creation
of a new capital to serve the new nation. Not until 1791 was an actual
site chosen. Largely a political compromise, Congress decided that the
new city should be built on the banks of the Potomac River. The final
decision as to where the exact site should be was left to President Washington.

Conegocheague (the Native American name for the junction of the
Potomac with its eastern tributary) was Washington's choice. In making
his decision, Washington strongly considered the commercial potential
of the site. Of primary consideration was that the Potomac provided a
more than adequate waterway to other regions.

The Conegocheague site was a source of amusement, and contention, throughout the nation. The poet Philip Freneau (1752–1832) found the topic to be more than ample fodder for his satiric pen. His playful poetic dialogue between two housekeepers arguing about the merits of situating the capital in New York, Philadelphia, or the Conegocheague illustrates the public's misgivings of the final choice:

> My master would rather saw timber or dig,
> Than see them removing to Conegocheague,—
> Where the houses and kitchens are yet to be framed,
> The trees to be felled, and the streets to be named.
> (in O.W. Larkin, 91)

But the seat of the new national government did move to Conegocheague. Washington selected a French-born engineer, Pierre-Charles L'Enfant (1754–1825) to draw up the design plans for the new capital. Washington was well acquainted with L'Enfant the man and L'Enfant the engineer. L'Enfant had served under Washington as a volunteer in the Revolutionary army where he distinguished himself as an engineer. (In 1783 Congress bestowed upon him the rank of major in recognition of his outstanding service to the country.)

L'Enfant was a commendable choice. Politically, his commitment to the United States was beyond reproach. As an artist and an engineer, he was respected and admired. His training was impeccable. (He studied under his father at the Royal Academy of Painting and Sculpture, where he was greatly influenced by Baroque architecture.[7]) His vision for the new capital was to be a provident and glorious one.

In 1791 L'Enfant's task was to transform the swampland along Goose Creek into a city of stately splendor, one that would match the vision of the young republic. But the task would not be an easy one to fulfill, or, in the case of L'Enfant, to complete.

L'Enfant's plan was fundamentally a gridiron of asymmetric blocks intersected by diagonal avenues. The chief focus was to be the Capitol (that would be at one end of the city), the presidential residence, and the monument (that would be at the other end). Between the Capitol and the monument would be the Great Walk (in the style of the Champs-Élysées). Various geometric forms would be created at the intersections, providing a showcase area for fountains and other monuments. (L'Enfant emphatically advocated that the city should have numerous statues and other monuments to honor great national heroes and statesmen.) New streets would be plotted so they would form aligning squares. L'Enfant's plan was not only one of elegance aesthetically, but one of rational forethought and planning. The plan transformed the ignominious Goose Creek into a grand canal for present needs while simultaneously devising a schematic approach to address future transportation requirements.

As secretary of state, Jefferson furnished L'Enfant with many metropolitan maps of the great cities of Europe (as well as his own ideas of where major buildings should be erected). L'Enfant's plan was a combination of several ideas that he gleaned from these maps. (Thus no one city served as the model for the new capital city.) He did not rely on a set architectural school of thought, although his training and predilection for the Baroque is evident in his plan.

L'Enfant did not, however, have the opportunity to see his plan come to fruition. He vehemently disputed with Jefferson, the city commissioners, and President Washington over costs and the removal of citizens' property to make way for construction; and because of this, the president felt it necessary to discharge him. L'Enfant's successors generally followed his original design. However, by the latter half of the nineteenth century, the harmony of his initial city plan had been undermined by a barrage of additional streets.

After L'Enfant's ignominious dismissal in 1792, numerous and diverse engineers and architects descended on the slowly emerging capital, all vying for the chance at making a substantial contribution to the design of the new city. Some were eminently more talented and experienced than others. The subsequent architectural history of Washington, DC, paralleled the political history of the nation (O.W. Larkin, 91). Conceptual conflicts, rivalries, and compromises resulted in the long drawn-out process of planning and building the nation's capital. Late Georgian advocates, such as Samuel McIntire and Charles Bulfinch, submitted drawings that were derived from either their own successes (in the case of Bulfinch, his design of the Boston State House can be seen in his plan for the Capitol) or their English progenitors.

Far less competent architects (notably William Thornton, a self-confessed amateur) became involved in the design of the Capitol.[8] By the time Jefferson had become president in 1801, the Capitol had devolved into a hodgepodge of different architectural conceptions. To remedy the situation, in 1803 Jefferson appointed Latrobe to oversee the design of the Capitol. The result was a streamlining of structure. Latrobe excluded an extraneous dome (of Thornton's design), retained the outer walls of the wings, added the House of Representative's oval chamber, and decorated the capitals (top portion of the columns) with corncobs and tobacco leaves. The latter details illustrate Latrobe's desire to reinvent Greek orders to reflect American nature (R. Hughes, 119). The devastating aftereffects of the War of 1812, however, resulted in another redesigning and rebuilding period that extended past the early nationalist period. It would be the responsibility of future generations to complete L'Enfant's magnificent plan.

## DOMESTIC ARCHITECTURE: SHELTER AND SECURITY FOR THE AMERICAN FAMILY

As dynamic as government buildings and city planning were during this period, architecture and planning were not limited to buildings on a grand scale. Though the more academic architects and builders were inspired by lofty ideals that they expressed through their designs, ordinary builders worked in the same style of the colonial period (Kimball, 145). Americans were concerned with the shelter and the security of their families and holdings. Domestic architecture (that is, buildings produced for the family unit) reflected the changing times and fortunes ushered in by the new nation.

Innovations in domestic architecture, by nature of its form and function, are often slow. Family domiciles and outer buildings have four elemental requirements: protection from the elements and forces of nature; preparation of food; provision for working space, preferably with a good light source; and allocation of sleeping quarters. In Colonial America, settlers were concerned initially with the bare essentials. From the beginning, American settlers followed the architectural styles from their homelands (Hunt, 259). Therefore, there was not a set domestic architectural style in Colonial or Federalist America. Habitations followed ethnic partialities and environmental constraints. Domestic building in America was an intricate mixture of ethnic, historic, and economic factors (St. George, 1827). Structures on the eastern seaboard were built by colonists who had migrated from Great Britain, Germany, France, Sweden, Switzerland, and the Netherlands (ibid). Some examples of this multinational influence could be seen in the almost austere, simple lines of medieval English building, especially the design of the small, clapboarded house or stone cottage. The log cabin, which dotted the American landscape, was the legacy of the Swedes and the Germans. Scandinavian design can also be seen in the steep roofs of many homes. The Dutch Colonials had a significant influence on New York building. The Dutch love of brick and stone and steep, pitched gabled roofs (and, in the late eighteenth century, the gambrel roof) were easily modified for the New World's buildings (Blumenson, 17). In addition, in the Northeast and the East temporal forces of climate, moral reform, historical survival, and adaptive reuse of structures had a major impact on the design of domestic architecture (St. George, 1827). This pattern had marked American domestic architecture for the past three centuries.

American domestic architectural styles lagged several years (even decades) behind those in Europe. In addition, American planners, when emulating European styles, erected buildings that were not as large or as grand as their European counterparts. There were fundamental differences between American architecture and the European styles American builders imitated. The differences arose from the availability of materials (for example, American builders preferred wood simply because it was readily available), the machinery available, the number and expertise of carpenters and other craftsmen, the differences in the American climate and social conditions from that of Europe, and the consequent diverse needs for protection (Hunt, 259).

Nevertheless, there were some particular styles that were prevalent throughout this period. The "hall-and-parlor" type of house (also known in various regions as "Colonial," "Early American," or "Cape Cod") became the most prevalent type in republican America (Glassie, 1898).[9] An American house type derived from English models, the hall-and-parlor house began as a four-room domicile. In the beginning, simple floor plans allowed for a daily living room space, a kitchen area, sleeping quarters, and a room reserved for polite visits or rituals, such as for courtship or funerals (St. George, 1827). In some cases, the limited room number often necessitated the family sleeping in one room. (Children were accommodated with "trundle beds," a low bed that was rolled under a larger bed when not in use.)

By the eighteenth century, the four-room house was the quintessential American floor plan. However, expansion and innovation allowed for three smaller rooms behind the main hall (or primary living area), making the plan two rooms deep (Cook, 1836). The back of the house now was reserved for storage and food preparation, thus permitting the primary living space to be used for sitting and dining (ibid.). In rural communities and on larger estates, a rear entranceway provided access to kitchen needs, such as smokehouses, bake ovens, and icehouses. (Ice boxes and refrigeration would come later in the nineteenth century.)

Urban homes, however, did not have the luxury of outer buildings (with the exception of privies). Despite the fact that New England farmers and the wealthy had installed icehouses since the seventeenth century, most American families could not afford the expense of ice storage as a form of food preservation. The more perishable items that required cooler storage were usually kept on the cooler side of the kitchen or in the cellar. (Although Marylander Thomas Moore had patented a refrigerator in 1803, most American families could not afford the cost of ice cutting that such a refrigerator required.) Food storage was often limited to pantries.

As in England, sanitation was problematic, handled almost primitively in the new republic (Morrison, 297). Even the homes of the wealthy did not have running water. In the country, water was carried from wells or springs by bucket. City residents were more fortunate. Houses were sup-

Mount Vernon, residence of George Washington. Courtesy of the
Library of Congress.

plied with water from private or public wells equipped with pumps.
Bathing was subsequently handled by portable tubs and basins with
pitchers.

Other personal sanitary issues were dealt with more publicly. In the
city, outdoor privies were the order of the day. On southern estates the
outdoor privies (referred to as "necessaries") were reserved for young
men and white servants (ibid.). Many times the estate necessaries were
octagonal brick buildings with multiple accommodations. At Washington's Mount Vernon, the necessaries enhanced the Palladian symmetry
of the estate, as the two octagonal necessaries flanked the courtyard that
led to the main entrance (ibid.). Most family members, however, chose
to handle bodily functions by use of commode chairs with pottery receptacles. (Because in the homes of the wealthy servants were responsible for the emptying and washing of the receptacles, servant stairways
were separate from the main staircase for this very reason.)

On the whole, the main and outer buildings were primarily wooden
or, in some areas, stone or even brick (again the Dutch influence). The
home itself generally included a central chimney or fireplace. Supple-
mental heat for other rooms sometimes included tile heating stoves,
Franklin stoves, and box stoves.[10] Box stoves were often built into the

chimney so that the open front served as a fireplace and the back extended into the room directly behind the chimney. This way the box stove heated two rooms. Coal, rather than firewood, was the primary fuel for home heating. The building boom after the Revolution drastically increased the need for wood, thus making wood far more costly than in the past (ibid., 298). Coal costs proved to be more in line with modest incomes.

Houses were generally compact, one-storey structures with partial or full underground cellars that furnished cool, frost-free storage for more perishable foods (Cook, 1835). The first versions had a stairway from the front entry that led to the attic. In the latter part of the eighteenth century, stairs were added from the exterior and the rear of the house (ibid.). Windows often had small panes to provide needed exterior light and ventilation from the summer heat (in the Northeast and East). Interior lighting—both fish and whale oil and candle—was handled by the use of wall fixtures, chandeliers, and portable candle and oil lights (McClelland, 111). Interiors were plastered and papered in an effort to decrease wind infiltration (Cook, 1836). Weathered shingles or clapboard, for the most part, covered exteriors.

Eighteenth-century Long Island and New England migrants to the Hudson River Valley brought with them variations of the hall-and-parlor or Cape Cod type house (Ryan, 1841). These ranged from three-room arrangements found in their native Yorkshire or a variation of the Cape Cod, called a "saltbox" (ibid.). Saltboxes got their name from their similarity in shape to the wooden salt box (hinged, sloped cover) found in almost every American kitchen (Cook, 1836).

One area marked by a unique architectural style was central Pennsylvania. The significant migration of German-speaking settlers (Pennsylvania Germans) to the rich farming area in the mid-eighteenth century resulted in an architectural style that was well adapted to the rugged landscape of mountain and river valleys (Bronner, "Pennsylvania Dutch," 1845). These immigrants from the Rhineland (now part of southern Germany and parts of Switzerland) incorrectly referred to as "Pennsylvania Dutch" (the term comes from the phrase "Pennsylvania Deutsch," meaning "German") brought with them a familiarity and expertise in designing and building central European structure types.

The Pennsylvania German house fundamentally was a three-to-four-room structure. The one- or two-storey house was usually built of stone or log with the distinctive Pennsylvania German roof that was long side-lapped shingles with a steep pitch (ibid.). Other characteristic features included a side entranceway (rather than the front of the facade), leading into a "Kich" (long kitchen) equipped with a central fireplace, "stupp" or "stube" (a front room) on the other side, behind it a smaller sleeping or storage room or "kammer" ("softest room") (ibid.). Many times the long kitchen was divided into a fourth room, which was used as a pantry or for storage (ibid.).

The outer buildings of the Pennsylvania German farm were also distinct. Built from the same material as the family home, the presence of the outbuildings evinced the focus of the family industry. Outbuildings were numerous and various; they included smokehouses, icehouses, springhouses, hay barracks, dry houses, and outdoor bake ovens (Bronner, "Outbuildings," 1846).

Southern domestic architecture was similar to many of the styles found in the Northeast and East. Regardless of the ethnic backgrounds of their builders, southern homes were wood dominated (Glassie, 1897). The building types were, though, reminiscent of building types found in the English West Country (ibid.).

Like their northern counterparts, southern domestic structures were at first one-storey, with either a square- or rectangular-shaped primary living area and a smaller bedroom. Later, the one-storey domicile was transformed into a two-storey hall-and-parlor house. The enlarged appearance was interpreted as a conspicuous sign of the improved financial and social status of its owner (ibid.).

Size and renovations to display a rise in fortune was not limited to southern citizenry. In the northern states as well, scaled-down neo-Palladian houses became all the rage among the professional classes, such as lawyers, magistrates, the clergy, and merchants (St. George, 1828). Late eighteenth-century builders frequently incorporated Greek revival motifs into eighteenth-century linear stone houses (Ryan, 1841).

The design and construction of American homes was not limited to the form and function of the building itself. How and with what they chose to furnish their homes is indicative of American taste and a testament to the skill of American cabinetmakers. In many cases, American furniture was equal to the best of the English in skill, design, and ingenious variation (R. Hughes, 61). This was an era in which American furniture making was the epitome of craftsmanship and imagination.

The wealthy furnished their homes with exquisite designs made from mahogany, which complemented the late Georgian and neoclassical interiors of the great houses (McClelland, 49). One of the most distinguished American cabinetmakers, the Scottish-born Duncan Phyfe (1768–1854), gained renown for the high caliber of his workmanship, the outstanding grades of wood that he used, and his delicate and graceful carving. Phyfe's work serves as the quintessential example of American furniture making during the early nationalist era.

Phyfe's true genius was in his interpretation of established European designs, translating them into an Adamesque style befitting the impressive homes of affluent and intellectual republican citizens. The low relief of Phyfe's carvings mirrored the motifs found in the work of Robert

Adam. In the early years of the republic, Phyfe's delicate, graceful pieces were often adorned with the usual period ornamentation, such as acanthus leaves, ribbons and bows, and harps and lyres.

Phyfe's contemporaries also excelled in design and skill. Philadelphian William Savery (1721–1787) worked in the Chippendale style (a furniture distinguished by its rococo decoration and flowing lines). The New England–based Goddard family founded the Newport (Rhode Island) School of American Furniture. The Goddards were known for their variations of Chippendale and Queen Anne styles (the latter is characterized by the use of cabriole legs—legs shaped in a double curve ending in a paw or claw and ball foot), styles that incorporated shell carvings. The Goddards also developed a unique surface treatment of wood that heretofore did not exist. Other American furniture makers adapted Hepplewhite designs (marked for their simple, elegant modifications of Robert Adams's designs) and Sheraton (a variation of the Adamesque style noted for its delicacy and finesse) quite successfully as well.

Although the less affluent could not afford the mahogany masterpieces of Phyfe, Savery, or the Goddards, they, nonetheless, furnished their homes with well crafted wooden pieces. Even the most pedestrian of American artisans was known for his skill in woodworking and carving. Pine and oak were readily accessible and fit into modest budgets. Furniture for all became more elaborate. (For instance, the chair now replaced the more rudimentary stool of the colonial period.) Many pieces were decorated and painted to enliven the living quarters.

Some Pennsylvania Germans crafted a unique style during this period as well. (Though some Pennsylvania Germans rejected decorative arts altogether, others, whose religious beliefs were less austere, engaged in ornamentation to brighten their surroundings.) These artisans, known as the "Gay Dutch," created pieces exemplified by dynamic inlay work and stylized painting adapted from their native folk art. Thus, the Pennsylvania German propensity for design and expression of domestic bliss could be found on the exteriors and in the interiors of their holdings.

As a matter of course, the rising incomes of the working class and the growing affluence of the professional and merchant classes were showcased by the renovations to and the new building of homes (and the furnishing of these homes) of peoples from various regions, histories, ethnic backgrounds, and financial standings. Albeit less impressive than the premier examples of neo-Palladianism (such as Monticello and the University of Virginia), these adaptations of Jefferson and Latrobe's neoclassical vision demonstrated the public's vision of what the new republic represented in their minds. Others chose to include the classical elements of the late Georgian style into their renovations or new buildings, thus alluding to the democratic ideology of the ancients while acknowledging their British heritage.

Framed by two wars (the American Revolution and the War of 1812), this formative period in American architecture was one in which political ideology and architectural theory were often interconnected. Overall, the architecture of the early nationalist period represents the American vision of government and self. Despite the disparate viewpoints of what form of republicanism the new nation should adopt (whether that would mean governance by an educated elite, a mercantile approach to the well-being of the republic, or a more populist sentiment), Americans were united in their belief that their architecture should perpetuate the idea of a virtuous republic. Defined by aesthetics and influenced by political theory, the architecture stands as a testament to the deliberation and beliefs of a new nation, one circumscribed by the Enlightenment era principles of balance, rationality, and benevolence.

# 5

# Fashion

Assuredly, the early republican era was one that was characterized by immense change—politically, socially, and culturally. But in no one area was this more visibly evident than in the fashions of the day. Within this relatively brief period, the making of cloth and clothing had radically changed. Before the war the finer fabrics, such as satin, damask, brocade, wool, and cottons, had to be imported (Nye, *Cultural Life*, 132), and only the very wealthy could afford these. Even after the war farmers and laborers and their families made do with homespun (a coarse woolen fabric), linsey-woolsey (a coarse fabric of wool spun with cotton or linen which was popular in the North), or fustian (a coarse fabric made of flax and cotton which was popular in the South). Jeans, fustian-made with wool instead of flax, was particularly popular with the less-privileged classes because of its durability.[1]

The making of cotton and linen was extremely labor-intensive. Most American homes had a loom and a spinning wheel to process natural fiber and make it into cloth. (By this time women, rather than men, took up the loom. Prior to the war, weaving was the male purview of textile production.) Linen, too, proved to be a tricky fabric to process. To get the desired shade of whiteness, linen needed to be bleached up to 30 times. Until Eli Whitney (1765–1825) invented the cotton gin in 1793, the cleaning of cotton was extremely tedious and thus expensive. (The seeds embedded in the lint had to be removed by hand. Because Whitney's invention greatly accelerated the cotton-cleaning process, cotton growing swiftly became an extremely profitable enterprise for southern plantation owners.) Although cotton clothing was considered stylish and therefore highly desirable before the war, it was relatively scarce for two reasons:

the high price and England's restrictions on the American textile industry. (The British had relentlessly discouraged the development of American textile mills primarily in an attempt to protect its own textile
industries.)

Once the War for Independence had ended, Americans increased their
efforts to establish a thriving textile industry on their own shore. Enterprising (and stealthy) textile manufacturers smuggled out of England
closely guarded schematics for carding machines, looms, and spinning
jennies. The availability of domestically loomed textiles, heretofore only
obtainable through importation, was a boon to American clothing making and fashion. By 1790, Americans were donning American-made
checks, ginghams, and cotton sheeting (Train, 252). By 1810, Americans
were able to commercially produce silk. (Prior to then, silk was spun
and woven in the home.) Cotton, however, became the fabric of preference.

The patriotic mood of the period also led to the rejection of the more
luxurious fabrics (satin, velvet, brocades, and silks). In an effort to promote American industry, the wearing of these fabrics (associated with
the English textile industry) was regarded as unpatriotic. A true son or
daughter of the republic wore domestic fabrics, such as cotton or kerseymere (a twilled woolen cloth). As one cultural commentator of the
period observed, "A pair of satin breeches would attract the observation
of every beholder almost as much as a maroon colored coat" (qtd. in
ibid., 235). (Shades of red, of course, were associated with Britain. Buff
and blue were considered to be more American colors.)

By their example, political figures of the day led the movement away
from English fabrics in favor of the domestic. Benjamin Franklin, who
for most of his public life dressed simply and plainly, was constantly
admonishing his daughters to shun opulent materials and dress themselves in more modest (and more American) calico (Earle, vol. 2, 725).
George Washington (who loved fine clothes—even to the point of having
his uniforms custom designed and made) adopted clothing made of
American fibers and by American hands. For his first inauguration,
Washington was outfitted in a suit of honest Connecticut brown broadcloth. Martha Washington not only wore domestic fibers, but wove and
knitted them as well (ibid.). Other presidents followed Washington's example. In one case, the choice of wardrobe was a political statement. A
chronicler of the times reported that for his presidential inauguration in
1801, Thomas Jefferson wore a "blue coat, a thick drab-colored waistcoat
with a red under-waistcoat lapped over it, green velveteen breeches with
pearly buttons, yarn stockings, and slippers" (qtd. in Train, 236). Jefferson's rejection of buckled shoes in favor of the more French slipper drew
much criticism from those who were suspicious of everything French.
His ensemble, as a whole, clearly violated the high fashion standards of

the time, aligning him with a more egalitarian mode of dress (paralleling his more egalitarian political theories).

The emerging middle class also influenced the more egalitarian movement toward dress. High fashion and luxuriousness was no longer the prerogative of the privileged classes. As some members of society (such as Jefferson) used clothing to establish a political point (thereby dressing more simply), prosperous merchants, traders, and entrepreneurs wore clothing that revealed their economic and social aspirations. In other words, the wealthy began to dress more in line with the middle class and the middle class emulated the wealthy. Class lines based on clothing became increasingly blurred.

Americans, like their European counterparts, were enamored with archaeological discoveries. The late-eighteenth-century findings at Pompeii and Herculaneum (Roman cities destroyed by the eruption of Mt. Vesuvius in A.D. 79) transformed western aesthetics. Jewelry reflected this shift. Simplicity and an emphasis on composition predominated jewelry design. The cameo, once regarded as passé, was en vogue.

British pottery manufacturer Josiah Wedgwood (1730–1795) was the predominant contributor to the popularity of the cameo. Wedgwood's cameos were fundamentally reproductions of Greek and Roman models, thereby catering to the late-eighteenth-century proclivity for antiquity. Cameos soon became the centerpieces of brooches, belts, bracelets, medallions, and rings for men and women on both sides of the Atlantic.

Precious gems were also popular, especially diamonds. Earlier in the century Brazil began exporting great numbers of diamonds to Europe. This led not only to the rise in the popularity of the diamond, but also to the spawning of countless imitations for those who could not afford the real item. Whether the genuine article or not, Americans treasured their jewelry. Demand for rings, watch chains, and pins resulted in the conversion of Spanish dollars and doubloons into jewelry. Enterprising New Englanders developed "filled" work (precious metal on the outside, pewter or lead on the inside) to meet the market's demand (ibid., 238). Yankee peddlers traveled the countryside having great success selling filled jewelry items, so much so that within the early years of the nineteenth century the supply could no longer meet the demand (ibid.).

Textiles, color, accessories, and jewelry definitely evinced Americans' shifting tastes in fashion during the republican era. The most striking change, though, was in the fashions themselves. Heavily influenced by European styles, American clothing dramatically changed. Men, historically the more flamboyant of the sexes when it came to fashion, adopted more somber fabrics and colors. By the end of the War of 1812, men had forsaken elegant knee breeches for more utilitarian trousers. Women eagerly abandoned the highly contrived, structured dress of the 1780s and early 1790s for the scanty "Empire" fashions that were sweeping Europe.

Perukes (or periwigs, the terms are interchangeable) became relics of the past.[2] The dressing of hair became more artless, thus less contrived. For a relatively short period of time, men tied their unpowdered hair back in a queue with a black ribbon. Sometimes the hair was netted in a black bag at the nape of the neck. Other times the queue hung unadorned down the wearer's upper back. Soon even that fashion went by the wayside. (Madison was the last president to wear his hair in a queue. Subsequent presidents wore their hair shorter and styled less ostentatiously.) Even children's dress underwent a small transformation. Up until the last part of the eighteenth century, children had been dressed in the same mode as their elders. Now their dress had been altered so that it was more age- and activity-appropriate. Overall, fashion in the new nation exhibited a more egalitarian and utilitarian approach to appearance and outlook following the lead of their third president.

## HAIR AND HEADDRESSES: THE FREEING OF AMERICAN SENSIBILITY

By the end of the seventeenth century, wigs were universally worn—especially by men. In the eighteenth century, wigs and hairdressing were of prime importance to the gentry in Europe and America. Even those with lesser means adopted wig wearing, although their hairpieces were shorter and of lesser quality than those of their wealthier contemporaries. Americans had no qualms about wearing secondhand wigs. The quality of the wig depended on the budget of the wearer. Lawyers, clergymen, merchants, and even slaves wore wigs. For years to wear one's own hair was considered déclassé. Even the poor covered their hair, usually with woolen caps.

For that reason, wigs were deliberately artificial-looking. The wig itself was attached to the head by a colored ribbon, accenting the natural hair peeking from underneath. Often powdered, elaborate wigs precluded a gentleman from wearing the eighteenth-century de rigueur tricorn hat (a low-crowned hat with a broad brim cocked on three sides). Of course, hats were—for those who would never go without an ornate wig—carried. For these men, the hat served more as an accessory than a functionary. Barbers and peruke makers did a brisk business because the care and maintenance of wigs was time-consuming and required much skill.

The initial cost of a wig was expensive. Because the common perception was that English wigs were of much higher quality than American-made ones, the wealthy willingly paid high prices for an imported London-made wig.[3] The upkeep was pricey as well. Barbers would make house calls to curl and dress a gentleman's peruke. Those who could not afford the services of a barber wore bag-wigs, wigs that were tied up in leather bags as a quick and easy means of caring for them.

In the early days of the republic, some of the aristocracy still wore powdered wigs, an additional expense. Not only was wig powder expensive, but also to achieve the desired snowy appearance, copious amounts of the precious powder had to be used (up to two pounds worth). The heaviness of the wig and the untidiness due to the addition of powder made wig wearing an uncomfortable and messy enterprise. Sometimes the wig was ill smelling because of the adhesive used. Pomatum (a form of pomade used to affix the powder) had animal fat as its chief ingredient. Soon the fat became rancid, emitting pungent fumes. A desire to be at the height of fashion sometimes ran the risk of the wearer being malodorous—thus unintentionally offensive. (Highly scented waters, colognes, and perfumes were used as a means of masking any odors due to lax hygiene or other causes.)

By the 1780s wigs were still worn, but these were smaller, less ornately styled than those earlier in the century. Men and women began showing their own hair, especially in the years following the French Revolution (1789–1799). For a time, women's hairstyles were so elaborately constructed that a wire structure beneath the hair supported fantastic motifs of curls, postiches (small hairpieces), and outlandish shapes. By the 1790s, women's coiffures used far less artifice. Like her male counterpart, the republican woman's hair was long (around shoulder-length). It was set in loose curls and drawn back either by a ribbon or by combs. On occasion, a woman might lightly powder her natural hair. Older women wore mobcaps (a large cap adorned with ribbons and trimmings) rather than expending the effort to dress the hair. At the turn of the century, women wore their hair shorter in tighter curls held in place with pomade. Men also had their locks shorn at much shorter lengths that had not been seen for centuries. There is a direct correlation between the length of a man's hair and the amount of hair on his face; when perukes and long hair were the fashion, men were beardless (Earle, vol. 1, 351). Consequently, in the nineteenth century, as men wore their hair shorter, they began to grow beards. But beards were unusual in the early nationalist period except, perhaps, on the frontier.

As hairstyles radically changed at the turn of the century, so did hat styles. Throughout the seventeenth and eighteenth centuries gentlemen wore tricorns or bicorns (the same as the tricorn except only two sides were cocked). During and after the Revolution, cockades (a rosette worn on the brim) adorned a tricorn. Originally soldiers wore cockades to differentiate themselves from the opposing side. For instance, a black cockade signified those who fought for the patriot cause. By the late 1780s, the French Revolutionaries had adopted red, white, and blue cockades. Americans who sympathized with the new French order wore the tricolor cockade to show their alliance. The Federalist, who generally mistrusted the French, soon appropriated the black cockade from the

Revolutionary War as their party badge. After 1810, the tricorn was replaced by the silk top hat as the customary headwear for a gentleman. Although sometimes the height and shape could be somewhat exaggerated, the top hat was more streamlined than the more flamboyant tricorn.

The women of the republic indulged in a love of fanciful hats as well. The calash (a large bonnet that resembled the calèche, a French carriage top, hence its name), the favorite of eighteenth-century American women, in due course gave way to more streamlined millinery. But during its heyday (the 1700s) the calash accommodated the immense hairdos of the time. Unlike the men, women chose to wear their hats rather than carry them. The calash offered some versatility for its wearer. It was sometimes worn so that the brim provided an overhang, shading the face. Other times it was pushed back so that it merely touched the back of the head. Long after it was considered stylish, the calash remained the favorite of older women into the latter part of the nineteenth century.

Women's hats were not at all limited to the calash. This was a time when female hat fashions changed rapidly and with much variety. Between 1784 and 1786 women's hats changed 17 times, ranging from close-to-the-head coverings to pouf hats decorated with military ribbons to large bonnets to black crownless gauze hats (Earle, vol. 2, 574). In the waning years of the eighteenth century, hats became more and more highly wrought. Large, black beaver hats bedecked with feathers were also the rage. Soon after, the riding hat came into vogue (ca. 1786–1790). Riding hats had large, heavy brims, often gracefully sweeping downward, and elaborately decorated with ribbons, feathers, and scarves. Some even had lace frills.

In 1794 "The Duke of York's Nightcap" made its appearance. Worn as a means to announce one's sympathy with the French Revolutionaries, it was an adaptation of the French peasant bonnet with a large, rounded crown. Pointed crowned felt hats, decorated with narrow, tricolor ribbons, were also a nod toward approval of French fashion and sympathy with French politics.

Women began to wear hats more often and for more occasions. In earlier years, the hat was a protective covering for the head—or used to shade the face. By the early nationalist period, hats were no longer worn for just protection or for comfort. Even though the elaborately decorated large hats were uncomfortable, women wore these hats indoors as well as outdoors. The beautiful but unwieldy hat had become part of formal dress which meant that they were also worn while dancing.

Women of the working classes still wore bonnets of calico and straw. Straw hats, in fact, were also highly prized by aristocratic women. At first, straw hats were expensive (usually imported from Italy). During the embargo, they became scarce because foreign goods could not be imported. Based on demand, straw making and braiding eventually became an American cottage industry.[4] American women found that they could work out of their homes making and braiding straw as a means of adding to the family income. Soon most American women could afford, and chose to wear, the lighter, more comfortable straw hat.

At the turn of the century and the years following, hats diminished in size. The meteoric rise of Napoleon in France and then on the Continent led to an emulation of French fashions, which were considerably simplified. Hats were now worn closer to the head, accommodating the shorter hairstyles. The Bonapartian hat, a satin, helmet-like affair circled with laurel and worn to the side, was extremely popular as early as 1802. Another popular hat, the "Lavinia," made its appearance soon afterward. A broad-brimmed hat sometimes adorned with a feather, the Lavinia gave the wearer a jaunty appearance. Other early nineteenth-century fashionable bonnet types included the "gypsy" (broad-brimmed with the brim dipping down in the front and center back), the "beehive" (high, rounded crown with small, upturned brim), the "Polish fly-cap" (a decorated turban-like affair), and the "cottage" (a slightly peaked, close-fitting hat worn over a cap).

Probably the most admired female hat style after the turn of the century was the "Polish casquette" or military hat. The Polish casquette was distinguished by a boxy, slightly elevated crown (often pleated) worn toward the back of the head. A small, matching pleated brim framed the face. Atop the casquette was usually a decoration of feathers or bows. A ribbon beneath the chin held the casquette in place.

On the whole, American hair and hat fashion expressed a visual breaking from English culture. As Americans became more aware of their national heritage and their uniqueness in the world, they opted to cease emulating British fashions. Instead, by the nineteenth century, American hair and headdress fashions looked to France, an ally in the Revolution and a country that had also undergone a revolution (albeit far more bloody and terrifying). The French influence would continue to profoundly influence American fashions for years to come.

## MALE DRESS: SIMPLIFICATION AND SOPHISTICATION

After the Revolution male dress (like hair and millinery fashion) in the United States still followed the styles of Great Britain. American citizens dressed in the same manner as their British counterparts according to social class and occupation (Nye, *Cultural Life*, 132). A well cut suit distinguished a gentleman from a laborer, farmer, or frontiersman. Clothes, in this case, did make the man.

Some modes of dress had been established during the war. In 1776 the branches of the military firmly established standard uniforms for line regiments: Naval officers wore blue coats with red lapels, their marine counterparts green coats with white facings. The Continental army originally used homespun coats and long trousers, or in some cases, buckskins. Later, an army uniform was designed: blue or black coat, red linings, black cocked hat, and gilt epaulets. Ribbons of various color differentiated rank. By 1779 a regular uniform was adopted; the facing color of the coat represented the colony to which the soldier was commissioned or enlisted. The military uniform was by this time firmly entrenched in the culture of the republic. In fact, military dress was not even altered much in the years following the Revolutionary War.

Frontiersmen continued to wear the buckskins they had worn for utilitarian purposes for decades before the war and as a form of uniform during the war for a few key reasons. First, it was extremely durable, protecting the wearer from the environment. Buckskin was warmer and heavier than most materials available at the time. Often it was finely tanned to the equivalent of a chamois. (Americans had learned an effective tanning technique from the Native Americans to achieve such high quality, mainly by using animal brains in the tanning process.) Second, it was readily available. (The material was usually bought from or traded with the Native Americans.) Third, because it was not dyed, buckskin provided excellent camouflage for hunters. The soft, earthy grayish-yellow of buckskin easily blended with woodland flora. For that reason (and because of its availability) the ordinary Revolutionary American soldier often wore buckskins in place of a uniform. After the war, those who returned to the frontier continued to do so.

Laborers and tradesmen also adopted buckskin because of its strength and comfort. A typical laborer or tradesman wore breeches made of buckskin, a leather apron and cowhide shoes with leather buckles, woolen stockings, and a flannel jacket, topped by a felt hat (ibid., 132). Shoes and boots were still largely made by hand although the first shoe factory had been in existence since 1760 in Massachusetts. Farmers, on the other hand, wore homespun: homespun breeches and jackets, shirts made from linsey-woolsey or deerskin, woolen stockings, moccasins or leather boots; only for special occasions did a farmer don a broadcloth or corduroy suit (ibid.). Industrious wives and daughters made most of these articles of clothing at home.

Those who had high social aspirations (such as the merchant class) or who had already attained the respect and admiration of the upper echelon of society, dressed much as their British counterparts (although a year behind in styles). In the late eighteenth century, an American gentleman's day costume (sometimes referred to as habit à la française) might consist of a cutaway coat (preferably blue), striped waistcoat, linen stock nattily tied under the chin, buff breeches, high-cut Hessian boots (with the tops turned down), and high-crowned beaver hat (Train, 235). For daytime wear, the republican gentleman fastened his watchcase with an ornately wrought chatelaine (a pendant made of embossed components with designs fastened by a hook to a belt or waistcoat pocket). His evening dress was more decorative. The double-breasted coat would have large, gilt buttons. A white waistcoat, light-colored breeches that ended two to three inches below the knee, white stockings, and buckled shoes completed the ensemble. A gentleman's clothing was custom-made, usually by a favorite tailor.

For the wealthy, gloves, canes, and walking sticks completed a gentleman's costume. Gloves were usually immaculately white, sometimes trimmed in gold fringe. Canes and walking sticks not only set off an outfit, but also were used in a gesture of greeting. The more courtly gentlemen would raise their canes to salute friends and acquaintances (Woodward, 146). The canes themselves could be rather costly. Made from *rodin*, a wood found in India, canes had decorative heads of gold, silver, ivory, or agate, sometimes set with small precious stones (Pistolese and Horsting, 239). Some men continued the pre-Revolutionary custom of carrying small swords or sword canes (Nye, *Cultural Life*, 132). In the event of inclement weather, a gentleman might carry an oiled silk umbrella, a mid-eighteenth-century American trend.[5]

By 1800 a French import, the pantaloon (slim trousers extending from waist to ankle, often held under the instep with a strap) began to replace knee breeches. (By 1810, they had done so entirely.) The first trousers were loose and fully cut, but by 1810 the slim-cut trouser was the rage. Trousers were now the male accepted form of dress—except in full-dress assemblies where knee breeches and silk stockings were still required. A man's political sympathies could often be determined by his dress. Federalists tended to hang onto the more conservative knee breeches and shoe buckles. Republicans favored the more French dress of pantaloons and slippers.

Trousers, in fact, were more popular with laborers and farmers; and in the 1790s the common man's preference for trousers over knee breeches predated that of the gentleman by decades. (Prior to 1789, the common man wore knee breeches, although farmers wore an earlier form of trousers called "skilts." Skilts were below-knee-length brown trousers that were very loose-fitting and about a half yard around the bottom.) This may have occurred for two reasons. First, the French revolutionaries had begun wearing trousers (known as the *sans-culotte*, meaning "without breeches") as a way of distinguishing themselves from the despised aristocracy. American middle and lower classes were sympathetic to, and some identified with, the French Revolutionaries. Adopting the sans-culotte might have been a symbolic gesture of allegiance with France. Second, trousers were more comfortable and infinitely less restrictive of movement than breeches. These trousers were short (usually three inches above the ankle). Thus, they covered most of the leg from briars and brambles but skirted the ground by several inches.

In keeping with the more egalitarian movement in male dress, Madison became the first president to wear trousers. By the War of 1812, trousers were popular with men of all classes. But with all trends, there was a reactionary backlash against the more democratic trouser wearing. President Monroe attempted to bring back knee breeches as the male form of proper dress.

Although a Jeffersonian Republican, Monroe insisted on wearing the clothes of post–Revolutionary America. In 1817 when Monroe entered the White House, he decreed that for all state functions men must wear knee breeches and silk stockings. Monroe himself still wore the cocked hats, aligning himself more with the style of the Washington administration than with the fashions of post–War of 1812. However, it is safe to say that Monroe's dress reflected a more nostalgic than political view—and one that was briefly lived.

Long trousers were a nineteenth-century phenomenon and it spawned others. In 1804 the first patent for suspenders was issued, signifying the eventual extinction of knee breeches. Trousers were not the only radical change in men's fashion. Men's coats became more broad-shouldered with a fitted waist and rolled collar. The redingote (a long, fitted coat designed to show off elaborate waistcoats) became very popular. Shirts were even showier than before. Cravats and frills replaced the simple linen stock. Waistcoats practically stood away from the body, padded from within by ruffled and frilled shirtfronts.

Wealthy men (and women) were also concerned with their facial appearance, notably their smiles. Americans had notoriously bad teeth. Diet and lack of dental hygiene were the primary causes of early tooth decay, rot, and the inevitable loss. Those with money chose to improve their appearance by purchasing false teeth, which, for the most part, were ill-fitting and uncomfortable.[6] (Often dentures slipped out of the wearer's mouth at inopportune moments, causing much embarrassment.) The enterprising Paul Revere, capitalizing on this drawback, advertised his dental services in the *Boston News Letter*:

PAUL REVERE—Whereas many Persons are so unfortunate as to lose their fore Teeth by accident, and otherwise, to their great Detriment, not only in looks, but speaking both in Public and Private:

"This is to inform all such, that they may have them replaced with false ones, that look as well as the Natural, and answer the End of Speaking to all intents by PAUL REVERE, Goldsmith, near the head of Dr. Clark's Wharf, Boston—

"All persons who have had false Teeth fixt by Mr. John Baker, Surgeon-Dentist, and they have got loose (as they will in Time) may have them fastened by the above, who learnt the method of fixing them from Mr. Baker. (see in Train, 177)

The most famous of denture wearers, George Washington, probably acquired his stern, non-smiling demeanor because of the ill fit and discomfort of his false teeth (which were costly). Washington's false teeth were not made of wood, as popular legend would have it. The president had only two or three of his natural teeth. Fitted around them was a denture plate made of gold. The upper and lower plates were affixed together with springs that cut into the cheek. The teeth implanted into the dental plate were mostly hippopotamus ivory, although a few were human teeth. Most assuredly, other republican denture wearers suffered the same discomfort (and probably the grim appearance) as the president. Only the poor went without teeth. Affluent Americans were willing to endure acute discomfort for the sake of appearance. But half of the American people found fashion to be liberating as the new nation grew, and that half was the women of the new republic.

## FEMALE DRESS: LIBERATION OF THE BODY

As women's roles increasingly became more important in republican society, their dress came to represent that change. American women, noted for their cleanliness and orderliness in appearance, increasingly took more interest in fashion. Following their European counterparts, some American women enhanced their look with powder and rouge and darkened their eyelashes. (The prejudice against "powder and paint" was a mid-nineteenth-century phenomenon. In the eighteenth and early nineteenth centuries, there was no stigma against using artifice.) Fashion was becoming an obsession that was passed from mother to daughter. A Hessian officer of the period observed

the daughters keep up their stylish dressing because the mothers desire it. Should the mother die, her last words are to the effect that the daughter must retain control of the father's money-bags. Nearly all articles necessary for the adornment of the female sex are at present either very scarce or dear, and for this reason they are now wearing their Sunday finery. (qtd. in Earle, vol. 2, 734)

As Americans as a whole had looked to Europe for inspiration in the arts, philosophy, and government, so did American women look to Europe for guidance in dress and deportment. In the early years (1783–1795) American women's dress followed English styles. Unlike men's fashions, women's dress was awash in vivid colors, celestial blue being a special favorite of fashionable women in the republic. By and large, women's fashions in the latter quarter of the eighteenth century were much simpler than in the past. Gowns were more simply constructed, using a petticoat for fullness rather than rigid wire frameworks. The result was a softer, more graceful style.

One popular costume of the early period (after 1770) was the polonaise, which was distinguished by its absence of a hoop skirt and panniers (a framework used to expand a woman's skirt over the hips). The skirt length was shorter (around ankle-length), allowing the wearer to show off an elegantly shod foot and providing more mobility. The bodice was fitted, usually trimmed in lace or ruffles. Flowing from the bodice was an overskirt that cut away in the front and was gathered in back by a small bustle or in three large festoons. The overskirt served to draw the eye to the very ornate underskirt. Some of the more popular fabrics used in the polonaise were rich brocades and damasks (a patterned fabric, usually cotton, silk, wool, or linen).

By 1795, the dress of fashionable American women became even more simplified. Like men's fashions, the sumptuous fabrics of prewar America made way for less pretentious materials. Following French, rather than British, fashion, American gentlewomen now chose fashions made from lightweight fabrics such as gauze or muslin. Such materials clung to the body, emphasizing the form. Necklines were lowered. (Often a gauzy scarf or handkerchief covered the shoulders in an attempt to maintain past years' modesty code.) The most radical factor of all was the absence of whalebone supports and petticoats. Even the arms were in full view because of the preference for sleeveless and puffed-sleeved dresses.

By 1806 the French "Empire" fashion was firmly ensconced in the annals of female fashion (Nye, *Cultural Life*, 134). The Empire dress was long and narrow and sometimes had a train. The neckline was cut low and the waistline quite high (directly below the bosom). Sleeves were tightly fashioned. This more neoclassical style was designed to accentuate the gracefulness and femininity of the wearer. Décolleté was the order of the day, to the despair of the more conservative. Sheer and clingy materials were also still in vogue. One wag commented that "in one year eighteen ladies caught fire and eighteen thousand caught cold" (qtd. in Train, 238).

Because dresses were so sheer and thin, additional articles of clothing began to appear at this time. The chilly North American climate (as well as Parisian winters) required warm outer garments. Jackets, overdresses, scarves, and wraps protected the scantily clad from the elements. These were often as carefully designed and worked as the dress underneath. But outer garments were not the only clothing that became important to the wearer. Translucent dresses became the catalyst for the appearance of a new female garment: the pantaloon.

Women adopted the pantaloon (or pantalets, usually used in reference to girls' pantaloons) as a form of underclothing. Before this period, women wore petticoats and corsets but no "drawers" as they came to be known. The pantaloons served as a means to retain modesty under the sheer Empire dress. Soon the pantaloons became a fashion statement themselves. For formal occasions, pantalets were made of satin and were heavily ruched with lace and other frills. Fashion plates (engravings of costumes) from 1811 show calf-length dresses in which the lacy pantaloon is seen from hemline to the ankle.

The few pieces of other undergarments worn beneath Empire dresses were close-cut and of light consistency (Earle, vol. 2, 785). Most women wore a lightweight chemise (a loose shift). The whalebone corsets were considered fashion relics of the colonial era. Certainly, the female body was freed from constraints. Thus, the Empire dress was at least healthier, if less modest, than the fashions of the late eighteenth century.

An alteration of the Empire dress, the chemise dress, came out of the need to wear a chemise beneath the thin Empire dress. Chemise dresses were usually made of sheer percale or a linen lawn. They were straight-lined and close to the body and had minimal trimming. The empire bodice was tight, drawn low at the corners of the neckline. The idea was to accentuate the breasts.

Some of the chemise dresses were cut so low that the wearer needed to place a "modesty" or "modesty bit" around the neckline and shoulders. Modesty bits used bits of thin muslin or lace as coverage. Chemise dresses, although not very warm, liberated women and celebrated the female form.

Shoes and gloves were important parts of a woman's dress and often revealed much about the social status of the wearer. Women of the lower classes wore more substantial shoes of leather with heels (although women of all classes were not expected to walk any great distance). Those of wealth and property wore slippers indoors and outdoors. Slippers were always thin-soled and made of fabric (usually to coordinate with a dress) such as silk, brocade, damask, or soft kid and had no heels. Thus slippers were extremely impractical for outdoor wear.

Heeled shoes had appeared earlier in republican society. (The heels were dainty, thus insubstantial.) By 1790 the heeled shoe had disappeared, replaced by slippers or sandal-like footwear. All footwear was worn with silk hose (in the case of the wealthy) or worsted wool or cotton (for those whose lifestyles required more practical stockings).

As impractical as footwear appeared to be, there were some devices designed to protect shoes from certain ruin. Pattens (an overshoe device), clogs (wooden-soled shoes), and goloe-shoes (from which galoshes evolved) protected the shoes or the feet from mud, stones, and puddles. Pattens had rough wooden soles and attached to the foot with buckles and straps. A patten had a thick sole, elevating the wearer (protecting not only shoes but stockings and hemlines). Clogs were similarly constructed but had wooden soles tipped in iron. Children wore clogs rather than pattens to protect their feet. The goloe-shoe was simply another name for a clog, although today there is a distinction between a clog (shoe) and galoshes (overshoes).

Pattens, clogs, and goloe-shoes were awkward and noisy, especially the high-soled patten. The noise made by pattens was so disconcerting that many churches posted signs barring the wearing of pattens during services. The high soles caused the wearer to wobble, sometimes resulting in ankle injuries or falls into the very mire they were trying to avoid. Not until later in the nineteenth century did women's footwear offer any substantial support or protection to the wearer.

Gloves and mitts (fingerless gloves) were also part of a well dressed woman's apparel (as well as men). Elegantly fashioned gloves came in various lengths and colors. Short gloves were made of linen or wool. Some were embroidered as well. Longer mitts that reached the shoulder were sometimes made of kid leather. The young daughters of the republic held "glove-bees" where they cut out and stitched together gloves for themselves and others. Like their elders, children also had a keen interest in presenting a stylish appearance.

## CHILDREN'S DRESS: BREAKING WITH TRADITION

Until around 1770 children dressed in miniature adult styles, but that tradition slowly began to change. In the early republican era girls dressed as their mothers: puffed-sleeved, high-waisted, narrow-skirted dresses reaching the ankle (Train, 238), but there were significant deviations in children's and adults' dress. Infants, of course, wore loose-fitting sacques and dainty bonnets. All children (babies, boys, and girls) wore aprons (called "pinners") that covered the waist, sleeves, and skirt. These had a practical purpose: to protect the clothes from tears and soil. Some aprons were ornamental as well. Children were also outfitted in sunbonnets and wore masks to protect them from the burning rays of the sun. (Their mothers and grandmothers had affected the wearing of masks for this reason as well.)

Young girls, like their fashion-forward elders, wore pantalets. At first the pantalet was an awkward garment with loose frills tied on with drawstrings below the knee extending to the ankle (Earle, vol. 2, 775). Because the strings often snapped, resulting in the garment trailing in dirt and entangling the feet, the pantalet was quickly modified to resemble the woman's pantaloon (that is, decorative trousers that served as drawers).

Following the lead of their mothers, girls made and wore gloves, often of nankeen. These were tied to the sleeves of the dress or the spencer (a waist-length jacket worn by women and children). Nankeen and linen gloves were stiffly starched, making them uncomfortable for the juvenile wearer. A mother's wish to present her children as having a clean, smart appearance superseded any discomfort starched gloves may have caused.

The young sons of wealthy citizens were dressed in high-waisted suits of kerseymere or its equivalent. Young boys were also outfitted in nankeen breeches. Because nankeen was lightweight, it offered limited protection and warmth during the long, severe northern winters. Thus, in winter, young boys wore breeches of yellow flannel. During their early childhood, philosopher, poet, and essayist Ralph Waldo Emerson (1803–1882) and his brother William were dressed in yellow flannel both day and night. Like other boys their age, the Emerson brothers were eventually allowed to wear trousers at the age of seven. These trousers were often a part of homemade nankeen suits.

Nonetheless, older boys emulated their elders in the dress. When knee breeches were the fashion, boys donned knee breeches and white silk stockings. As male fashion preferences moved toward trouser wearing, boys followed their elders' example. Boys also wore highly decorative shirts, heavily frilled not only at the neck, but also at the wrists (Train, 238).

But unlike the dress of their elders, which eventually was heavily influenced by French fashion, American children's dress was less artificial and restrained. Although there are instances of children wearing wigs, elaborate coats, unusual ruffles, and carrying small swords (as the children of wealthy European families did), American children's dress was a far more scaled-down version of adult fashions. With the introduction of the pantalet for girls and the pantaloon (trousers) for boys, American children had more freedom of movement than ever before.

## COLLEGIATE ATTIRE

Collegiate attire in the new nation deserves special mention. University students were held to strict standards of dress, including admonitions concerning detail and color. The Oxford gown (the academic regalia, gown and hood—the remnant of this tradition is still an integral part of commencement ceremonies today) as decreed by the governing body of the college was the appropriate apparel for students and faculty. For example, at Harvard dress codes were based on the student's year of study. In 1784, all Harvard undergraduates could don blue-gray coats and black, nankeen (a buff or yellow cloth), or olive waistcoats. Underclassmen, however, were restricted to plain buttonholes. Juniors were permitted more finery: frogs (but only on the center front, not on the cuffs). Seniors were given the most latitude: buttons, buttonholes, and frogs. Gold and silver lace and cords and edging on hats and waistcoats incurred fines for all those who indulged in such frippery (Earle, vol. 2, 741). Moreover, prescribed necktie colors and appearance were severely imposed. White and black were the only colors permissible. Hats, caps, boots, and shoes could only be black. In cases of a family tragedy, only seniors could wear mourning clothes, a severe imposition considering the rigid societal constraints regarding dress for special circumstances such as bereavement.

## DRESS FOR SPECIAL CIRCUMSTANCES

Some specific instances demanded a departure from the norms of everyday dress and formal wear. Although most citizens' wardrobes were limited (except, of course, those of the very wealthy), Americans proved to be resourceful in dressing for special occasions. Two milestones in a citizen's life required unique dress: weddings and funerals.

Weddings were an integral part of a community's social life, regardless of geographical location. For over two hundred years Americans in city and country, North and South, delighted in a custom called "Coming Out Bride" (ibid., 631). Coming Out Bride was a lengthy affair. On the first Sunday after the wedding and the four Sundays after the honeymoon, the newly married couple would attend church services in the finest clothing they could afford. If the couple were very wealthy, the new bride might have a new elaborate costume for each Sunday. (The groom would wear a new suit as well.) Often the new husband and wife were given the most prominent seats in the church, a place where all could admire their new finery.

The bridal dress and coming-out-bride ensembles were of various colors. White was not the set color for bridal costumes until the nineteenth century. The first recorded instance of an American bride decked in an all white bridal dress, complete with a wedding veil, was in 1800. A portrait depicts Mrs. James H. Heyward of Charleston, South Carolina, in all white wearing a tulle veil, pearl tiara, and pearl earrings (ibid., 639).

In the late eighteenth century brides wore the most expensive dress within their means, the color and fabric based on preference and availability. Silk brocade was one favorite material with republican brides. Portraits and accounts from the period record that brides wore dresses of gray, pink, yellow, and lavender. Headdresses were often made of lace, matching the color of the dress or the ornate lace trimmings. (Veils were a nineteenth-century development.) Some brides carried leather-framed fans as an accessory. Silk shoes completed the ensemble.

Like wedding clothing, funeral and mourning dress played an important role in society. For all Americans the correct and appropriate mourning attire was crucial when the necessity arose. The outward appearance of mourning was taken with the utmost seriousness in the new republic. Dark or dull colored clothing was compulsory for bereaved family members. Men sometimes wore black armbands to denote their sorrow. Widows especially were held to stringent standards of mourning attire. Known as "widow's weeds," the mourning costume was composed of black clothing from head to foot. All widows regardless of age or class wore heavy black veils to signify their grief.

Overall, citizens carried mourning attire to the extreme. Black gloves (known as mourning gloves) were distributed at funerals. Even the soles of shoes were blackened as a measure of grief. All children—even the very smallest—of a family in mourning were forbidden to wear lace or embroidery. Instead, a girl would wear three bands of dark crepe as trimming on the bottom of her pantalets (ibid., 777).

Mourning jewelry, although sometimes expensive, was popular. Since societal dictates precluded the bereaved's wearing of the heavily encrusted jewelry and decorative cameos that were so well favored by citizens, male and female mourners created and wore unique jewelry items for the occasion. The hair of the deceased was the preferred material for such memorabilia. Sometimes a lock of the dearly departed's hair was encased in a locket. Other times the hair was plaited, forming a ring, bracelet, brooch, or watch guard (ibid., 656).

Engraved gold rings were given out to mourners at funerals, usually at great expense to the family of the deceased. (The cost was approximately one pound apiece. If the funeral was a large one, this could be quite costly.) These rings, known as "mourning rings," bore dire adages such as "Prepared be/To follow me" and "Death parts/United hearts" (ibid., 655).

A nationwide phenomenon occurred in December 1799 with the news of the death of George Washington. The death of the beloved icon of the new republic sparked a national outpouring of grief, some of which was manifested in mourning dress. All Americans were expected to wear a crepe badge as a symbol of their sorrow. In addition to the mourning badge, saddened Americans wore black cockades, sashes, belts, slippers, and gloves (ibid., 748). Men and women carried handkerchiefs imprinted with Washington's image and a list of his virtues.

Hence, the republican insistence on virtue was literally manifested in the clothing of the day. Regardless of occupation, social or economic class, age, or gender, Americans' love affair with fashion had many cultural and economic consequences. Political independence may have precluded industrial and economic independence, but all three led to a sartorial independence that ushered in a freedom from bodily constraint and a celebration of the human form.

# 6

# Food

At first glance the new republic was a land of plenty for most citizens in both city and country. A relatively sparsely populated nation resulted in vast lands available for cultivation and grazing. Rivers and the ocean provided an overabundance of seafood for the nation's needs. The United States was rich in its production of food sources. Although the harsh climate played a significant factor in the quality and sometimes the availability of food, the American farmer was, in fact, virtually self-sufficient. Those in villages and cities also benefited from this plentitude. And in times of crop devastation, farmer and city dweller alike suffered.

## MEAT, POULTRY, AND FISH

At this time no other nation in the world had the quantity and variety of foods available to it than did the United States (Nye, *Cultural Life*, 130). Americans primarily raised hogs, cattle, and poultry for their meat sources. Pork and fish became the basis of the American diet since both were easily smoked and/or salted as an efficient means of preservation. Hogs, especially, were an economic boon for the American farmer. An abundance of hogs on the American continent made them easily and cheaply acquired. In contrast, in Europe, pork and other meats were at a premium because livestock in general required much land and grain for grazing (Cummings, 15). Americans had the necessary land and grain. Hogs also presented no additional work for the farmer since they usually were allowed to roam, finding their own food on their way (Train, 239). Furthermore, hogs increased in size rapidly—within the first eight months a young hog could increase its size 150 times (Kephart, 46).

Unlike other meats, the flavor of pork was enhanced by the smoking and salting processes (Cummings, 16). Americans loved the taste of a savory smoked ham or a side of bacon. In the Western Territories farmers preferred salted meats to that of fresh meat; for example, Kentucky settlers were known to eat salted meat three times a day. Some even believed that fresh meat was "unwholesome" (ibid., 16). Although wilderness families often supplemented their meals with game (such as deer, squirrel, and wild fowl), pork was still the staple of the diet. As one frontier wife and mother asserted, "Game's good as a relish and so's bread; but pork is the staff of life" (qtd. in ibid., 12).

Pork was also an inexpensive option for city laborers, especially in the Mid-Atlantic states. Often a famished worker would have a meal of butter crackers and a pound of "blood pudding" for the sum of three or four cents (ibid., 28). Blood pudding was a flavorful mixture of hog blood (occasionally beef blood might be used as a substitute) and chopped seasoned pork packed in a casing. Sometimes laborers bypassed the butcher and created their own fresh meal. Scavenger pigs roamed city streets, feeding on offal (the waste parts of butchered animals) and slops. Laborers, rather than paying pennies for a meal of blood pudding, would cut the ears of the scavenger pigs to bleed them, thus supplying a fresh ingredient for blood pudding.

The New England diet, on the other hand, was a little more balanced. New Englanders enjoyed both pork and beef, although their meals were as monotonous as those on the frontier. (The working-class New England family feasted three times a day on meals of salt pork, cornmeal mush, and pea and bean porridge. The only deviation came from beef or dried or salted fish.) In the South, mutton was a desired dish, although because of the preservation problems, it was considered a luxury.

As a rule, American farmers preferred not to raise sheep and goats because these animals were prone to disease and required constant supervision (Nye, *Cultural Life*, 129). With the exception of pork and game, all other meats were only available for consumption at the time of slaughter, particularly in the summer. In the city, cattle were driven through the streets to the slaughterhouse. Since there was no refrigeration in the latter part of the eighteenth century and only the wealthy could afford to maintain icehouses, farmers had to resort to hanging meats in wells or springhouses with less than desirable results. A Long Islander remarked in his journal that after slaughtering a lamb in August and hanging the meat in his well, he was "resolved to have no more fresh meat till cooler weather comes. Those who have a mind to swallow or be swallowed by flies may eat fresh meat for me" (qtd. in Cummings, 17). City people had to either eat the meat almost immediately or have it salted or smoked.

Poultry, like hogs, were easy to care for since they, too, foraged for food unattended. Because of their small size, a chicken or turkey could serve as the main course for a single-family meal. This was no problem in the country. In the city this presented a problem because fresh chicken lasted about 18 hours in New York City (Nye, *Cultural Life*, 131). In general, the wealthier classes in the city included more poultry in their diet than their less-affluent counterparts.

Fish was readily available on the eastern seaboard and, like pork, easily preserved. Cod was the first choice for New England appetites. A variety of other fish found in rivers appealed to republican palates. Seafood, primarily lobster and eel, was often a main course on eastern tables. Salted and smoked fish became a principal part of the eastern diet. Prosperous citizens sometimes included shellfish on the menu as well.

## GRAIN

Grain (which included wheat, rye, barley, oats, and maize) was probably the American farmer's primary crop. Americans did not want for bread. Although the frontier farmer suffered crop failure, his eastern counterpart was successful. Wheat crops yielded ample harvests. (Wheat grows and thrives within a wide range of climates. Thus, wheat fields predominated the landscape in the North and the South.) Where there were wheat fields, there was bread on the table.

Corn (or maize) became the indispensable grain crop in America.[1] Corn served both as livestock feed and the American main dish. In New England—with the exception of Connecticut where the wheat crop had been seriously damaged by smut (fungus)—corn was a frequent substitute ingredient in many dishes. Hasty pudding, the homey dish that became the subject and title of Joel Barlow's mock epic poem, graced many American tables.[2] By the early republican era, hasty pudding had become a Yankee institution, so much so that in John Adams's home it was served every Sunday as part of the evening meal (Jones, 10). Harvard's Hasty Pudding Club, founded in 1795, took its name from the students' own cooking of the dish in fireplace pots.

Essentially, hasty pudding (sometimes known as "Indian pudding") is cornmeal mush sweetened with maple syrup or brown sugar. It was an adaptation of the English recipe for porridge that required wheat flour as its main ingredient. Because cornmeal was less expensive (and more plentiful) than wheat, colonists had substituted cornmeal in the mixture. Its ready availability, cheapness, and sweetness made it popular fare.

American ingenuity revealed itself in the variety of other recipes that used corn as the main ingredient. "Rye and Injun bread" was a mixture of rye and corn, another republican favorite. To make hominy, another popular dish, corn kernels were hulled, dried, then soaked and boiled. Grinding hominy into a coarse white meal produced hominy grits. Cornmeal was often used in baking different kinds of cakes such as hoecakes, johnnycakes, and cornpone. Remarkably, popped corn became the only snack food of the early nationalist era.

## SPIRITS

On the frontier farmers had found a new use for corn. Isolated settlers, although industrious, longed for a break in the dreariness of frontier life. Liquid refreshment was a welcome relief, especially alcoholic refreshment. In the backwoods the refreshment of choice was corn liquor because of its accessibility.

On the eastern seaboard alcoholic beverages were easy to find. For many years breweries had been an eastern institution. Bountiful eastern apple orchards supplied the operators of cider mills with their main ingredient. But for those in the western part of the states and the territories, ales, beers, and ciders were rare. In the West, there were few natural apple trees. Malt liquors were hard to preserve. But corn was plentiful and could easily be converted into the prized elixir.

Unfortunately, excessive drinking of corn liquor (and other spirits) became a problem as a result of the abundance of corn liquor. Several possible causes for this include a diet of heavily salted meat prompted drinking hard liquor; the common misperception that hot summers made drinking cold springwater dangerous (alcohol was a safer alternative); hard labor precipitated hard drinking; and heavy drinking broke up the monotony of life on the frontier (Cummings, 15–16). After the turn of the century, subsequent settlers did plant orchards and brewed malt liquors. By this time corn liquor lost some of its popularity with the newer inhabitants of the frontier. Visitors to the United States noted that these settlers were far more temperate in their imbibing than in the past (Melish, 51–52). Perhaps the cause was that the potency of the corn liquor led to more drinking, not just environmental and psychological factors.

Excessive alcohol consumption was not perceived as a problem on the frontier and by the best of families in cities and villages. It was not unusual after a dinner party to find one or more of the guests sleeping off the effects of over-imbibing (Woodward, 177). The anecdote that follows, from Senator George F. Hoar's *Autobiography*, succinctly sums up the American apathy toward excessive drinking.

The habit of excessive drinking was then universal in this country. Even the clergyman staggered home from his round of pastoral calls, and the bearers partook of brandy, gin, and rum at funerals. It was not uncommon to see farmers, highly respected in the town, lying drunk by the roadside on a summer afternoon, or staggering along the streets. I have heard Nathan Brooks, who delivered the first temperance lecture in Concord at the request of the selectmen, say that

A DRUNKEN MAN.                              *From Lavater.*

Illustration of a drunken man, circa 1800.
Courtesy of the Library of Congress.

after it was over he and some of the principal citizens went over to the tavern
and each took a drink of flip. (qtd. in ibid., 178)

The republican propensity for drinking eventually led to political
problems. During the war whiskey production had risen significantly.
Because whiskey making had seriously depleted grain stores (corn,
wheat, and rye), the wartime governments had to curtail the amounts of
grain distilleries could use in liquor production. Also, there was no tax
on liquor or licensing of distilleries. Anyone and everyone could make
and sell whiskey. For many, distilling was a lucrative sideline.

In 1791 Congress enacted a nine-cent-per-gallon excise tax on whiskey.
The whiskey tax had been proposed as a viable means to raise money
for the national debt. Irate backwoods distillers reacted very violently to

the federal revenue officers who came to collect the tax. By 1794, well organized farmers in western Pennsylvania led an armed rebellion (the Whiskey Rebellion). Fortunately, no battle ensued between the army and the insurgents, partially because the farmers had no desire to bear arms against the militia. Some were brought to trial; two were convicted for treason but pardoned by Washington. The end result was that Congress eventually repealed the whiskey tax. Whiskey, in fact, was not taxed in the United States from 1792 to 1862. Obviously, Americans guarded their right to distill and consume whiskey as a fundamental right (as well as their right to resist taxation).

## VEGETABLES

Although pork and grains were the basis of American food and drink, vegetables provided some variety in the republican diet. Farmers grew the usual English vegetables: peas, beans, vegetable marrow (a large, green squash found in the British Isles), and cabbage. To that they added vegetables indigenous to the American continent: yams, pumpkins, and the American variety of squash. Americans also grew root vegetables such as potatoes and turnips. Early American cultivation did not, however, include cauliflower, eggplant, and rhubarb since these were unknown at this time (Train, 239).

The tomato, today a mainstay in the American diet, was not particularly popular with Americans during this time. Called "love apples," tomatoes were primarily grown alongside other plants in American gardens for their color, not necessarily because of their tastiness.[3] The French, on the other hand, had become adept at using love apples in their cuisine. American gentry, many enamored with all things French, introduced French cooking in their households and with it the tomato into their diets. (Jefferson was particularly fond of tomatoes.) But these were the exceptions, not the rule.

Americans also resisted eating leafy vegetables, somehow equating them to being less nutritious than other vegetables. Unlike root vegetables, squash and leafy vegetables were difficult to preserve. (Most potatoes and beans could be either stored in bins or dried.) Though farm families enjoyed wild greens such as dandelions, turnip tops, and wild plants (cowslips and pigweed), these were handily picked from the wild. No labor-intensive cultivation was involved.

If a family chose to grow green vegetables, that chore was usually left to the farmer's wife. Farmers saw little reason to invest their efforts and time in growing vegetables that were less substantial (that is, less filling) than the usual staples of the American meals (meat, grain, and root vegetables). Many times the farmer would not even allow his wife to purchase seeds to start a garden since farmers generally regarded gardening as a waste of time. In one documented instance, a Maryland farmer refused his wife's request for money to buy seeds, mainly because he thought it more prudent that money be spent on whiskey and tobacco instead (Cummings, 21).

## FRUITS

Although many Americans did not eat fruits regularly, there were huge varieties available to American palates. Berries grew wildly and abundantly. American orchards yielded pears, cherries, peaches, plums, and apples. Most fruits were, however, extremely perishable. The exception was the apple, which could be kept for months after the growing season had ended. As prized as the apple may have been, it was not available to all.

Apple trees took many years to mature and so there was a scarcity of them, especially on the frontier. Prior to the settlement of the North American continent, there were hundreds of apple varieties available in Europe. The original settlers had brought the apple to North America where it quickly adapted to the American climate. In the initial stages of the westward movement, trappers and Native Americans carried apple seedlings into the frontier, but apple trees were still relatively uncommon on the frontier. Fortunately, due to the extraordinary efforts of a practical nurseryman, western settlers were able to own and maintain their own apple orchards.

John Chapman (1774–1845), also known as Johnny Appleseed, was instrumental in bringing apples and books to the frontier and in the process became an American cultural hero. Chapman's original plan was to make a profit from his apple seedling sales. Indeed, the demand for his product was apparent. At the turn of the century, territorial law required that all newly established homesteads needed to plant a minimum of 50 apple trees in the first year of settlement. (The law was designed to guarantee the stability of western homesteads.) Apples, then, served a dual purpose for early western settlers: to establish homesteading rights and to supplement their diets.

With this in mind, around 1800 Chapman began collecting apple seeds from cider presses in western Pennsylvania. From there he planted apple nurseries from the Allegheny Mountains into what is now known as the Midwest. Folk legend maintains that it was Chapman's dream to cover the United States and its territories with apple trees so that no one would ever go hungry because apples were so plentiful.

Chapman was a colorful figure. His appearance was, to say the least, eccentric. Historical accounts record that Johnny Appleseed was a small, wiry man with long, unkempt dark hair and a scanty beard. He was usually barefoot, even in the middle of winter (although he had money to afford boots). His cast-off, ragged clothing had been acquired as payment for his apple seedlings. A self-professed missionary of the Church of the New Jerusalem,[4] Chapman shared the Bible and the writings of Emanuel Swedenborg (1688–1772) with settlers along with his seedlings. Often he would separate the books into sections, leaving one section with a family. On his next visit, he would pick up the section and exchange it with another.

Although destitute in appearance, Chapman owned thousands of tracts of land throughout what is now Ohio and Indiana. He used this land to plant his apple seeds, transplant the seedlings, and then set out orchards. Although he sold many of his seedlings to the settlers, he also gave away thousands of seedlings to settlers who could not afford them. The profuse apple orchards that exist in the Midwest to this day are largely due to his efforts.

While apples became a staple of the frontier diet thanks to the efforts of Johnny Appleseed, back East tree fruit was used for the making of brandies and ciders rather than for eating. More exotic fruits, such as pineapples, bananas, and figs, were imported from the nearby West Indies but were reserved for the tables of the more affluent. Strawberries and raspberries were readily picked from wild bushes and plants, eaten in spring and summer, but rarely were they preserved.

Regrettably, fruit was difficult to preserve at a moderate price. Canning and preserving required large amounts of sugar, which was quite costly. Heat canning was in very limited practice. (Not until the 1840s would heat canning be widely used commercially and domestically.) Cider and brandy making were the exception. Although initially expensive, cider and brandy often yielded a tidy profit for those with an entrepreneurial spirit. On the whole, much fruit rotted on the ground, providing fodder for rummaging hogs. Throughout the country apples that were not turned into cider served as pie filling. Above all, fruit was seasonable. In the spring and summer, Americans had fresh fruit. In the colder seasons, they usually went without.

This was true for city dwellers and country denizens alike. Because transportation during this period was rudimentary (that is, pre-railroad), Americans found it difficult to ship fresh fruits and vegetables to cities. In the winter and early spring, there were virtually no vegetables or fruits to be had in the major cities such as Boston and New York. (Fruits and vegetables were acquired from growers whose gardens or farms were at the perimeter of the city limits.) In the summer when produce was available, it wilted and rotted very quickly.

## DAIRY

Dairy products were, in many cases, subject to the seasons as well. If pastures were green, milk was plentiful. In New England milk was abun-

dant. Pastures were green, and the climate was more conducive to preservation. But in most parts of the country milk spoiled quickly. Having
milk on a regular basis was a luxury only the wealthy could afford. The
ice and the icehouses used to keep milk preserved were expensive. For
those in the city of modest incomes, milk was carried in from outlying
areas in tin cans. By the time the milk reached the city, it was no longer
very fresh.

In the South the lack of availability of milk was a serious problem.
The much warmer climate made it virtually impossible to keep milk in
city and country. As a beverage it was in short supply. Milk did, however, have the advantage of being processed into other forms that could
be kept for long periods of time, namely, butter and cheese. Most country
homes were equipped with churns and cheese presses for this purpose.

In addition, there were times that milk was scarce throughout all the
United States, not just the South. Americans had adopted the English
practice of open pasturage (open grazing). In England where the climate
was milder, this did not present a problem. Grass was available most of
the time. But the harsher American winters often killed off the grass,
forcing the cows to roam through the woods to look for food. Subsequently, there was little or no milk available in winter for anyone.

## HEALTH AND FOOD QUALITY

Overall, Americans suffered from seriously ill balanced diets due to
the scarcity or absence of such essential foods as dairy, fruits, and vegetables. Mortality rates in many parts of the country were quite high.
(The exception was Massachusetts where many lived to be septuagenar-
ians and octogenarians.) Both young and old had terrible dental problems: decay, rot, and tooth loss. Children were given meat to eat before
they had teeth, perhaps resulting in stunted growth and lifelong poor
health. The lack of essential vitamins and minerals found in fresh, leafy
vegetables and milk contributed to many health problems. Many suffered from skin conditions caused by poor nutrition.

In the city ill health was often at crisis levels. The causes of many
deadly illnesses that repeatedly plagued urban areas, such as typhoid,
cholera, and yellow fever, were regarded as mysteries.[5] The inability to
preserve food, especially in the summer, presented real problems for the
city. Poultry could not be killed more than four hours before cooking.
Milk soured within one or two hours after milking.

But American diets were not without some merit. Because bread was
made from whole grain, rather than refined, flour, it was far more nutritious than twenty-first-century fare. Some homemade recipes supplemented diets and added much need vitamins. Spruce beer, a fermented
concoction brewed from spruce twigs and needles with sugar or molasses, was known to stave off scurvy. In mountainous frontier communi-

ties, children often chewed on twigs, perhaps as an instinctive means of replenishing much needed vitamins (Cummings, 24).

Despite the unevenness of quality and availability of food, Americans were renowned for their hearty and indiscriminate appetites. In 1796 a visitor to the New York marketplace recorded 63 types of fish, 14 varieties of shellfish, 52 types of fowl and meat, and 27 varieties of vegetables (Nye, *Cultural life*, 130). The famous quote below from the French philosopher Comte de Constantin-François de Chasseboeuf Volney (1757–1820) provides a vivid description of American eating habits and the quality of the prepared food: [6]

In the morning they deluge their stomachs with a quart of hot water impregnated with tea, or so slightly with coffee that it is mere colored water; and they swallow, almost without chewing, hot bread, half-baked toast soaked with butter, cheese of the fattest kind, slices of salt or hung beef, ham, etc., all which are nearly insoluble. At dinner they have boiled pastes under the name of puddings, and the fattest are esteemed to be the most delicious. . . . To digest these viscous substances they take tea bitter to the taste. . . . Supper again introduces salt meats or oysters. As Chastellux says, the whole day passes in heaping indigestions on one another. (qtd. in Nye, 130–131)

Americans were almost oblivious to the abysmal quality of their food because it was often poorly prepared and preserved. Stoves were largely a luxury—most food was cooked in a fireplace. Utensils, dishes, and cookware had not changed much from colonial days. (The materials used for utensils and dishes reflected the social class of its owners. Ordinary folk used wood or pewter utensils and dishware; the aristocracy preferred silver-plated utensils, imported china, and crystal.) Because most cooking—baking, broiling, roasting, and boiling—was done in a wide kitchen fireplace, the colonial standard implements were used: griddles, hanging pots, trivets, Dutch ovens, trammels [the links and hooks used to raise and lower kettles], cranes, and long-handled peels [shovel-like tools] used to retrieve food or pots buried in the coals (Jones, 5). Preservation methods were primitive. Consistency in quality was hard to achieve. Food was many times undercooked or burned.

European travelers often commented on the stomach-churning quality of American cuisine: the bitterness of the coffee and tea, the rancidity of the produce, the saltiness of the meats, the fattiness of the pastries. Rich and poor alike ate spoiled food ravenously. Jefferson deemed that in Virginia humans and livestock were "illy fed" (qtd. in Cummings, 13). Ingredients that might have made the food more palatable (such as refined sugar and spices) were too expensive. Molasses and brown sugar were the substitute-sweetening agents for the common person's tea or coffee. Also, the high price of sugar precluded any canning of fruit. The republican housewife was too often burdened with other more demanding household chores to spend the time and effort to prepare a tasty, well prepared meal. Meals were hastily concocted. In some parts of the country (such as New England and parts of the frontier), families had the same meal three times a day.

The wealthy were more fortunate in the preparation of food. Because they could afford sugar on a grander scale, republican gentry were treated to jellies, syllabubs (a dessert of sweetened cream mixed with liquor and gelatin), fruits, and nuts. John Adams remarked that the Philadelphia dinners he attended were "elegant" and "sinful feasts" (qtd. in ibid., 30). Fashionable tables were elegantly decorated with flowers and small statuary.

Southern tables were even more richly laden—at least those of the plantation owners. Money and plentiful labor (slaves) afforded the southern gentlefolk a more varied table. A southern dinner frequently included many kinds of soups, meats (poultry, beef, mutton, and pork), sweet potatoes, hot breads, biscuits, muffins, and cornbreads topped with assorted jellies and relishes, numerous pastries, and wines and other spirits (Train, 239).

## ICE CREAM

For those who could afford it, "iced creams" were a delectable treat. Such prominent figures as Washington, Jefferson, and Dolley Madison served ice cream to their distinguished guests. In 1784 Jefferson, in fact, had purchased a "cream machine for ice," one of the few Americans to own such an invention. A European import, iced fruits and creams have had a long and impressive history. Marco Polo first introduced these desserts to Europe from the Far East. By 1670, iced desserts were sold in Paris with great success. When the early settlers came to the New World, they brought their desire for this frozen dessert with them. By the early nationalist period, frozen desserts (ice cream and fruit ices) were extremely popular, but very expensive to make.

The cost and availability of cream and sugar were lesser concerns for wealthy ice cream devotees. The ability to acquire and store ice was the chief worry. Ice was not readily available, particularly in the summer months. New York, Pennsylvania, and New England were the primary sources of ice. During the winter, enterprising northerners would cut large blocks of ice from frozen streams and ponds for shipment to outlying states. The holds of the ships were insulated and hermetically sealed. Well-to-do southerners had icehouses built to store their shipments of ice. Usually built under a shade tree, the brick (or sometimes wooden) icehouse was double-walled (the space between stuffed with moss) with a foundation laid six feet deep (Woodward, 130). Many of these icehouses were so solidly constructed that the ice would last for three months even in the middle of summer, assuring that the popular dessert would be on hand for important dinner parties.

Transporting ice to those who lived away from the coast presented a problem. At this time, there was no practical means of shipping ice inland (Woodward, 130). Instead, country residents stored what ice they had acquired in the winter months in springhouses. Springhouses were constructed much like icehouses except that water diverted from a spring flowed through them, which created a pool of cool water in the springhouse (ibid., 130). Containers were then placed in the water in an effort to keep their contents cool. Obviously, springhouses were not as effective as icehouses in maintaining the necessary frigid temperatures. Thus, citizens living near ports had more access to ice—and to ice cream and other perishables.

## EUROPEAN CUISINE

After the French alliance of 1778, fashionable citizens took up French cuisine. The influx of French émigrés in the 1790s (and with them their knowledge and talent for cooking) altered American food sensibilities. Soups, salads, ices, bonbons, and fricassees became the order of the day. At least two American presidents, Washington and Jefferson, indulged in the new cuisine. (Patrick Henry used Jefferson's propensity for French cooking to attack him politically. Jefferson, Henry told a political rally, had "abjured his native victuals.")

Jefferson almost single-handedly established French cooking as a part of American culture. Even though he never lost his taste for the southern cooking of his youth (Virginia dishes and French cuisine were both served at the White House on a regular basis), the third president was the first to employ a French chef in the White House. But he was not content to turn over the responsibility of selecting the type of food and preparation of menus to the staff, no matter how impressive their qualifications. When it came to food, Jefferson took a hands-on approach.

Historical accounts reveal that as president, Jefferson, along with his steward, would drive out in a wagon early in the morning to the Georgetown market. There Jefferson would select only the finest meats and produce. Edmund Bacon, his overseer, recorded that Jefferson's marketing bills were often in the $50 range for that day's purchases (Jones, 38). By post-Revolutionary standards, that was an exorbitant amount.

Jefferson was also an inveterate collector of recipes, both foreign and domestic. Surprisingly, far before the great immigration of Italians to the United States, Jefferson had introduced pasta to America (ibid., 39). He had Parmesan cheese shipped to the United States because he felt that it would be a fitting accompaniment to his macaroni. Found among his papers was a drawing and description of a machine especially designed to shape macaroni (ibid.). Jefferson's pasta recipe, which calls for two eggs, a wineglass full of milk, a teaspoon of salt, and hard flour to make a firm dough, surprisingly resembles current recipes for pasta (ibid.).

Jefferson was instrumental in introducing rice into the American diet as well. In his travels abroad, at great personal risk, he had smuggled out rice (in his pockets) to America. He also had paid an Italian mule driver to smuggle a sack of rough rice out of northwest Italy. Later, he was able to import African dry rice to Virginia—a crop that did not require swamped fields (ibid.). Rice soon became a part of many American diets.

## COFFEE AND TEA

Haute cuisine was not the only gastronomic phenomenon in the new republic. American beverage preferences began to change at this time. Tea, a by-product of America's British heritage, was still the most popular drink. But coffee drinking was quickly on the rise. Tea drinkers during the war began to turn to coffee as a patriotic alternative to the British practice of tea drinking. By 1800 twice as many pounds of coffee were consumed per capita than tea (Cummings, 34). (However, tea produces twice as much per pound than coffee.)

The War of 1812 radically changed the drinking habits of Americans. Because Great Britain had been America's primary source of tea, the interruption of the tea trade due to the war caused high price inflation. Concurrently, Brazilian ports were now shipping coffee throughout the world. Coffee prices were much more in line with modest American budgets. After the war, tea prices soared from 80 cents per pound to $1.13, in comparison to the relatively stable coffee price of 20 cents (ibid., 35).

## COOKBOOKS

This was also the period marked by the appearance of the American cookbook. Up until this time, recipes had been handed down from generation to generation or found in oft-reprinted English cookbooks. Even though newspapers and periodicals carried food news, they seldom devoted any space to cooking matters (ibid., 70). But in 1796 a Connecticut woman, Amelia Simmons (a self-described "American orphan"), published the first cookbook by an American. Its title, albeit a very wordy one, proclaimed the author's ambitious agenda: *American Cookery, or the Art of Dressing Viands, Fish, Poultry, and Vegetables, and the Best Modes of Making Pastes, Puffs, Pies, Tarts, Puddings, Custards and Preserves, and All Kinds of Cakes, from the Imperial Plumb to Plain Cake. Adapted to This Coun-*

*try, and All Grades of Life*. This impressive, all-encompassing-sounding tome was a mere 46 pages in length. Its small size aptly illustrates the lack of variety in the American diet (ibid., 42).

*American Cookery* was so popular with the public that it was published in four editions from 1796 to 1808. In the later editions, Simmons included recipes that reflected the national zeal for the patriotic-sounding dessert: Independence Cake, Federal Cake, and Election Cake, the latter a highly spiced fruity cake reserved for town meetings (Jones, 31). *American Cookery* also advocated a distinctly American way of cooking by including recipes for American dishes such as Jerusalem artichokes and pumpkin slapjacks (pancakes made by adding cornmeal and pureed pumpkin to the usual recipe). *American Cookery* was the foremost cookbook of the age, its impact not eclipsed until 1829 with the appearance of Lydia Maria Child's *The Frugal Housewife*.

## PENNSYLVANIA GERMAN COOKING

Sometimes dishes reflected the culture and heritage of a particular immigrant group, creating a style of cooking that predominated (and still does) American fare. Although many immigrant groups brought unique recipes with them, thus increasing the offerings on the national menu, one group in particular stands out in its contribution to American cuisine. The Pennsylvania Germans, known for their devotion to hearty and substantial meals, developed recipes and techniques formulated to make preserved food taste as appetizing as fresh food, usually by the use of spices, primarily as preservatives rather than seasoning (ibid., 82).

Moreover, these immigrants had a unique view of healthcare. The Pennsylvania Germans felt that feeding the body to maintain health was far more prudent and economical than paying the doctor later on (Weaver, 10). Retaining the fundamentals of the original German cooking while using American ingredients, Pennsylvania Germans created a cuisine of one-pot meals, a very family-centered approach to dining. Their objectives were to keep the body strong and functioning, to satisfy the enormous appetites of hardworking farmers, and to produce meals that reflected Old World skill and New World tastes. The result was a very distinctive cuisine that spread quickly into other areas.

Washington reportedly enjoyed Pennsylvania German cooking. His wartime campaigns in Pennsylvania had introduced him to this distinctive regional cuisine. Like many other Americans, Washington had initially eaten Pennsylvania German cooking in roadside taverns.[7] The bill of fare probably included such specialties as raisin pie, shoofly pie (a breakfast cake made of molasses and dough crumbs), and scrapple.

Scrapple (or *panhaas*), a simple breakfast side dish, became a culinary favorite even among the most urbane citizens of Philadelphia. It is a mixture of ground pork scraps (heart, liver, and rib meat), cornmeal, buckwheat flour, and seasonings. The meaty mixture is then cooked in a pan until it reaches a thick consistency. The mixture is then poured and cooked in loaf pans. After cooling, the loaves are sliced and broiled or fried. The Pennsylvania Germans served scrapple hot with an assortment of condiments: molasses, pepper hash (a canned pepper and onion relish), or pepper vinegar (which was developed from Caribbean cooking after 1800).

The popularity of scrapple was not limited to Pennsylvania. In Maryland, scrapple was made from cornmeal and pork sausage. In Ohio (then part of the Northwest Territory) oats, rather than cornmeal, was used as the binding agent. German immigrants who settled in what is now the St. Louis area altered the recipe even more substantially. Scrapple in this area was made by mixing pork with oatmeal and either barley or rice.

By and large, American eating habits were as diverse as its population and its climate. Though some fare was uniform throughout the United States and its territories, climatic conditions often resulted in problems of spoilage, contamination, and shortage. Americans attempted to resolve these problems with ingenuity. Sometimes (in the case of food preservation), the results were less than desirable. But in other cases, tasty and nutritious new dishes were created, many reflecting the unique character and national origins of their creators. In essence, American cuisine was as republican as the society from which it came.

# 7

# Leisure Activities

During the Revolution the spirit of republicanism and the qualities associated with it—namely, virtue and rationality—checked Americans' innate love of physical entertainment but did not eradicate it entirely. After all, virtuous living and indulgence in sport seemed to be theoretically at odds. There were many vocal critics of games and sports, but the majority of Americans chose to scoff at them. Republican America, a nation that valued hard work and industry, was also a nation that engaged in play, game, and sport whenever possible.

This was not the first time in American history that Americans' love of play willed out over moral objections. Despite Puritan intervention in the North, from colonial days onward, Americans had eagerly adopted primarily English pastimes. Though many English games and sports had grown out of pagan rites and religious customs, God-fearing Christian Americans had participated in them nonetheless. Since English customs and pastimes were components of a "festive culture," that is, one that was characterized by eating, drinking, game playing, and dancing (Rader, 2), Colonial America also had a festive culture, especially in the more remote areas.

But a festive culture was in direct opposition to the national republican notion of virtue. Spirited republicans considered the vain diversions of profligate Europe to be unworthy activities for a free citizenry. Gambling, drinking, cockfighting, and other amusements (particularly those held on Sunday) were to be discouraged at all costs. As a republic of virtue, the United States needed to eliminate any activity that smacked of immoderation. An ideal citizen should be frugal, industrious, and abstemious.

Jefferson succinctly voiced America's fears of undue English influence on its citizenry, especially in regard to recreation. In a letter dated October 15, 1785, to John Banister Jr., Jefferson decried the nefarious influence England had over unsuspecting young Americans. He wrote, a young English gentleman

learns drinking, horse racing and boxing. . . . He is led by the strongest of all the human passions, into a spirit for female intrigue, destructive of his own and others' happiness, or a passion for whores, destructive to his health, and, in both cases, learns to consider fidelity to the marriage bed as an ungentlemanly practice. . . . [H]e retains, through life, a fond recollection, and a hankering after those places, which were the scenes of his first pleasures and of his first connections. ("Letters," 838–839)

Others shared Jefferson's concerns. The idle pastimes of the British aristocracy were perceived as a threat to the national vision of a republic of virtue, or, as patriot Samuel Adams had called for, a "Christian Sparta." During the Revolutionary War, the "states" had each passed sumptuary laws to restrict individual extravagance. In fact, the Sons of Liberty tried to enforce the First Continental Congress' resolution that all types of diversion, such as gambling, cockfighting, and horse racing, be restrained.

The attempts at curtailing sports and games by such well-meaning patriots ultimately failed. Even during the Revolutionary War, soldiers did not forgo amusements. In fact, the austere General Washington gave orders that "games of amusement" be part of army life. Thus the Continental army frequently engaged in bowling (using cannonballs), wicket (a form of cricket), shinny (a field hockey–type game), fives (a type of handball), and the medieval form of football (Rader, 16). Gambling, on the other hand, was strictly forbidden—but engaged in anyway.

Although the ideas of a Christian Sparta and a republic of virtue were noble ones, they were difficult to enforce. After the war, the United States progressively became more a part of the North Atlantic marketplace. America began to move rapidly from a relatively isolated set of colonies to a nation that increasingly interacted on a culturally global plane. With the influx of English theatrical troupes and other entertainments, Americans became more and more preoccupied with European activities—and these grew to include more games, hobbies, sports, and the like. Even on the frontier, where life was harsh and isolated, settlers reached out for companionship by holding sporting and gaming contests (Dulles, 69). The altruistic republican impulse was soon superseded by the profligate and speculative. Americans held fast to their festive culture, despite the admonitions of the nation's leadership. Consequently, fads, games, toys, hobbies, and sports were an integral part of American culture in the early nationalist period.

## FADS

As part of a festive culture, fads (activities or fashions briefly taken up by the public with great enthusiasm) are an expected occurrence. A fad, by nature, is a collective obsession that might stem from various motives. The impetus for fads in the early nationalist period was chiefly the ebullient patriotic spirit that followed the successful war for independence and an interest in the culture and activities of the ancient republics of Greece and Rome.

Expressions of patriotism appeared in home decorations, clothing, and artifacts. The eagle, now a national icon, was everywhere: on furniture, pottery, draperies, bedspreads, mirror frames, and even in the intricate inlays of Hepplewhite and Sheraton tables and furniture frames (Train, 232). In art and advertising ventures, the eagle was usually depicted with wings spread and talons outstretched, as crushing its enemy (analogous to the nation vanquishing its foes). Savvy innkeepers and shopkeepers also incorporated eagles in their signs, designed to appeal to patriotic patrons. In keeping with Americans' fascination with the eagle, after the adoption of the Great Seal of the United States in 1782, the obverse side of the Great Seal (technically, the coat of arms of the United States) adorned many domestic arts[1]: quilts, needlepoint, and crewel crafts.

Icons were not limited to the eagle. President Washington was also an icon; his visage was found everywhere and anywhere. Portraits and other graphic reproductions of the great man hung in countless American homes. After his death in 1799, pictorial renditions of Washington included mourning symbols, such as funeral urns with the inscription "Washington" and lamenting Goddesses of Liberty or Columbia (the allegorical female figure representing America). Most of the population made some show of grief, whether it was by wearing black armbands or carrying handkerchiefs embossed with Washington's face. It was considered the height of insensitivity and disloyalty not to offer some outward sign of mourning at Washington's passing.

Other outward displays of patriotism included the wearing of cockades (rosettes worn on hat brims) and liberty caps and erecting "caps of liberty" (descendents of the "liberty pole"). At first, the cockade signified the wearer's alliance with the Revolutionary forces. Later, it served as a symbol of the wearer's political party allegiance. Liberty caps were worn as a sign of being sympathetic to the French Revolutionary cause. Originally worn in France, the liberty cap was rather popular in the United States until 1800. The cap was brimless and fit neatly on the head, an

The Great Seal of the United States. Courtesy of the Library of Congress.

explicit departure from the traditional tricorn and bicorn hats worn at the time.

Liberty poles had a longer history in the United States than cockades and caps; the pole originated in the pre-Revolutionary era. Originally, the liberty pole was a point of assembly used by dissident colonists. (The colonials would gather beneath the pole—originally a tree—to hear speeches, sing rebellious tunes, and, most important, hang unpopular officials in effigy.) Later, poles were used to celebrate acts of defiance and were gaily decorated in accordance with the act commemorated. After the war, liberty poles were transformed into caps of liberty, poles that proudly displayed the American flag and a Phrygian cap (a soft, forward-peaked hat commonly depicted in ancient Greek statuary). Even

Allegory of American Liberty. Courtesy of the
Library of Congress.

the most disenfranchised of society (illiterates, wandering mariners, the impoverished who could not vote or hold office) appropriated the liberty pole and cap symbols in tattoos, thereby expressing their hatred of everything British and their love for democracy (Newman, 170). By and large, the cap of liberty combined two American passions: the love of national symbols and an interest in antiquity.

The archaeological digs at Pompeii and Herculaneum had sparked Americans' interest in ancient Greek and Roman artifacts. Jewelry, art, and architecture all reflected the late-eighteenth-century interest in the ancient. Cameos, depicting graceful Greco-Roman goddesses, were all the rage. The predominance of the Goddess of Liberty and Columbia figures in fine and domestic art was an outgrowth of American passion for the classical. What began as a collective fascination, however, transcended fad and fashion. American appropriation of classical lines and allegory became an integral part of its culture, establishing a distinctive architecture and a national iconography.

# GAMES

Although their leisure time was dear, Americans enjoyed devising and playing games. Games were not only amusing, they also challenged the intellect and logic skills of the player. For adults, games allowed participants to test their physical and strategic skills, depending on the game. In some cases (especially games of chance), playing the game was another opportunity to gamble. Even in straitlaced Boston, men and women played cards and dice, wagering substantial sums (Nye, *Cultural Life*, 144). For children, games presented an outlet for invention, memorization (many children's games involved the recitation of a rhyme), and the development of interpersonal skills. Games were relatively inexpensive to play (omitting the gambling element). The only limitation was time. Middle- and upper-class citizens had more time to indulge in game playing than the poorer classes, whose average working day exceeded ten hours. Games in the early nationalist period can be placed in roughly four broad categories: those that require physical skill, those based on chance (dice and coin tossing), those that focus on the use of strategy (card and board games), and children's games.

## Games of Physical Skill

The citizenry of the new nation relished the opportunity to exhibit their physical skill and dexterity in games. Games of physical skill, such as quoits and ninepins (two of the more widely played games of this type), were inexpensive to play and gave the player(s) a sense of satisfaction in performing well. Unlike the sports of the period that were adversarial (physical or strategic attack of an opponent), these games depended on a participant's surmounting obstacles inherent in the game. (For example, a quoits player may have competed against another player, but his challenge was to improve his own throwing skills.)

Quoits, the precursor of horseshoe pitching, required players to throw three-pound flat iron rings (quoits) at a stake (the hob). A quoit that encircled the hob counted as two points, one that was closer to the hob than an opponent's was worth one point. Because the participants threw these heavy rings at distances up to 60 feet, the game required both strength and skill. Rich and poor, young and old were keen quoits players. Premier American colleges, such as Princeton and Maryland Washington College (founded 1782), had organized quoits teams that had many enthusiasts. Players found the game to be relaxing, yet challenging.

Ninepins and skittles (the English variant of ninepins) were the fore-runners of modern-day bowling. Both were very popular in the northern states, especially in New York (largely because the Dutch colonists had brought the sport to New Amsterdam in the seventeenth century). Nine-pins and skittles were usually played at inns and taverns. Inn guests found a game of ninepins relaxing. Unlike bowling, ninepins and skittles were played outdoors, thus enabling the player, while taking in fresh air, to practice the skills necessary to become a proficient player, because ninepins and skittles required good hand-eye coordination. A player also needed to be strong (or could build up his strength) because hefty wooden balls were used to knock down the heavy wooden pins.

## Games of Chance

In games of chance, the probability of the outcome is the deciding factor. That is, the outcome of the play has an equal chance of taking place again. Unless a player cheats (by altering the playing piece or by sleight of hand), he or she has no control of the outcome of the play. Thus, games of chance lend themselves to gambling. Since gambling, despite the continuous outcry by moralists throughout the nation, was popular in all the states and territories, games of chance were played frequently for large and small sums.

Dice games, one of the oldest games in the history of humankind, were the most common games of chance played. Mathematical probabilities in a dice game are determined by the combination of the six spots on the die that are rolled. Republican dice rollers might play hazard (the English forerunner of the American game of craps that dated back to the fourteenth century) or simply bet on the probability of a roll. Another game of chance that was casually played was coin tossing (heads/tails call), a game of chance with a 50/50 ratio of probability.

## Games of Strategy

Games of strategy sometimes are a combination of chance and strategy (some card and board games) and sometimes are based on pure strategy alone. As in the case of games of chance, game-playing citizenry some-times used games of strategy as an excuse to gamble. In other cases, the incentive was purely the sense of triumph from outsmarting an oppo-nent. During the early nationalist period, the most commonly played games of strategy were card games, billiards, and board games, many times at the neighborhood tavern or inn.

Whist, which had been very fashionable in England by the mid-eighteenth century, was one of the most popular card games in Federalist America. George Washington was an inveterate whist player, hosting whist parties that lasted until the early hours of the morning. (Whist required four players who would be divided into two sets of partners.)

Billiards had been popular in Colonial America, and many taverns had a billiard table on the premises for the pleasure of patrons. (The wealthy, of course, owned their own billiard tables and equipment.)

Intense backgammon games and checkers matches were played everywhere, in the backwoods, elegant parlors, village taverns, and city inns. However, chess provided the most intellectual diversion of all games of strategy. Its most vocal enthusiast was none other than Benjamin Franklin who earlier had devoted an entire essay (entitled "The Morals of Chess" [1779]) to its virtues. Anticipating the usual arguments concerning game playing (idle amusements, undue competitiveness, weakening of the intellect), Franklin expounded on how playing chess taught the player foresight, circumspection, caution, and optimism. Chess, said Franklin, was "useful in the course of human Life. . . . For Life is a kind of Chess, in which we often have Points to gain, & Competitors or Adversaries to contend with" (ibid., 928). For a nation concerned with virtue and moral principles, Franklin's perspective was espoused. Americans became serious chess players, relishing the game for the intellectual challenges it presented and also for the prudence that it taught.

## Children's Games

American children mainly played games that involved rhymes and very little additional equipment. For those games that required some physical ability, a ball was the usual piece of equipment used, the exceptions being kite flying, mumblety-peg (played with a knife and also called "stick knife"), and marbles. Most children's games originated in the British Isles although a small number could be traced to France and Germany (Newell, 2). The emphasis in most of the games at the time was on mental skills, whether that was manifested in the form of memorization (rhymes) or by presenting a series of challenging questions (guessing games).

Popular rhyme games at the time included games that children still play today, such as "As We Go Round the Mulberry Bush," "Threading the Needle," "Ring Around the Rosy," "The Farmer in the Dell," and "London Bridge." Children also engaged in dances popular with their elders such as the Virginia Reel, which began as an imitation of the adult activity of weaving (ibid., 80). The first movements of a Virginia Reel imitate the moving of the weaving shuttle from side to side, the second the passing of the woof over and under the threads of the warp, and the third the tightening of the threads.

A particular favorite guessing game was Odd or Even, which involved guessing whether the number of beans a player held in his or her hand was an odd number or an even number. Other favorites included How Many Fingers and Thimble in Sight, a game in which an object (usually a thimble, hence the name) is hidden and the seeker is given clues to its nearness (one "freezes" when far from the object, "warm" when closer, "burns" when almost on it).

Children also loved games that involved chase and search, such as tag, Blindman's Bluff (the American derivative of the English favorite Drop Glove), and Hunt the Squirrel (a game of pursuit similar in its goal to musical chairs). Because children of the period were very physically active at work, games that involved running, jumping, hopping, and ball playing were also very popular. Both girls and boys played Hopscotch, whereas more vigorous games such as Tag and Den (a game of chase in which each boy represents a wild beast that captures other players and drags them home to his den) were the province of boys.

Ball games, with a few exceptions, were relegated to masculine play since girls were perceived as being too delicate to withstand the roughhousing that went along with ball games. Like their fathers and older brothers, young boys played quoits; ninepins; and one-cat, two-cat (precursors of baseball). Leapfrog, marbles, and mumblety-peg were also great favorites of little boys. Thus, by the early nationalist period, games defined by gender were ensconced in society.

## TOYS

Historically, through play and through the choice of toys used at play, children develop interpersonal skills and, in some cases, learn about the world and how to survive in it. Toys fundamentally function as props in play activities, activities that can involve competition, fantasy, entertainment, learning, luck, and even doing nothing at all (Mergen, 163). This was as true during the early nationalist period as it is today. Because parents realized the importance of toys in a child's development, republican children played with toys that were educationally and morally instructive.

As in the colonial era, American children during this period mostly played with homemade toys. Dolls were made of rags, cornhusks, leather, wood, and even twigs. A large variety of toys were carved or fashioned from wood by American craftsmen: rocking horses, pull toys, doll cradles, blocks, small sleighs, small animal figures, boats, skates, wagons, and even tiny furniture. In one known instance, a doting father provided his daughter with a miniature wooden coffin so that she could stage mock funerals for a beloved doll. Artisans who worked in metal fashioned whistles, rattles, horns, blades for skates, and pewter tea sets.

Stick coral was often used to make baby toys such as whistles, rattles, and teething rings (McClintock and McClintock, 32). Those citizens who could afford to do so had teething rings carved from costly ivory.

Wealthier families were now able to purchase imported manufactured toys (which were readily available) for their offspring. During the war, trade between Britain and her rebellious colonies had abruptly ceased (except for the period when British troops occupied New York), thereby severely cutting into British trade profits. Affluent Americans who had been loyal customers of British manufacturers could no longer buy expensive imported toys for their children. At the end of the Revolutionary War, British toy manufacturers began to export large inventories, much to their advantage. Thus, British exportation of toys was considered a boon for exporter and customer alike—except by American toy manufacturers who saw this as an infringement on their market. But as the nation moved into the nineteenth century, the fledgling American toy manufacturing industry eventually prospered and was able to compete successfully with European imports.

The overall emphasis on toys was their instructive value. Dolls helped to foster the maternal instincts believed inherent in little girls. Rocking horses, no matter how intricately carved or rudely fashioned, were seen as a means to teach small ones how to ride. Push toys were used for exercise and to develop coordination. English wooden puzzles, when put together, revealed names, portraits, and brief biographies of royalty, thus preserving cultural ties to the mother country even after the Revolution (B.C. Smith, 73). Alphabet blocks enjoyed great popularity before and after the war. Well educated progressive parents embraced John Locke's theory that children's learning should be congenial. Alphabet blocks aided children in learning their letters at a very young age, while also proving to be an amusing activity for the child.

Although generally not considered toys, children's books were considered to be an integral part of their recreation. They had been part of American childhood from the early eighteenth century. *Mother Goose* (first published in 1719) was a mainstay in American homes. American publishers reprinted many popular illustrated children's books at a reasonable cost (between four and 20 cents per copy). By the end of the eighteenth century, American children's books were highly entertaining but also instructive (McClintock and McClintock, 66). Often they contained bleak moral lessons. An example of the genre is *The History of King Pippin* (published in Boston in 1793), a rousing story of four bad boys who met their fate at the jaws of ravenous beasts.

Not all children's books of the period contained such dire endings. *Juvenile Pastimes, or Sports for the Four Seasons* was a compendium of games for children.[2] Among the games listed were time-honored children's amusements such as leapfrog, shuttlecock, Hopscotch, Blindman's

Bluff, kite flying, and Maypole dancing. More obscure games by today's standards included King Am I, chuck-farthing, peg-farthing, and knock out and span.

Of course, schoolbooks were a fundamental part of a child's library. Primers and spelling books were shelved next to cherished illustrated storybooks. Noah Webster's *The American Spelling Book* (published in 1783 and also known as "The Blue Back Speller") promoted a distinctive American culture. Webster's work emphasized the use and spelling of "Federal English" (American English) over established British usage and definitions. Hence, an American child was literate not only in letters, but also in cultural usage.

As the nation moved into the nineteenth century (beginning the shift from an agricultural to an industrialized society), children desired toys that were more realistic. To meet public demand, manufacturers greatly improved the craft of toy making. Toy trains, boats, and tools became miniatures of the real article. Doll furniture manifested exquisite cabinetry and carving. Mechanized toys, such as music boxes, clocks, and warbling birds, were cleverly manufactured and readily purchased by indulgent parents. Dolls became much more realistic looking. By 1790, American artisans were creating jointed wooden dolls, making them more lifelike. Imported dolls, often very expensive and thus treated with care, had glass eyes, wooden or porcelain heads, and human hair. Highly wrought wooden toys revealed the imagination and talent of their makers. One of the most popular children's toys of the early nineteenth century was a Noah's Ark set, complete with ark, Noah's family, and miniature pairs of unusual animals. Domestic artisans rendered to the best of their abilities (and imaginations) exotic animals that never had set foot on the American continent—even in exhibition.

## HOBBIES

Most American hobbies, like other forms of recreation, grew out of utility rather than a special interest to investigate at leisure. Women, as part of their household duties, were expert spinners, seamstresses, and cooks. Their exceptional skills eventually developed into hobbies—activities that extended over into leisure time. Many were gifted in assorted types of needlework (crewel, embroidery, cross-stitch). Upper- and middle-class women, who had more leisure time than poor or working-class women, decorated furniture and sundry items by stenciling, gilding, and painting. An accomplished few painted landscapes to mat and hang in the home.

Only the wealthy (men and women) had the time and means to explore the arts as an avocation. Those who could afford lessons were schooled in singing, dancing, painting, and playing musical instruments—and often performed quite well. There were many amateur musicians and artists in the genteel classes whose efforts were applauded for their entertainment and aesthetic value.

As life improved through economic and industrial means, one specific group developed a hobby that had a great impact on American culture then and to come. Middle- and upper-class women now had the time, and thus the inclination, to read novels for amusement. (Although men read novels, women made up the largest percentage of novel readers.) Writers began to tailor their works to garner the interest of a largely female audience, which later in the nineteenth century would lead to the rise of the domestic novel.

Sleighing, considered to be one of the most popular hobbies of the period, was limited to those who could either afford a horse-drawn sleigh or rent one for three to five dollars an hour. Unlike games and sports that required the skill, strength, and dexterity of the individual or strategy or just plain luck, the appeal of sleighing resided in the frolics that ensued. The large cutters slicing through the snow made the vehicles very fast and the ride revitalizing for the passengers. Sleigh parties often involved music, drinking, eating, and often a bit of courting as well.

In the latter years of the eighteenth century, sleighing was commonly viewed as a healthful enterprise. Breathing in fresh, cold air on a sleigh ride was seen as beneficial to pulmonary health. But by the nineteenth century, sleighing had acquired critics who thought that the hobby contributed to the high incidence of consumption. Despite the dire warnings of such detractors, Americans continued to hold sleighing parties throughout the period and throughout the nineteenth century.

## SPORTS

The United States, from its inception, had always been a sporting nation. Although the days of most citizens revolved around work, Americans took what precious leisure time available to them to engage in sport. A moralistic undercurrent within their communities sometimes hampered the efforts of those in the northern and Mid-Atlantic states. Religious leaders frequently decried what they saw as the moral erosion of American citizens because of sports. Sports, they warned, led to dissipation (gambling, drinking, undue competition, and brutality). Southerners, however, participated in sports freely with clear conscience, fully indulging in gambling, drinking, competing, and, in some cases, brutality.

There were also critics throughout the country who were skeptical of physical exercise, particularly when it came to women's participation. Women of this period were still regarded as fragile creatures whose constitutions could only tolerate no more physical exertion than lifting a

needle. (Those who held this opinion apparently overlooked the stren-
uous nature of housework.) Moreover, women were expected to spend
most of their time maintaining households and caring for their families.
Sports would take away time from their familial duties.

But women did participate in sport, albeit on a limited basis. Most
women could ride, and those of the upper classes prided themselves on
their equestrian abilities. (The mark of a true gentlewoman was her elegant appearance and graceful "seat" on and expert handling of a horse.)
A few progressive-minded women participated in other sports (such as
swimming), and young girls were encouraged to toss balls as part of
childhood play. But for the most part, women were spectators for most
early nationalist sports.

Not all authorities were critical of sport. Liberal thinkers such as Benjamin Franklin and Dr. Benjamin Rush spoke out in favor of sport—and
Americans considered their views carefully. Franklin was a sincere advocate of the sporting life, citing its healthful benefits to body and soul.
His philosophy was that proper recreation taught valuable lessons in
patience, caution, circumspection, and prudence. These were vital attributes that served all people well throughout life. Rush, on the other hand,
was more guarded in his advocacy of sport. For Rush, sport had voca-
tional value only. The strength, dexterity, and skill acquired in sport
could easily be carried over into performing occupational duties. Competition in sport translated easily into profit from labor.

American sports were, for the most part, diverse in nature and number. Some grew out of utility. Others originated as a source of amusement only. Most American sports of the period originated in Europe or,
in some case, were learned from Native Americans. Some eventually
were modified, resulting in uniquely American sports. Fundamentally,
sport in the early nationalist period can be broken down into two broad
groups: participant and spectator.

## Participant Sports

Participant sports focused, with few exceptions, on the accomplishment and skill of individual performance rather than teamwork. Most
sports during the period did not require, and often did not have, an
audience. This is not to say that Americans were not interested in skill,
dexterity, and strength in physical recreation. Americans were avid
sports enthusiasts, but the majority of sport was limited to individual
participation and interest. Participant sports in the early years of the
republic can be classified as those that evolved from necessity to amusement (hunting and fishing) and those that had a strictly recreational basis
(archery, swimming, skating, etc.).

## *Hunting and Fishing*

From the era of discovery and colonization, Americans had to hunt and fish to survive. Game was plentiful in the New World, and colonists became crack shots and expert anglers. As colonial settlements grew, emerging into thriving towns and cities, hunting and fishing became lucrative enterprises. No longer were hunting and fishing for sustenance only; many accomplished sportsmen killed for profit. Eventually sportsmen developed a partiality for a type of hunt. Some preferred to hunt one by one, tracking for the most part small game (rabbits, squirrels, birds); others liked to hunt in groups (wild fowl, foxes, deer); still others formed companies to hunt larger game (bears, deer, wolves) (Holliman, 14).

With the importation of sporting dogs in the latter years of colonization, Americans began to regard various types of hunting as sport. Dogs were imported, bred, and specially trained depending on the type of hunting sport (gun dogs: pointers, setters, spaniels; hounds: bloodhounds, foxhounds, terriers, beagles; other sporting breeds: Newfoundlands, shepherds, and mixed breeds). Training of sporting dogs became almost a pastime in itself. Much care was given to a dog's diet and health (in some cases, more care than that given to humans). Sporting dogs were given the best of water and plentiful amounts of meat mixed with mush or bread. If a veterinarian was not available when the animal fell ill, its owner—who was often very knowledgeable in canine diseases and treatments—treated it.[3] Owners also spent a great deal of time training and exercising their animals, much in the same way they would train their children. Even the naming of the dog was of prime importance. One-syllable names were preferred—and never should they end in a long "o" sound. (The command "toho," used to order the dog to stand or bark, might cause the animal to confuse the command with a name ending in "o.") The exception to monosyllabic names was in the naming of foxhounds. Foxhounds were given names that reflected their character, such as "Caesar," "Sweet Lips," or "Clarion" (ibid., 41). No matter what its name, the sporting dog soon became indispensable in the hunt, and the care and training of a hunting dog was regarded with the utmost importance.

Whether hunting was for necessity or sport, the right equipment was imperative for success. Most Americans owned at least one gun—and for a hunter, the gun was one of his most prized possessions. Often the gun (like the dog) was named. A then-young New Hampshire lawyer, Daniel Webster (1782–1852), named his guns "Learned Selden" and "Mrs. Patrick," in the tradition of early American hunters. A hunter's gun was also kept in pristine working order. No matter how tired a shooter was at the end of a day of hunting or participating in a shooting match, he cleaned his gun almost immediately. Barrels and stocks were rubbed down. In the case of flintlocks, the flints were changed in anticipation of the next day's firing.

During most of the early nationalist period, the single-barrel flintlock rifle was the gun of choice. Flintlocks weighed between 11 and 12 pounds, had barrels of four and one-half to five feet in length, had bores of five-eighths to three-fourths of an inch, and carried leaden balls (made from molten lead) from 30 to 60 in a pound (ibid., 15). They were heavy and cumbersome to carry but were used almost religiously by frontiersmen even after the appearance of the percussion ignition system in 1807.

Although percussion ignition eventually revolutionized hunting in the United States, it was not widely used until the 1830s.[4] Percussion ignition was more reliable than flintlocks, but only the well-to-do could afford the new expensive guns. Most people continued to use the single-barrel flintlock rifle for shooting. Flintlocks were imported from England but were also made and purchased in the United States, especially from the Pennsylvania Germans who had established themselves as superb gunsmiths.

Because success in the hunt was dependent on the ability to shoot, shooting matches that tested a participant's ability to hit a target cleanly and accurately began to spring up around the country. Sometimes the target was an animal (small birds tossed in the air, a staked turkey, ranging cattle—called a "beef shoot"), sometimes a challenging inanimate target. Two particularly popular contests of the latter type were "snuffing a candle" and "driving a nail." In a snuffing-a-candle contest, the marksman was to shoot at a burning candle approximately 50 yards away. The object was to snuff the candle without putting it out (and of course not to hit the candle itself). In a driving-a-nail contest, a nail driven two-thirds its length into a plank of wood served as the target. The principal goal was to fire at the nail, hitting it directly on its head, driving it into the board. Prizes ranged from cash awards to the target itself (in the case of fowl, small animals, and beef) to a round of drinks at the local tavern (which often sponsored the shooting match). But the ultimate prize was the esteem and respect a marksman received from his peers.

Fishing, like hunting, quickly became a recreational diversion. Americans had always been avid fishermen, at first as a means of putting food on the table, then as a sport. People from all walks of life fished, and fishing was universally viewed as an edifying pursuit. Even the most stern and puritanical of Christian preachers approved of fishing. (After all, Christ and his disciples fished.) Fishing was seen as restorative. It encouraged the angler to meditate, ruminate, and speculate, all while waiting for the proverbial bite.

But fishing was not just a solitary activity. Villagers and farmers often formed "fishing parties," groups that agreed to fish together on a given day—usually a Saturday. Occasionally the party would divide itself into two rival groups, the objective being to see which group could catch the most fish. In early afternoon the two groups would meet to clean and cook the catch.

Organized fishing clubs were rare, though. The notable exception was the venerable Schuylkill Fishing Company (Philadelphia) founded in 1732. The oldest sports club in the United States, the Schuylkill Fishing Company was established to provide its members with fresh-air exercise and conviviality. Membership benefits included tackle and bait, bateau (a small, flat-bottom boat), and hat and apron (the appropriate fisherman's garb of the time period). Club activities centered around angling, cleaning and cooking of the catch, and speeches and songs. Fishing clubs such as the Schuylkill Fishing Company offered anglers an outlet that incorporated exercise, skill, and social amenities.

### Recreational Contests of Skill

Along with sports that evolved from activities that were essential to survival, Americans also enjoyed sports that were purely recreational in conception, but emphasized the strength and skill of the participants. Although an audience was optional, the participants' sense of accomplishment was often aligned with self-assessment, that is, the goal in these sports was to surpass one's personal best. A few of the more popular types of these contests of skill were archery, swimming, and skating.

For Americans, archery may have had its roots in England, but it was from the Native Americans that the Anglo citizenry learned to be skilled with bow and arrow. Although Americans may have originally used bow and arrow to hunt, they soon began to hold informal archery contests to test their skills. Again, class distinctions were not evident at this point. (Exclusive archery clubs did not appear in the United States until later in the nineteenth century.) In the early republic, an archer who owned even the most primitive of equipment would try his skill against his neighbors.

Even though many Americans, like their European counterparts, viewed regular bathing (and thus wetting the body unnecessarily) suspiciously, swimming began to grow in popularity during this period, partly because of the earlier efforts of Benjamin Franklin. Franklin, a great supporter of all water sports, concurred with John Locke's emphasis on the importance of swimming in a young person's curricula. In his early essay "The Education of Youth" (1749), Franklin admonished parents to instruct their children in swimming because it would "keep them in Health, and to strengthen and render active their Bodies" and that swimming offers "some Advantage besides, to be free from the slavish

Terrors many of those feel who cannot swim, when they are oblig'd to be on the Water even crossing a Ferry" (327–328).

Franklin was not only America's first swimming master, but also its first skin diver and the world's first designer of water skis (Twombly, 39). Outfitted in a wet suit and webbed sandals of his design, Franklin often braved the depths of powerful, cold currents of the Schuylkill River. He advised all Americans to swim for two hours an evening to ensure a restful night's sleep and good digestion. By 1790 his treatise on "The Art of Swimming" had been widely published in the United States. Americans read what the great statesman had to say about the healthful benefits of swimming, studied it, and put it into practice.

Floating baths were instituted in all the major cities so that Americans could learn to swim in safe environs. To accommodate patrons' preferences, the floating bathhouse was divided into two major sections: one for women, one for men. (Very few women learned how to swim. Bathing, however, was viewed as being beneficial to them, as long as it was not for a long period of time.) These were further subdivided into sections designated for learners, another for experienced swimmers, and finally for bathers.

Swimming was not limited to indoors. Many followed Franklin's practice and swam in rivers and the ocean. A few intrepid souls tested their aquatic mettle and swam long distances, to the amazement and disbelief of the public. (Such attempts were generally considered foolhardy, but the public was fascinated with accounts of long-distance swimming feats just the same.) In the summer months swimmers frequented resorts, such as Cape May, New Jersey. But only the wealthy could afford a week at Cape May. (The cost: $7 per week for lodging and meals. Towels were not provided.) A visit to a resort for the purpose of swimming or bathing was seen as being therapeutic despite the cost.

Finally, individuals often indulged in the cold weather sport of skating. Skating was one of the more "democratic" sports, since all that was needed was a frozen pond or river and a pair skates (which could be had for as little as 25 cents). As in the case of the political process, women were excluded from such democracy. (A woman on skates was considered scandalous.) But American men and boys from all walks of life could be seen gracefully gliding over a frozen river, cutting figures into the ice or intensely chasing a ball.

## Spectator Sports

Although all sports are participatory, spectator sports differ from participant sports by the role the audience plays in the event. In participant sports, performance before a crowd is a secondary, even tertiary, element. For example, hunters and fishermen engaged in their respective sporting pursuits because of the sense of personal accomplishment. Even as hunters perfected their marksmanship skills and participated in shooting matches, the focus of the contest was on the individual's sense of achievement, not the amusement of the audience.

On the other hand, in spectator sports the interest shifts from the participant to the onlookers. Often onlookers become minor participants in the event, customarily by cheering and booing, at times by placing bets on the outcome. In certain cases, the onlookers reward the winner and punish the loser. During the early nationalist period, crowds were extremely interactive in spectator sporting contests. Bets were placed at a fevered pitch. Winners were carried on chairs through the town or village, hailed as local champions. Losers were humiliated further by punitive crowds. All in all, the excitement of the contest was inside and outside the sporting arena.

### Foot, Walking, and Boat Races

Until the 1820s, racing was a spontaneous sport, not likely to draw huge crowds, but had its champions and challengers just the same (Holliman, 152). Those fleet of foot seemed to be always up for a local challenge, usually with a small wager involved. Men and boys raced down country lanes and roads for the honor of being acknowledged local champion.

Surprisingly, walking races drew larger crowds than foot races. A walking race varied in length from town to town. Many walking races were only a mile long, but others exceeded the ten-mile mark. Many turned out to see how the local challenger would fare and to cheer him onward. The goal of a walking race was to establish a record time. On occasion success in a walking race transcended local or even regional interest. In one case, it became a matter of national pride. In 1809 a Georgia man was clocked at seven and one-half minutes a mile, breaking all records previously published in the *English Sporting Magazine* (ibid., 151).

The United States was a country that produced tough and resilient boatmen, especially in cities and villages on the Atlantic seaboard, and soon their natural competitive impulses prevailed. Races (both sailing and rowing) between rival boatmen arose. By 1811 public interest in rowing races had reached its peak with a race between rowers from Long Island and New York City. But spectator interest in the strength and ability of the rowers was now superseded by their interest in the make of the boat. National honor was now at stake.

The Long Island/New York contest featured boats from two manufacturers: Chambers of London and Baptiste of New York. Chambers had challenged the Americans, playing on a national sensitivity to the widespread English contempt of anything American. Thus, the boat itself rather than those manning it became the locus of the race. By the next year, war put an end to boat racing—the battleground of war now replaced friendly competition on the sea to settle the issue.

## Horse Racing

Horse racing has enjoyed global popularity since prehistoric times and essentially the rules have not changed (that is, victory is awarded to the swiftest). The British, in particular, were (and are) passionate horse racing enthusiasts and their American cousins were (and are) no less devoted to the "Sport of Kings." Gentry and working class alike indulged in the racing of and betting on horses. In small villages and in the territories, short quarter-mile races were a common occurrence. Since even farmers of reduced circumstances owned a horse, there was no shortage of riders or horses available for an impromptu race.

Those with the means to breed and race horses seriously did so. English horses with impressive bloodlines had been exported to American shores as early as the colonial period. Americans, through careful breeding, worked to improve on these lines and were often successful. With the importation of the great thoroughbred sire Messenger from England in 1786, American thoroughbred horse racing rivaled any in the world.[5] Other thoroughbreds had reputations of legendary stature as well, notably Top Gallant, Wrangler, Peacemaker, Potomac, Truxton, and their sire, Diomed. When Diomed died in 1808, his passing was mourned in some places with the same intensity and passion as Washington's in 1799 (Holliman, 108).

The appeal of racing varied in intensity by area. As expected, racing was heavily criticized in New England. The puritanical mind-set was still evident in regard to morality. (The chief objection to horse racing was that it encouraged gambling, in particular, and dissipation, in general.) There were, nonetheless, some New Englanders who bred and raced horses. In 1808 Timothy Dwight, president of Yale (founded 1701), noted that horse racing was the premier spectator sport in the state of Rhode Island. Races were promoted and well attended in various cities and towns in Massachusetts. However, New Englanders' primary interest in racing was in the breeding of horses, rather than in the racing itself.

Horse racing had been an established sport in the Mid-Atlantic since the mid-seventeenth century. Although horse racing never caught on in New Jersey and was essentially banned in Pennsylvania for many years, it was very popular in New York. The Catskill and Poughkeepsie regions, in particular, were known for offering exorbitant purses, especially in light of the economic structure.[6] Even after horse racing was prohibited by state law in 1803, New Yorkers persisted in holding races.

Nowhere in the United States was horse racing more quickly and tightly embraced than in the South and the southwestern territories (such as Kentucky). Southern planters had the means to maintain stables of expensively bred thoroughbreds. Southerners historically were zealous in their love and appreciation of fine horses. Unlike Northerners, Southerners never had to contend with high-minded legislators who objected to racing on moralistic grounds. In fact, many southern politicos bred and raced horses themselves. In the autumn months, horse races were held throughout the South, drawing crowds from all walks of life. Bets were energetically placed and whiskey liberally consumed by all.

Jockey clubs were established in all major southern cities and many villages. The most prominent men in society held the office of president or vice president of the local jockey club. Membership dues were steep—frequently in excess of $20—but racing supporters willingly paid them (ibid., 114). The jockey club played a vital role in the administration of races. Stewards were chosen from the club membership to manage the race. The horses and the stable colors were assiduously recorded. Horses were weighed before the race and fees of approximately $20 were collected from non-club entrants; entrance fees were waived for club members. Generally speaking, southerners were united in their passion and pride in horse racing.

### Wrestling, Gouging, and Boxing

Wrestling (or "wrasslin" or "russlin" as it was pronounced in the backcountry) was extremely popular on the frontier, where hand-to-hand combat skills were held at a premium, and in towns and cities as well. Young boys were introduced early to the wrestling arena and the rewards that it held. To be declared village wrestling champion was a high honor. Powerful wrestlers were afforded the respect of the village elders and the admiration of young, unmarried females.

The fixation with one's wrestling prowess was not limited to the young. Even those in position of power continually honed their wrestling skills. In 1791 Judge William Cooper of New York (father of novelist James Fenimore Cooper) had a formidable reputation as a wrestler (ibid., 149). Legend has it that when the elder Cooper came to Cooperstown to receive his first judgeship, he proclaimed that he could throw any man in the county and immediately challenged all to a match (the prize: one hundred acres). A local strong man challenged Cooper. Cooper accepted the challenge but lost the match. The honorable Judge Cooper awarded his opponent with one hundred acres, demonstrating that sport and virtue were not disparate concepts.

A typical wrestling match involved two contestants in a ring facing each other. Often wrestling matches commenced after the raising of a building. Plied with strong spirits, young and middle-age men began wrasslin' matches on the green. The combatants met face to face, arms locked around the other and chins tucked under each other's right shoulder. The wrestlers inveigled to throw each other to the ground. The first man whose body part (with the exception of the feet, of course) touched the ground was considered "thrown."

In some areas, mainly the western regions, wrestling was an unusually brutal sport. More often than not, no referee was present. No-holds-barred was the rule. Brutality in the ring and outside the ring was often expected. Many times the loser was mutilated. Eye-gouging, biting, cutting off limbs, and slitting of noses and lips were accepted methods used to dishonor the losing combatant—and were often expected at the end of a match. Although some colonies had outlawed such outrageous punitive measures by the mid-eighteenth century, these repugnant activities remained a problem in Georgia and North Carolina until 1899 (Twombly, 26).

One particularly gripping firsthand account from 1806 aptly illustrates the brutality of the backwoods wrestling match. Two county wrestling champions from Virginia and Kentucky faced each other in an especially sadistic contest as the bloodthirsty crowd cheered on its favorites:

The crowd roared in anticipation of what it was about to witness. Many of them had been present at such sporting events. The Virginian did not let them wait. Placing his thumbs in the proper place, he gave his opponent's eyeballs an instantaneous start from their sockets. . . . The people cheered, their minds being hardened in advance as to the mercilessness of the event. The gouged man was simply an animal, like the bear chained to a tavern wall and set upon by baiting dogs. He was there for their amusement. (qtd. in Twombly, 26)

Gouging was a sport in itself, usually used to settle gambling disputes over cockfighting or horse racing (although political arguments were sometimes the impetus for engaging in a brutal eye-gouging, jaw-breaking, and nose-biting match). Not limited to the lower classes, gouging was an unfortunate English custom finely honed by Americans (Holliman, 138). The powerful and educated were just as prone to engage in gouging as the poor and illiterate. Combatants throughout the nation were held in high esteem for their ability to gouge out eyes and bite to the bone. A well placed kick could shatter a jaw; an ear could be ripped from the side of a head by a vicious bite. Skilled gougers grew their thumbnails long for the express purpose of scooping out the eye of an opponent. Carefully preserved eyes, ears, noses, and fingers were treasured as trophies from successful gouging matches.

Gouging matches were held much in the same way as wrestling matches. A crowd would gather around the two combatants, eventually forming a ring. Unlike wrestling matches, which began as exhibitions of strength and agility and regrettably could degenerate into acts of gross brutality, gouging matches were exercises in mutilation. A combatant's skills were measured by his facility to disengage eyes, bite ears and noses, break jaws, and bite to the bone any part of his opponent's body—and his efficiency in doing so.

In contrast, boxing was a more refined sport—and not nearly as popular with early nationalists. Late eighteenth-century attempts to introduce the "manly art" to American shores were relatively unsuccessful. Even in Britain boxing had declined in popularity from its heyday earlier in the century. Pugilistic bouts could not compete in the public arena with the more violent, hands-on wrestling and gouging contests. But in 1798 a Boston school advertised instruction in the more genteel art of fencing and "the scientific and manly" art of boxing (qtd. in ibid., 140), signaling the beginning of an American interest in a more regulated physical combat.

American interest in boxing was sparked by the 1810 London match between Tom Cribb, a celebrated bare-knuckled fighter, and Tom Molyneux, the great African American heavyweight champion from New York.[7] Molyneux had gained national fame as the "Champion of America" in 1809 after defeating numerous opponents in the sporting district of New York City. The British aristocracy and American newspapers alike avidly followed the Cribb-Molyneux match. Though the decision was in favor of the Briton, American interest in boxing did not wane. Americans continued to be interested in reading graphic accounts of British boxing matches. American newspapers, in reporting the Cribb-Molyneux match and others that followed, were, of the most part, severe in their criticism of boxing, judging it brutal and immoral. This did not deter Americans' growing fascination with prizefighting. But not until the 1820s did boxing become an important part of the American sporting scene.

### Ball Playing

Ball playing was a popular sport since the era of colonization. American men, women, and children were known to toss a ball around for recreation since the seventeenth century. The earliest English settlers played rounders, a form of the English game of cricket. Native Americans were also ardent ballplayers. Even prior to the Revolutionary War, Americans were known to play "base ball."[8]

American baseball had its origins in a children's game called "cat" or "old-cat." Old-cat required, at minimum, three players (pitcher, catcher, and batter) and two bases. The object of the game was to hit the ball at such a distance that the batter could run to the other base and return before being put "out," either by the ball being caught on the fly or by being hit by a ball thrown by one of the other players. The game's name changed to reflect the increase in the number of players and bases (two-old cat = five players, two bases; three-old cat = six players, three bases; four-old cat = eight players, four bases).

Four-old cat quickly evolved into a predominantly New England game called Town Ball. Although the rules varied from town to town, it was immensely popular. Town Ball, unlike four-old cat, was a team sport. Each team captain was chosen on the strength of his personality, not necessarily his skill (Twombly, 46). The captains took turns selecting teammates until every player was chosen. This made for irregularly sized teams. Sometimes a team would have eight players, other times as many as 20. Every player on a team had a turn at bat during an inning, so Town Ball was a fully participatory sport.

Town Ball required four bases. Originally wooden stakes were used for bases, then stones, finally stuffed canvas sacks. (The use of the sacks—now called "bases"—led to the two-word appellation "base ball.") Americans also improvised their choice of bats. Sometimes the bat would be similar to a cricket paddle. Other times an old ax handle would do. The ball was a bullet entwined in yarn and covered in deerskin or cowhide.

The basic rules of Town Ball are similar to those of baseball, although Town Ball was far more brutal than baseball is today. To "plug" or "soak" a base runner (the equivalent of an out in baseball), overly eager opponents often hurled balls aimed at the spine of the runner. Runners careening into stone bases and wooden stakes were subject to broken bones and dislocated joints. Brawls often broke out after particularly vicious "pluggings." Despite the hazard to life and limb, Americans persisted in playing "base ball" whenever possible.

### Cockfighting, Animal Baiting, and Gander Pulling

Brutality and cruelty in sport was not limited to humans. Sadly, the early nationalist period was punctuated by the exploitation and abuse of animals. Cockfighting, animal-baiting (usually bulls), and gander-pulling contests drew substantial crowds. Although some observers voiced their revulsion of these practices in print, such objections did not deter most spectators from watching (and betting on) bloody animal sports. In many cases, spectator games involving animals were heralded as contests that showcased strength and vigor.

Cockfighting, like many popular violent sports, was brought to the colonies from England where it flourished in all areas. Its reception varied from area to area. In New England the sport was publicly denounced, but determined Yankee cockfighters pitted their birds surreptitiously. In the Mid-Atlantic states, societal judgment was not as harsh. Although cockfights were not advertised in newspapers (which would have indicated some acceptance by the norm), they were prevalent, especially in New York City. In the western territories cockfighting had almost fanatical devotees. The most famous of the western cockfighters was none other than Andrew Jackson, whose behavior at cockfights was recorded as vociferous and passionate.

In the South, however, cockfighting rivaled horse racing in respectability and popularity. Rich and poor, master and slave, male and female, upright and disreputable, all went to see the "feathered gladiators" fight to the finish. Newspapers regularly ran advertisements and announcements of local cockfights, which were heavily attended. Sometimes the feathered combats raged for days. This, of course, increased the business of local inns and taverns since cockfighters and bettors rarely left a "cock main" (a series of cockfights) early. Professional gamblers found cockfights extremely lucrative as well. Thus, the cock main was a frequent haunt of the seedier types. But even the most esteemed southerners eagerly embraced cockfighting.

Detractors argued that cockfighting stimulated the baser passions. Indeed, the fights were particularly gory. The combatants, equipped with steel gaffs (pointed spurs) fought to the death. Feathers and blood were sprayed everywhere. Often uninitiated spectators were sickened, covering their eyes from the bloody spectacle. Moralists denounced the sport, saying that cockfighting led to drunkenness, sloth, and debauchery.

But no sermon or essay could deter cockfight aficionados. Cock mains were generally viewed as great entertainment. Spectators cheered on their favorite feathered gladiator, raising and taking bets, and drinking spirits as the battle raged on. Some gaming birds' reputations were raised to mythic proportions, their images immortalized in paintings. In rural areas the local champion was often honored as the subject of weathervanes.

Cockfighting in itself became a small industry. Birds were carefully bred, lineages painstakingly recorded. The wealthy employed special handlers to care for and train the birds, and owners spared no expense in feeding and training. Some of the southern gentry owned as many as 70 or 80 gamecocks expressly raised for the cockpit. The gentleman who possessed a valiant and winning gamecock was the object of envy. Overall, gamecocks were viewed as an investment.

Animal baiting was another grisly contest patronized by Americans. As with cockfighting, animal baiting was a sport that Americans had adopted from the English who had indulged in it for centuries. All parts of the United States held animal-baiting contests with bulls and bears serving most often as the main wretched attraction of the day. Sometimes more unusual animals, such as buffaloes and tigers, were baited. (Americans were fascinated with the more exotic animals, so a tiger-baiting contest was considered to be a special treat.) Such vicious contests were extremely popular everywhere. Contests were heavily advertised, drawing in large crowds who were eager to pay admission prices from a quarter to a dollar (Holliman, 131).

An animal-baiting contest was held in a specially built fenced-in arena, designed to seat approximately two thousand spectators (ibid., 132). In the center of the arena, the starved animal (starved to increase its ferocity) was chained or tied to the ground. Specially trained bulldogs were set upon the hapless animal. The exhibition was especially fearsome.[9] The dogs, trained to kill, tore into the baited animal's flesh, often ripping off its ears immediately.

The appeal of animal baiting was not based on an American lust for gore and cruelty. Rather, Americans were fascinated by the power and agility of an animal, hindered by chains, to fend off six to eight well trained English bulldogs (ibid., 134). Animal-baiting advertisements of the day attest to American interest in the battling skills of wild animals. In a tiger-baiting ad from 1809, the news copy proclaimed that the "Tyger, generally in fighting, falls on his back and whilst he seizes his adversary by the throat, endeavors to rip him open with his hind claws" (qtd. in ibid., 133). The tiger's ingenuity in counterattacking an adversary was the real attraction for Americans, not necessarily the gore that followed.

Gander pulling was one of the oldest of American sports, brought to New Amsterdam by the Dutch. As with other cruel and bloody sports, gander pulling spread to other parts of the colonies and remained popular in the United States and its territories until the mid-nineteenth century. Unlike cockfighting and animal baiting, gander pulling was popular with only the lower classes.

In gander pulling, a goose (sometimes a hare was substituted) was suspended on a bar or rope that spanned a road. The live animal's neck was clipped and then greased. Contestants on horseback charged down the road, hoping to grab the bird and pull off its head. The audience doused those who missed with buckets of water. Often a gander-pulling contest lasted for hours, making for many wet contestants and one tortured bird.

The prize in a gander-pulling contest was trivial. Sometimes the purse consisted of contributions by the audience, approximately 25 cents a head (ibid., 136). Other times the winner was treated to rounds of drinks at the local tavern. Frequently, the prize was the bird itself. The true draw was the betting that ensued, sometimes for money but more often than not for liquor (a great favorite with the common people).

Regardless of how cruel gander pulling and other games and sports may seem, they are evidence that republican America, despite the warnings and fears of the national leadership, remained a festive culture. Hardworking Americans could not forgo their innate love of play and competition. As much as they adhered to the idea of a virtuous republic, many times their love of the speculative and of amusements (especially amusements that led to drinking, eating, and other forms of conviviality) prevailed over their idealism. The new nation was a country that loved a good contest, no matter what form it took.

# 8

# Literature

Having successfully attained political and economic independence, Americans after the Revolutionary War now declared a literary independence from Great Britain (and, to a lesser extent, Europe). But this cultural war would not be as handily won as the political one. Unlike the creation of a new government, the creation of a new, national literature would necessitate some reliance on the great literary traditions of Europe—with the caveat of, in the words of American lexicographer Noah Webster, that there should be no "servile imitation of the language, manners, and vices of foreigners" (see Nye, *Cultural Life*, 243). Nonetheless, the quest for an American Shakespeare and an American literary set of standards had begun.

Undoubtedly precipitating this national interest in literature was the noteworthy rise in the literacy rate of post-Revolutionary citizenry. Americans had renewed their interest in education. The rising literacy rate and the renewed interest in education were reflected in the burgeoning publishing trade in post–Revolutionary America, a commercial enterprise that appealed to the needs of intelligentsia and populace alike.

As English colonists, Americans' reading habits had reflected those of their contemporaries in the mother country. John Usher, a Boston bookseller in the 1680s, recorded that his patrons had purchased 400 Bibles, 1,000 religious books, 1,000 schoolbooks, 162 romances, 81 poetry books, and 28 jest books (Nye, *Unembarrassed Muse*, 10). A century later, the reading preferences of the citizens in the new nation had not changed much from that of their forebears. In fact, the publishing trade thrived, more so than ever before.

The Revolution had produced a new group of readers, people who believed that industry and education were the keys to social and upward mobility. For these ambitious Americans, the written word in itself represented empowerment. Consequently, this new reading audience's desire to know was voracious. Newspapers grew in number and power, especially in light of the great political debates of the period (Federalist/Anti-Federalist and the subsequent Federalist/Republican conflicts). Citizens avidly followed the political debates that were assiduously reported by partisan papers. Technological advances, such as mechanical typesetting, were instrumental in the rise in newspaper circulation.

During the colonial period, newspapers used as their sources news items originally reported by the British press. Often these were lifted verbatim. Throughout the colonies, regardless of location, the reporting of the news was identical. Thus, a yeoman farmer in Georgia often read the same story word for word that would have been read in the local paper by a Bostonian merchant. After the Revolution, however, the look and nature of journalism in the United States began to change.

The passage of the First Amendment in 1791 assured freedom of the press. No longer fearing government intervention, newspaper publishers promoted and abetted the fierce partisan arguments of the period (particularly between the Federalists and the Jeffersonian Republicans). This ushered in what many journalism historians regard as "the Dark Ages" of American journalism (Tebbel, 55). Reportorial freedom was the order of the day. Newspapers quickly began to print more than reported material from Europe and smaller items of local interest (such as religious tracts, weather reports, so-called miraculous events, and advertisements for and reviews of popular novels of the day). Satires, lampoons, and exposés became standard features in post–Revolutionary American newspapers. Also, newspapers began to offer column space to all citizens, who, no longer afraid of government reprisals, wrote with astonishing candor on all issues of the day.

Two very partisan journalists exemplify the ferocity of newspaper reporting, both, coincidentally, editors of Philadelphia newspapers. The first, William Cobbett (1763–1835), writing under the name "Peter Porcupine," was a fiercely anti-Republican, pro-British editor and journalist. Cobbett, an Englishman, settled in Philadelphia where he launched his Federalist newspaper, *Gazette and Daily Advertiser* (1797–1799). Cobbett was renowned for publishing writings that argued against the practice and spirit of the American idea of a democracy. As a result, his enemies were legion. (His other writings—most conspicuously *A Bone to Gnaw on for the Democrats* [1795], *A Kick for Bite* [1796], and the defamatory *Life of Tom Paine* [1796]—provide excellent examples of his malicious and inflammatory pen.) Eventually, Cobbett's vicious diatribes were no longer tolerated even by a nation that had embraced the First Amendment. After paying a heavy fine in a libel suit, Cobbett returned to England in 1800.

The most famous of the republican journalists was the editor and poet Philip Freneau. A follower of Jefferson and Madison, Freneau took up journalism early in his career. After the Revolutionary War, Freneau returned to journalism, founding and editing the republican *National Gazette* (1791–1793). The semiweekly *National Gazette* almost immediately became the voice of a freethinking democracy. Radically anti-Hamiltonian in his politics, Freneau engaged in vicious battles with the Federalists, often vilifying the Federalist leaders of the day. Freneau particularly denigrated the policies of Hamilton, so much so that Hamilton felt compelled to accuse the *National Gazette* of being established for the political use of Secretary of State Thomas Jefferson (Hudson, 186). The *National Gazette* was, on the contrary, the creation and mouthpiece of Freneau, not Jefferson. (Under oath Freneau had testified that Jefferson neither suggested nor furnished any of the items published in the paper.) Under Freneau's editorship the *National Gazette* featured biting satires, burlesques, and discreditable revelations. His articles and columns were so acerbic in nature and content that Freneau earned the everlasting scorn of Washington, who called him "that rascal Freneau" and a "wretched and insolent dog."

But Freneau, to his credit, also published learned essays on government by Madison and Pennsylvanian jurist Hugh Henry Brackenridge (1748–1816). In one article, Madison eloquently argued that republican virtues and liberty itself could only be advanced in a nation where there was a "general intercourse of sentiment" facilitated by "particularly a circulation of newspapers through the entire body of the people" (qtd. in Davidson, 160). The press, obviously, concurred.

Federalists, too, offered temperate and learned essays on political issues. Dramatist Royall Tyler, with publisher Joseph Dennie, wrote the very popular "Colon & Spondee" columns that were widely published in New England newspapers. Although satiric—and definitely Federalist—the Colon & Spondee columns were extremely popular because of their wit and self-restraint (ibid., 197).

Unfortunately, not all political columnists were as responsible or as balanced in presenting their views as Brackenridge, Madison, Dennie, or Tyler. Many surpassed the invectives of Peter Porcupine and Freneau. Ordinarily, American publishers did not censor what appeared on their pages. News stories became increasingly more scandalous, rhetoric in columns more provocative. For example, in 1800 a writer who signed himself "Burleigh" posed the question in the *New York Commercial Advertiser*, "Do you believe in the strangest of all paradoxes—that a spendthrift, a libertine, or an atheist is qualified to make your laws and govern you and your prosperity?" (qtd. in ibid., 161). The spendthrift, libertine, and atheist? Vice President Thomas Jefferson.

Newspapers, on the whole, added to the polarization of American politics and pandered to a reading public's interest in the salacious. Newspapers exploited the people's interest in the acquisition of knowledge and the desire to make their voices heard. Although some journalists reported responsibly, a vast number resorted to sensationalism and inflammatory rhetoric to sell papers.

American magazines also played an integral part in the formation of the literature of the new republic, but this was a medium that had a better reputation than that of newspapers. Though often very short-lived, magazines began with loftier aspirations. Quality of content and writing in magazines was, in fact, superior to that found in most newspapers. In effect, the influence of the magazine industry was profound and wide-reaching.

Historically, magazines from the period performed three important roles in the development of literature and of the publishing industry in the United States: They were often the source of a democratic literature of high quality; they stimulated the book trade by instilling in their readership solid reading habits and by familiarizing the public with the works of writers of noteworthy reputation; and they today provide an indispensable history of the period (Mott, *History of American Magazines,* 2–3). Early nationalist magazines, by their very content, revealed the preferences and the interests of the literate public. To generate and sustain subscriptions, even the most specialized magazines had to appeal to the interests of their readers. Thus, these magazines simultaneously reflect the popular cultural interests of Americans and efforts of the literary establishment to influence (and manipulate) the tastes of the literate public.

The Post Office Act of 1794 resulted in a greater number of magazines being founded. (Basically the act granted permission to send magazines by mail. The postage, however, was rather costly, frequently increasing the cost of the magazine to the subscriber up to 40 percent more.) But subscription lists grew, and thus the number of magazines multiplied. In 1794, only four American magazines were in existence; by 1810 there were 40 (ibid., 120). The proliferation of the magazine despite its cost perhaps reflects the desire of all literate citizens to broaden their scope of knowledge. Magazines appealed to all classes, genders, and age groups. Some were targeted at a specific group. Some aspired to reach a broad spectrum of the population. But all reflected the collective interests and hopes of a new nation.

The most famous of the periodicals of the time were literary magazines. Published weekly and monthly, the literary-based magazines were characterized by judicious selections of tales, poetry, essays, "fragments" (sketches), book reviews, and meteorological tables. Literary magazines afforded young aspiring authors an outlet for their fledgling attempts. Some of the more prominent magazines of the period included the Philadelphia-based *Monthly Magazine and American Review* (1799–1800), the *Literary Magazine and American Register* (1803–1807) (both established and edited by novelist Charles Brockden Brown), *Port Folio* (1801–1827), and the *Analectic Magazine* (established in 1813 under the editorship of Washington Irving).

The desire to establish an American literary culture was not the only reason for the proliferation of the magazine as a medium. The religious fervor of the period led to the increase of religious periodicals. Most religious periodicals contained narratives of conversions, deathbed scenes, reviews, poetry, and accounts of remarkable providences. Some ventured into the political arena. One magazine, the *American Moral and Sentimental Magazine*, openly announced, in its preface, its campaign against "the torrent of infidelity," a decided reference to Jefferson's theological views during the 1800 presidential campaign (ibid., 132).[1]

Although most religious periodicals were organs of organized religions (such as the Congregationalists, the Presbyterians, and the Methodists), even the Deists had a magazine, the *Theophilanthropist* (founded in 1810 by the Society of Theophilanthropy). The *Theophilanthropist* was dedicated to interpreting the works of the late Thomas Paine (reviled by many Americans—mistakenly—as an atheist) and to disparaging the Methodists and Calvinists. Often the *Theophilanthropist* resorted to crude satiric attempts in their concerted efforts to oppose Methodism and Calvinism. One issue featured a woodcut of a Methodist preacher with "greasy locks hung down" and a quote: "Here all decency is outraged, and the most frantic bedlamites are considered as under the influence of the Holy Spirit" (qtd. in ibid., 132–133). On the whole, regardless of denomination or intent, religious periodicals were more prosperous and enduring than the more erudite magazines of the period.

Some periodicals began to focus their efforts toward groups heretofore ignored. Women and children soon became targeted audiences for magazine subscriptions. The *Lady's Weekly Miscellany* (1805–1808), which had the longest existence, contained short fiction, theatrical reviews, poetry, and announcements of marriages and deaths. Women's periodicals during this period had relatively short life spans. (The flowering of the woman's magazine was to come later in the nineteenth century.) More successful were magazines not necessarily targeted specifically toward women but included articles designed to garner female interest. Some of the more astute publishers openly solicited contributions from women. The *Literary and Scientific Repository* triumphantly declared "every man of sense and sentiment must view with hearty satisfaction the literary improvement of the females of his country" (qtd. in ibid., 140).

Aside from the expected articles and criticisms of female fashions of the day, some magazines addressed the issue of female suffrage and women's rights. Charles Brockden Brown's magazines, in particular, often addressed issues of importance concerning women's role in the new republic. Brown used his *Literary Magazine* as the means to discuss his own views regarding suffrage and political voice, under the guise of a fictional dialogue earlier published as *Alcuin* (1798). In the 1805 magazine reprint, Brown caustically observes (through one of his characters, the sage and eloquent Mrs. Carter) that in the United States women have no more rights than beasts. The dialogue also powerfully addresses the issue of women entering the professions and the education of women. For Brown, to neglect the education and training of women in the new republic was akin to wasting a valuable natural resource.

The question of education did not stop at the argument on female education. Americans were also very concerned about the education of their young, and the periodicals of the time reflected this concern. Juvenile periodicals began to appear. The first magazine for children to appear in the United States, *Children's Magazine* (1789), featured an introduction to geography, moral tales, and sentimental verses. One juvenile magazine had the distinction of being published and edited by a child. The *Juvenile Port-Folio* was the product of Thomas G. Condie Jr., who was 13 at the time he produced its first issue. The *Juvenile Port-Folio*, a four-page octavo published weekly, was a valiant attempt to emulate adult writing of the day. Young Condie even attempted a mock-heroic poem on apple dumplings: "The Dumplianiad." Those who taught American children were soon afforded a magazine that dealt with pedagogical matters. In 1811 the first American educational periodical, *Juvenile Monitor, or Educational Magazine*, appeared. *Juvenile Monitor* was soon followed by other magazines of its intent that would deal with pedagogical and educational themes.

Educational topics continued to grace the pages of most American magazines, not just those dealing with or designed for children. The more literary-based magazines also included articles and essays on the state of education in the United States. In 1817 an article in the *Analectic* offered an analysis by region of the state of education in the nation. (The author found New Englanders to be the most literate, New Jerseyites the least. Free schools in the poorer urban areas were not successful. Education in the western territories was also poor. Female education was basically ornamental.) Other magazines, notably the *Port Folio* and Brown's *Literary Magazine*, addressed the subject and nature of topics taught in the schools.

One of the most controversial of the educational topics was Noah Webster's *Compendious Dictionary of the English Language* (1806), the preparation for his *An American Dictionary of the English Language* (1828).

Webster's insistence on American usage and spelling over the more traditional British forms especially drew the ire of the editor of the *Port Folio*. Its owner, editor, and publisher, Joseph Dennie, wrote a scathing criticism of Webster's work. Dennie averred that, "We deem it our duty as good patriots, and fond lovers of provincial idioms, and colloquial meanness, and, in short, of every thing, hostile to English sense, and English stile, to furnish this great lexicographer with all the barbarous words and phrases which we can procure" (qtd. in Mott, *History of American Magazines*, 147). Dennie offered some of the following Americanisms as examples of "barbarous words and phrases": "evincial," "carniverosity," "hellniferous," "that's disingenus," "I coch it," "deadheartedness," "caucus," and "he laughed and gurned." A proponent of British English, Dennie eventually proposed that the nation establish an academy of authors who would uphold the British standard of English (Chielens, 320). Thus, the *Port Folio* became the advocate voice for political linguistic control.

American concern about the pursuit of knowledge was not limited to formal education, nor were magazines the only venue for self-improvement. Astute publishing houses also profited from the citizenry's zealous search for knowledge, particularly the pursuit of education and self-edification. Social guides, textbooks, self-improvement books, histories, captivity narratives, informational almanacs, children's books, travelogues, biographies, and novels were soon available to sate the reading appetites of the public (Davidson, 65).

The number of self-improvement books especially increased during the early republican era. In a new nation that, by its very conception, encouraged educational reform and the proliferation of literacy, self-improvement books furnished the masses with a means to improve their reading and writing skills. These books emphasized self-reliance, questioning of ideas and authority, open-mindedness, and inductive reasoning (ibid., 69). Due to the nature of American journalism at the time, these books offered timely and astute advice. Often readers were encouraged to write letters and reviews to newspapers, thus allowing them to enter the public forum. (But again the emphasis was on balanced reasoning.) Specifically, heretofore disadvantaged readers were now given the tools to improve not only their literacy skills but their reasoning skills as well—and advice on how to exercise them for the public good. This was sound advice in an era of the slanderous and the libelous.

As literacy rose in the new republic, libraries and reading groups also multiplied in due course. The majority of Americans, whose limited finances prohibited them from purchasing many books, turned to subscription (also known as "social") and circulating libraries to augment their reading. Initially, the subscription library was the brainchild of a young Benjamin Franklin in the 1740s. Franklin had the desire to read multitudes of books, but had not the purchasing power to acquire them. He reasoned that others of the merchant and trade class had the same wishes—and the same limitations. A subscription library would fulfill the need, yet not pose a financial hardship for those of modest means.

Subscription libraries operated on a shareholder basis. Shareholders in the library were charged an annual fee and were required to purchase shares in the library, often as much as $20 per share (ibid., 28). Eventually, the high cost resulted in the subscription libraries serving an affluent elite—a far cry from Franklin's poor tradesmen who paid ten shillings per annum for their subscriptions. Thus, circulating libraries (commercial libraries that rented books at a more affordable price) became the common people's access to books. Circulating libraries often made financial concessions for their patrons. For example, circulating libraries in major cities charged $6 per annum and offered flexible payment plans: monthly, quarterly, biannually, or annually (ibid., 28).

The growing library system had made obtainable materials heretofore unavailable to the masses. Community reading groups flourished as well, also in response to the national desire to improve literary skills. Informal reading groups afforded readers a chance to discuss and share impressions with others. During the early nationalist period much of the reading was for entertainment, but some was for edification. For although mass education was rapidly being systematized, many Americans were interested in self-education (ibid., 65). Books were purchased or lent—and then subsequently discussed within the community—because they proved to be a reliable source of instruction.

There was, however, a notable shift in the public's interest in texts that were highly esteemed for their edification purposes. Pre-Revolutionary America had regarded the Bible and the Psalter as the authoritative texts to be consulted in every aspect of life. Literate colonists often read religious books, such as the Bible and the Psalter, repeatedly to glean moral and spiritual truths. But at the end of the eighteenth century, Americans' perception of the sole importance of the Bible had dramatically shifted. Because of the availability of more books (and the variety of books), reading habits had changed. Americans still read the Bible, but it was no longer considered the only source of spiritual enlightenment. Rather than reading intensively (such as the practice of reading the Bible over and over), Americans now chose to read extensively (ibid., 72). The public's quest for variety and quantity was intense—and ownership became a priority. Many Americans were not content with merely renting or lending books. The serious reader's hope of acquiring a personal library was intense.

Books, though, were a dear commodity. A modern-day estimate determined that a typical novel published during this period (about 75 cents to $1.50 in price) would be about three or four times the price of a hardcover book today if measured against consumer indices and wages. As an example, a copy of Charles Brockden Brown's *Wieland; or, The Transformation. An American Tale* (1798) would have cost a Massachusetts day laborer two days pay; for that amount of money he could purchase a bushel of potatoes and a half bushel of corn (ibid., 25).

Thus, very few Americans of the middle and lower classes could afford to acquire expansive personal libraries—or even to own a single book. To assure a profit, most publishers relied on subscription sales arranged by a traveling agent. The agent would scour the countryside for subscribers who would be willing to pay for a book not yet published. He would return to the printer with subscription orders and from that number the publisher would be able to calculate the print run. The success of a subscription campaign would, however, depend on two key factors: the honesty of the traveling agent and the willingness of a skeptical public to purchase a book in advance. Often purchasers would rely on an author's reputation—thus predicating a preponderance of British writings rather than American since British authors had a worldwide reputation. But established reputation was no guarantee of subscription success. Even well-known European authors were not assured subscription success. At best, subscription campaigns were a weak marketing device.

American authors incurred additional difficulties because of the capricious nature of the literary marketplace. Not only did the public expect them to create a national literature, one that would distinguish American history, manners, and principles, but also works that would pique their interest. Thus, for an American writer's work to sell, he or she would need to be sensitive to the reading tastes of this discerning marketplace.

Astute authors quickly realized that what did sell was the novel, which was not considered to be a "reputable" genre. In spite of political leaders, academicians, and the clergy's condemnation of novel reading (the main objection was that it would inflame the baser passions), readers on both sides of the Atlantic clamored for this relatively new art form. Essentially, the first completely realized European novel was Samuel Richardson's *Pamela; or, Virtue Rewarded* (1740). (Interestingly, Benjamin Franklin was one of the first American publishers of *Pamela*.) Although the English novel evolved from a fertile literary tradition that harkened back to ancient Greece, the depiction of life in a fictional narrative (as constructed by Richardson) was considered to be a new genre. The novel quickly became a middle-class kind of luxury because the middle class identified with its plot and characters. Novels were generally set in middle-class surroundings in authorial attempts to depict life as realistically as possible. Leading arguments against novel reading included objections that the arts tell lies, that they are merely imitative of life, and thereby that they stimulate unhealthy emotions. Novel aficionados and authors refuted such objections by claiming that novelistic descriptions of seductions and other ethical failings served as moral lessons (that is, the novel was instructive rather than destructive to the moral fiber of the young).

Even though the novel had been in existence in Europe for approximately 50 years—increasing in popularity—in American literature the novel (as a genre) did not exist prior to the Revolutionary War. Colonial American literature was generally characterized by its imitation of British forms, such as the essay and the poem. Revolutionary America preferred literature that was derivative rather than innovative—and thus ignored novel writing altogether. But the post-Revolutionary rise in the literacy of the citizenry, especially among women, expanded the reading public, a reading public that demanded and voraciously read novels, both British and American.

For the most part, American ventures into novel writing, regardless of mode, slavishly emulated the British, and, thus, critics often dismissed these efforts. Even as late as 1820, Sydney Smith issued his now-infamous, disdainful inquiry in the *Edinburgh Review*: "Who reads an American book?" But contrary to Smith's belief, one shared by many Europeans, during the early nationalist period the novel flourished and developed significantly as a popular art form.

Many early American novels were less than stellar in their renderings of "American life and experience." American pens produced scores of lackluster novels. By any historical standard, some of the attempts were inept if not outright laughable. Yet a few American writers quickly transformed this new genre into a form of education, an entry for the reader into the realm of intellectual, political, and philosophical thought because serious novelists consciously viewed themselves as shapers of the character of America and of the American character. For those who had a feminist agenda and for women, especially, the novel became the ideal vehicle to reach an entire audience previously only slightly exposed to the realms of ideas and possibilities for social change.

Early American novels can be roughly placed in one of four categories: the sentimental (imitators of Richardson), the historical romance (emerging from the popularity of the novels of Sir Walter Scott), the gothic novel, and the satiric (along the lines of the works of Jonathan Swift) (Nye, *Cultural Life*, 252–253). Of the early nationalist period, the sentimental and the gothic novel were the most popular (and most often adopted by American authors), closely followed by the satiric. Still another form that evolved during this time was the slave narrative. Moreover, all forms became effective vehicles to instruct the new republic on the value of a virtuous life and a virtuous society.

# THE FIRST AMERICAN NOVEL

In 1789 William Hill Brown's *The Power of Sympathy; or, The Triumph of Nature. Founded in Truth* made its first appearance. Ascertained to be the first novel written by an American, *The Power of Sympathy* is a novel fraught with moral didacticism, as well as a resolute patriotic stance. The prevalent theme in the novel, however, is the seduction motif and the treachery of such actions. The dedication page to the first edition proclaims that the audience for the novel and its author's intent is "To the Young Ladies, of United Columbia, These Volumes. Intended to represent the specious Causes, and to Explore the fatal Consequences, of S E D U C T I O N; To inspire the Female Mind With a Principle of Self Complacency, and to Promote the Economy of Human Life, Are Inscribed, With Esteem and Sincerity, By their Friend and Humble Servant, The Author" (5).

The authorial directive clearly demonstrates its derivation from Richardson's *Pamela*. (Like Richardson, William Hill Brown used the epistolary format in developing his tale of seduction and sentiment.) And like most American literary practitioners at the time, Brown used an English form that an American public would find most appealing and would guarantee a place in the American literary marketplace.

*The Power of Sympathy* has a relatively complex plot structure. A young man, Harrington, makes plans to seduce the virtuous Harriot Fawcet. Eventually, Harrington falls in love with Harriot (virtue wins out over vice) and abandons his seduction plans. He proposes marriage. The lovers, however, are not united. A worthy matron, Mrs. Holmes, discloses that Harriot and Harrington are actually half siblings, thus sparing the couple the pain of unwittingly consummating an incestuous relationship. Harriot dies soon after the family secret is revealed. A distraught Harrington kills himself soon afterward.

Interwoven within the main plot line of the romantic relationship between Harrington and Harriot are several subplots: one a seduction/suicide motif, another of a suicide over the despair of an engagement interrupted, another of seduction and abandonment, and still another of the real-life story of the seduction and abandonment of Elizabeth Whitman.[2] The main plot and the subplots, nonetheless, underscore the theme of virtue and restraint.

Undeniably, *The Power of Sympathy* is a flawed book. Like many of its type, it is a weak imitation of a British form, utilizing an American setting in an effort to address issues facing American society. Its characterization is weak, cohesiveness in the narrative is lacking, often the plot is disjunctive, and the tone throughout wavers between unrelenting moralizing and exploitive sensationalism. Yet this earliest of American novels succeeds in addressing issues that preoccupied Americans, especially the issue of the nature of republicanism. Though the nature of what constituted republicanism was hotly debated at the time (ranging from the strict derivation of the word from ancient Greek to the more egalitarian ideas put forth by Thomas Paine), Americans did concur that American society was an enlightened society and, therefore, superior to the decadent society of Europe (particularly of Great Britain). European decadence, thus, should be avoided at all costs.

Thus, *The Power of Sympathy* at times digresses into a discourse on republican values. As a novel "founded in truth," it not only elucidates republican ideas of temperance and benevolence but democratic ideals as well. Brown succinctly propounds that this new nation is relatively yet uncivilized and therefore has not been corrupted by European immorality (Petter, 248). In several letters within the novel, the idea is advanced that Americans have opportunities to bring forth a new world order; among these would entail the abolishment of slavery and the creation of a noble literary tradition, one which would espouse honor and rectitude (unlike the perceived decadent nature of the European novel). These ideas would be echoed by other writers of the period.

## "WOMEN BEWARE" NOVELS

William Hill Brown may have been the first American writer to venture into novel writing, but he certainly was not the only one. Women, in particular, found the novel to be an effective outlet to raise issues specific to women. Even though they were not afforded a voice in the new nation (despite Abigail Adams's now famous plea to her husband to "remember the ladies" in the formation of the new government), women took up their pens in an effort to let their views be known and disseminated.

One of the most successful American women novelists was an English immigrant, Susanna Haswell Rowson (1762–1824). After immigrating to the American colonies, the Haswell family had returned to England after ten years of residing in Massachusetts. In London, Rowson (now married) embarked on a literary career. When she returned to the United States in 1793, she began republishing many of her books that had been published in England. (This, again, was a common practice in the United States. English books were the primary source of income for American publishers. Either publishers imported standard British editions or they reprinted them.)

Rowson's works offer a remarkable example of the skillful adaptation of popular British forms to expound a moral message, which was her impetus for writing in the first place. Although she publicly disapproved of most novels, feeling that they exerted an undue, and harmful, influence on young girls in particular who were prone to romantic and fanciful thoughts, Rowson used her pen to counteract their insidious effect. Her most successful (both financially and artistically) novel, *Charlotte Temple, A Tale of Truth* (published in England, 1791; republished in America, 1794) is, like *The Power of Sympathy*, a cautionary tale. The basic plot can be easily summed up as "seduced and abandoned in the New World."

A British officer, Lieutenant Montraville, seduces a 15-year-old English girl, Charlotte Temple. She willingly follows him to America where Montraville deserts her in favor of a much wealthier young woman. Charlotte, unmarried and pregnant with Montraville's child, is eventually forsaken by all her acquaintances. Her father arrives from England in an effort to take her back to her homeland, but unfortunately she dies in childbirth. (Her daughter, Lucy, is the subject of the sequel, *Lucy Temple*, published posthumously in 1828.) Rowson's message to the young women in America is clear: virtue and marriage offer women the only security they might have.

Hannah Webster Foster (1758–1840), another prolific and popular writer, also adapted the novel of seduction with some success. Her most famous novel—based on the real-life tale of Elizabeth Whitman (1752–1788)—*The Coquette; or, The History of Eliza Wharton* (1797), uses the epistolary form rather effectively. Superior in skill and theme to the earlier *The Power of Sympathy* (which also broadly alluded to the tale of Elizabeth Whitman), *The Coquette* in many ways transcends the tried and true apparatus of the novel of seduction. The hapless Eliza Wharton is seduced, abandoned, and dies an ignominious death in childbirth. The novel, like all others of its genre, ends predictably with a didactic conclusion, complete with a highly sentimentalized inscription from her tombstone.

Foster's work exhibits much more restraint than earlier seduction and sentimental novels. Strongly developed characterizations, rather than long, digressive moralistic narrative, reinforce Foster's moral lesson to the youth of America. In addition, in the novel Foster raises the issue of education for women in the new republic, the dichotomy of the issue itself. Many republican thinkers agreed that for a woman to play a responsible role in society, she needed to be educated. However, her very education excludes her from a society that has no place for an educated woman. Eliza Wharton (the coquette of the title) is depicted as an intelligent, able woman who carries herself with dignity. Yet she, like all women of the time, is circumscribed by societal constraints. She must choose to retreat into the stability that only marriage might offer women or to be a coquette, a woman who will not be fettered by the institution but elects to enter romantic dalliances. Eliza's imprudent decision leads to her fall.

Readers' responses to this novel were enthusiastic and intense. Perhaps American women recognized that Eliza's story was their story, a story of lost desire and identity (Davidson, 149). Consequently, *The Coquette* was immediately an enormous success with the reading public— a success that was sustained throughout the nineteenth century. (Within a four-year period [1824–1828] *The Coquette* was reissued eight times.) *The Coquette* was one of the most often purchased books of the early nationalist period, a time when books were hard to acquire and expensive (ibid., 150). In the preface to the 1855 edition, Jane E. Locke avers that "it is not surprising that it [*The Coquette*] thus took precedence in interest . . . of all American novels, at least throughout New England, and was found, in every cottage within its borders, beside the family Bible, and, though pitifully, yet almost as carefully treasured" (qtd. in ibid.).

Still another novelistic response to the role of women in the new republic was Tabitha Gilman Tenney's *Female Quixotism: Exhibited in the Romantic Opinions and Extravagant Adventures of Dorcasina Sheldon* (1801). Like Susanna Rowson, Tenney strongly decried indiscriminate novel reading. As the title suggests, *Female Quixotism* is patterned after Miguel de Cervantes's *Don Quixote* (1605), designed to lampoon romantic ideals and counsel against ascribing to the prevalent novelistic idyllic treatment of love. Tenney's audience is unequivocally young American women.

A widowed father has indulged her heroine, the foolish Dorcas Sheldon. Rather than reading edifying tomes, Dorcas has indiscriminately read scores of romantic and sentimental romances. A mild example of how novel reading has influenced Dorcas unduly is her decision to change her name (and thus her identity). She forsakes the sensible name of Dorcas for the more romantic-sounding Dorcasina. Because she mistakes romantic plots and conventions for depictions of real life, Dorcasina becomes involved in a series of romantic misadventures. At the end, Dorcasina, who has lost both youth and beauty, finally faces the truth. Somewhat repentant over her misspent youth, Dorcas dedicates the rest of her unmarried days to engaging in charitable activities.

The irony of *Female Quixotism* is that Dorcasina does not give up novel reading—and that Tenney circuitously shows that the novelistic form itself was not without merit. By her very example, novel reading (albeit satiric) could offer valuable lessons, especially to young women. Dorcasina has learned the difference between the fanciful and the real, as do Tenney's readers.

Accordingly, American writers adeptly adapted the established novelistic forms of the sentimental (seduction), the romance, and the satiric as a venue for shaping American mores, as well as a means of supplementing income. (Early American authors rarely could subsist on their literary earnings.) It was, however, their adoption of the gothic novel that led to the establishment of a truly American literary tradition.

# THE GOTHIC NOVEL

Another form of the European novel that American writers adapted for their own purposes was the gothic novel, a genre whose origins can be traced back to Sir Horace Walpole's *Castle of Otranto* (1764). The plots of gothic novels are infused with horror and mystery, and gothic novels are often laden with the following generic conventions: oppressive gloom, the underlying horror and dread of the protagonist or narrator (whichever may be the case), and a feeling of certain doom. Typical conventions found in gothic novels include moldering castles, labyrinthine passageways, glowering villains, and supernatural phenomena (such as witches, werewolves, and ghosts). Some (or all) are employed to create an atmosphere of suspense, mystery, fearful apprehension, and strangeness. Indeed, atmosphere is often foregrounded over characterization. Everything in a gothic world is highly significant—and charged with meaning—and events seem to be linked with a divine (or an infernal) logic.

Americans found that the gothic genre lent itself well to the American experience, especially what is known as the "explained gothic" (gothic romances that attributed a rational explanation for supposedly supernatural phenomena). While explained gothic, like gothic novels grounded in the supernatural, is characterized by the gothic pleasure principle (the reader's perverse pleasure in being terrified), it is devoid of supernatural events and devices. What merely appear to be supernatural phenomena are easily explained in rational terms, hence the qualifier "explained."

Especially popular were the explained-gothic novels of the English writer Ann Radcliffe (1764–1823). Radcliffe's innovations added an air of respectability to the genre. Using the apparatus of the romance (which, in the eighteenth century, had even less credibility than the novel), Radcliffe remarkably transformed the conventions of the romance—the extravagance of its settings, its heavy reliance on fancy rather than careful observation of nature, its use of coincidence—into instruments of didacticism (K.F. Ellis, 99). Not only did her five gothic novels[3] establish the explained mode of the gothic, but they also were immensely popular with readers on both sides of the Atlantic. Not surprisingly, she had many imitators in Europe and America alike.

For American writers Radcliffe's explained-gothic novel was the ideal form for exploration into individual psychology, and subsequently Americans transformed the genre into a means of examining and critiquing the American experience. Although the first American gothic novels retained the medieval, brooding atmosphere of their English counterparts, the Americans soon began to use American settings and devices (such as Native Americans and witchcraft, although the latter first appeared in German literature) in their gothic novels. In his preface to *Edgar Huntly* (1799), Charles Brockden Brown wrote, "One merit the writer may at least claim [is] that of calling forth the passions and engaging the sympathy of the reader, by means hitherto unemployed by preceding authors. Puerile superstition and exploded manners [, and] Gothic castles and chimeras, are the materials usually employed for this end. The incidents of Indian hostility, and the native of America to overlook these, would admit no apology"(3).

Many other writers followed Brown's pronouncement against the use of "puerile superstition" in their gothic novels, opting instead to use American settings and experiences, such as epidemics and Native American uprisings and attacks on colonial settlements. During this period the American transformation of the gothic genre proved to be rather successful, critically and financially. But the American gothic novel achieved distinction in the psychological gothic tales of Charles Brockden Brown, a would-be Philadelphia lawyer turned novelist and magazine editor.[4]

It is difficult, however, to separate Charles Brockden Brown the man from Charles Brockden Brown the myth. The fanciful commentaries of "observers" and early biographers of one of the preeminent novelists of the early nationalist period rival that of the gothic effects of Brown's four gothic novels.[5] For instance, John Neal, a prolific American writer in the early nineteenth century, described Brown as one who was "lost in thought, and looking like a shipwrecked man. . . . He went off in a lingering consumption, with a broken heart—and a spirit absolutely crushed" (see Axelrod, xi).

The "real" Brown came from a Quaker family, was educated in Friend's Latin School in Philadelphia, and studied law but never practiced it. Instead he wished to earn a living by his pen. At the outset of his literary career, Brown was greatly influenced by the radical writings of British philosopher and novelist William Godwin (1756–1836), as evidenced in much of his writing.[6] Later, he appears to have renounced Godwinianism (and fiction writing altogether), concentrating on his political pamphleteering efforts that espoused Federalism.

In his attempt to earn a living by writing, we might only surmise that Brown was aware of and interested in a particularly popular mode of fiction of the era—that is, the gothic novel. He did not, however, incorporate the supernaturally based gothic of established British gothicists such as Horace Walpole (1717–1797) and Matthew "Monk" Lewis (1775–1818). Rather, he found the more rationalistic explained gothic of Ann Radcliffe (whose American readership was numerous) and the German romancers Friedrich von Schiller (1759–1805) and Cajetan Tschink (1763–1813) more suitable for the intellectual ambience of the early nationalist period. Explained gothic permitted Brown to use the genre for ulterior purposes—that is, to explore the interiors and repercussions of an abnormal psychological state in a politically unstable nation.

Brown's first novel, *Wieland; or The Transformation. An American Tale* (1798), is (despite its flaws) generally regarded to be the finest early American gothic novel. Its suspenseful plot, approach to the genre, and unyielding movement toward the resolution are testaments to his artistic success. Unlike other gothic novelists of his time, Brown did not believe that the reader's horror was dependent on the author's manipulations of the standard gothic conventions (such as moldering castles, degeneration, and superstition). Yet the novel reveals Brown's adeptness at transforming Radcliffe's type of gothic into a mode that reflected early American experience and concerns. Clara Wieland, the unreliable narrator of the tale, in many ways parallels the typical Radcliffe heroine. She retreats in abject terror from what she perceives to be supernatural phenomena; she is confronted with the possibility of rape at the hands of a stranger, the insidious Carwin (although she is inexplicably attracted to and yet repelled by him); and she is separated from her true love until the novel's denouement. Undoubtedly, Brown's style is uniquely his own, yet his intention was to recreate the effects of the most successful of English gothicists of the time.

In his re-creation Brown refrained from employing the clichéd trappings and European settings of Radcliffe, preferring to use American social concerns and the environs of his native Pennsylvania. Rather, he sets *Wieland* on the banks of the Schuylkill River, not in Europe. The appearance of the supernatural phenomena in the novel, the spontaneous combustion of the elder Wieland and the projection of mysterious voices, are meticulously explained away, the former by authorial footnote, the latter by the use of ventriloquism by the villainous Carwin.

In *Ormond; or, The Secret Witness* (1799), Brown's second published novel, the author inverts the notion of the powerless gothic heroine. Constantia Dudley, probably the most formidable and resourceful of Brown's female characters, strikes back at her attacker, the sinister Ormond of the title, with a vengeance. Armed with a small, but lethal, penknife, she kills the would-be rapist.

In *Arthur Mervyn* (1799–1800), Brown uses a natural catastrophe, the yellow fever epidemic in Philadelphia of 1793, as the means of creating a gothic horror rivaling any horrific scene found in the genre before. Early in *Part I*, Brown has the young Mervyn encounter the most ghastly form of a friend dying from the fever. This terrifying psychological experience is tantamount to actually confronting a specter: "My heart's-blood chilled. If an apparition of the dead were possible . . . this was such an apparition. A hue, yellowish and livid; bones, uncovered with flesh; eyes, ghastly, hollow, woe-begone, and fixed in an agony of wonder upon me" (C.B. Brown, vol. 3, 167).

This particular passage epitomizes Brown's control of his material, a control even more remarkable when one realizes that in this passage (and others relating to the yellow fever epidemic), the author has not resorted to conventional literary devices. In his graphic depictions of the putrescence of the sights and smells of the Philadelphia hospital, the fear of death, and the psychological horror of the city's inhabitants, Brown was able to use gothic conventions to reveal the intolerable conditions of the epidemic to illustrate the nobility, and the depravity, of the human spirit under such conditions.

One of the themes of Brown's last gothic novel, *Edgar Huntly* (1799), is the much discussed (during this time) affliction of somnambulism. The "mysteries" of this novel are partially attributed to the sleepwalking of Edgar Huntly and Clithero Edny. But true to the one artistic merit Brown, as an author, lays claim to in his preface, he does not fall back on such old and tired clichés as "Gothic castles and chimeras." Instead, he incorporates "incidents of Indian hostility" and "the perils of the wilderness" (of what is now east central Pennsylvania) in *Edgar Huntly*. Gone are the abnormal phenomena of *Wieland*: the dramatic death scenes and the use of ventriloquism by the unscrupulous designed to perplex the participants and the reader. The world of *Edgar Huntly* is, instead, a wholly natural one. The terrors and mysteries the characters confront are not so much from the external world as from the internal world of the mind.

Brown's influence on later American gothic writers was profound, a pervading influence evinced in the writings of later authors such as Edgar Allan Poe and Nathaniel Hawthorne, as well as Washington Irving. His preference for American settings and themes, and his skillful use of such, led others to forsake the castles of Ann Radcliffe in favor of American materials. Brown's transformation of the explained gothic into a genre that used scientific explanations for what appeared to be the uncanny establish his place in the development of American gothic fiction. The logical, yet convincing, explanations for the terror generated in his novels mark Brown's invaluable contribution to American literature.

## OTHER AMERICAN GOTHICISTS (1790–1816)

Although Charles Brockden Brown admonished American writers to use American material in their writings (and thereby avoid "puerile superstition"), not all practitioners of American gothic followed his dictum. Notably S.K. Wood's *Julia, and the Illuminated Baron* (1800) and Isaac Mitchell's *The Asylum; or, Alonzo and Melissa* (1811) rigidly adhered instead to the European settings and devices established by British gothicists. In the former, Wood rarely resisted the impulse to incorporate in this work a gothic convention from the British strain. *Julia* abounds in

European settings, seductions, poisonings, castles, miniatures, and, of course, the reunification of the heroine and her true love. Wood did, however, apologize for setting her gothic tale in Europe, stating that "an aversion to introduce living characters, or those recently dead, rendered Europe a safer, though not a more agreeable theatre" (qtd. in Redden, 47).

In the latter, Mitchell incongruously sets his gothic romance in a medieval castle on Long Island. Replete with a band of marauders, a pair of maudlin lovers, violent storms, mysterious passageways and trapdoors, and precognitive dreams, *Asylum* is a prime example of American overdependence on the popular British form. Mitchell, in his preface, stated that the new republic could not provide material adequate for the "vesture of fiction" (vol. 1, xviii). To his credit, Mitchell did admit that Charles Brockden Brown was the "only one in this country who can lay much claim to originality" (vol. 1, xxiv), but adds "no writer, ancient or modern, has yet equalled Mrs. Radcliffe, in the field of Romance" (vol. 1, xviii).

Although the majority of American gothic novels were written much in the same style of Wood and Mitchell, there were writers who used American material to augment their novels, some exclusively. Ann Eliza Bleecker's *The History of Maria Kittle* (1790–1791) is an example of the exclusive use of American material and setting. Predating Brown's gothic novels by seven to eight years, Bleecker's work quite possibly is the first American gothic novel based on American experiences and themes. Much of the material in Brown's *Edgar Huntly* is similar to that found in *Maria Kittle*, with the exception of the sleepwalking incidents. Basically, Bleecker's epistolary novel used American settings and Native American atrocities to create a gothic experience. The evil deeds of Bleecker's Native Americans do, in some part, reflect the influence of the English gothicists on her work (Redden, 45). In fact, Mr. Kittle's remark at the beginning of the tale that "Oh! This gloom that darkens Maria's soul is supernatural!" (Bleecker, 17) illustrates Bleecker's use of gothic trappings. (Remarkably, *Maria Kittle* also employs the rhetoric, intent, and events found in the seventeenth-century captivity narratives. Although Bleecker's fictional account is a late representation of the narrative tradition based on a historical situation, much of the novel incorporates the apparatus of the sentimental novel as well.)

*A Journey to Philadelphia; or, Memoirs of Charles Coleman Saunders* (1804), published pseudonymously under the name Adelio, is a confessional narrative that manifests the influence of Charles Brockden Brown. The hero, Charles Coleman Saunders, has been unjustly accused of being a criminal and, on the basis of circumstantial evidence, sentenced to death. Saunders resembles Brown's dubious hero Arthur Mervyn on more than one count. Other events that exhibit Brown's influence are the appearance of a sleepwalker (as in *Edgar Huntly*), the use of a double (as in Brown's *Stephen Calvert*, published in his *Monthly Magazine and American Review*), and the suicide attempt of a young girl (echoing Welbeck's leap into the Delaware River[7] in *Arthur Mervyn*) (Petter, 325). More importantly, Adelio's use of Brown's technique of internal dialogue was a concerted effort to reproduce the thought process (ibid., 326).

*Laura* (1809) written by "A Lady of Philadelphia," also reveals the influences of Brown, and of Ann Radcliffe. Set in Philadelphia during the yellow fever plague (once more a novel reminiscent of *Arthur Mervyn*), Laura experiences the horrors of the plague, which the author recounts in graphic detail: the rumbling of the death carts, the moans and shrieks of the ill and dying, and the heart-rending pleadings of family members and loved ones. The use of the American setting and the yellow fever epidemic obviously illustrates the author's indebtedness to Brown.

The Radcliffean influence in *Laura* is evident in the characterization of Rosina (Laura's mother), an unhappy nun who had, against her wishes, been placed in a convent, her subsequent escape, and the heroine's separation from her lover, Belfield, a victim of yellow fever (ibid., 49). Other more traditional conventions found in the novel include a terrifying sequence in a cemetery, Laura's madness after the death of Belfield (he dies in a duel defending her honor on the eve of their wedding), and her escape from the unsavory advances of Melwood (a case of mistaken identity—he thinks she is a prostitute).

Still another example of the commingling of Radcliffean and Brownian gothic is George Watterson's *Glencarn; or, The Disappointments of Youth* (1810). Although *Glencarn* is set in Pennsylvania and Ohio, elements of the British gothic are present. For instance, after the title character is thrown into a cave by bandits, he discovers that the walls are smeared with blood and that human skeletons are scattered about the cave's floor. His grotesque couch is a casket that contains the mangled body of a woman. The Radcliffean horror chamber has successfully been transported to the banks of the Ohio.

Nonetheless, Brown's influence is much more evident than that of Radcliffe, both in setting and inspiration for subject matter and plot. Many events in *Glencarn* blatantly echo those found in Brown's novels. Although Watterson was, in some respects, an emulator of Brown, his work does not artistically approach the skill of the latter. In fact, as one twentieth-century literary critic has asserted, "*Glencarn* may serve as an example of the American novel at a very low ebb" (Cowie, 108).

Even though the majority of early American gothicists' works were not of the highest caliber, their use of the gothic represented the popularity of and the adherence to the works of more skillful gothicists (such as British practitioner Ann Radcliffe and the American Charles Brockden Brown). Sentimental and gothic romances were not, however, the only generic means authors had for exploring and questioning ideology in the new nation.

## CRITICISM OF THE VIRTUOUS REPUBLIC: PICARESQUE, ADVENTURES, AND HISTORIES

Sentimental and gothic novels provided writers with a framework in which to investigate and question societal and political issues facing Americans. But early republican writers did not exclusively use these forms to further their agendas. Critics of the new society found that the satire, too, was well suited for their purposes.

Satire, which uses wit and humor to point out human and institutional weakness, originated in ancient Greece. By the eighteenth century, satire had reached its apogee with the brilliant poetry and prose of English satirists such as Alexander Pope, Henry Fielding, Joseph Addison, and Richard Steele. American writers adhered to the English style of the satire, but modified its content and theme to address domestic political difficulties—with mixed results.

A Pennsylvanian politician and judge, Hugh Henry Brackenridge, embarked on an ambitious plan to adapt the picaresque (a loosely plotted, episodic satire that followed the misadventures of the rogue hero) to the American environs. His lengthy picaresque, *Modern Chivalry*, was nearly 30 years in the making.[8] Published in six successive installments (1792, 1793, 1797, 1804, 1805, 1815), *Modern Chivalry* chronicled the adventures of the rather aristocratic Captain Farrago (who represented republican idealism) and his sidekick, the Irish immigrant Teague O'Regan (who represented overreaching aspirations).

Somewhat modeled on Cervantes' *Don Quixote, Modern Chivalry* lampoons American politics. Indeed, Brackenridge pointedly disputes the notion of what he saw as the myth of the virtuous republic (Hedges, 199). *Modern Chivalry* afforded Brackenridge with a means to criticize the American political press (he views it as a national "disgrace") and the aristocratic pretensions of the Federalists (ibid.).

The early nationalist period also saw the emergence of the witty satire of Washington Irving (1783–1859). In 1807, the young Irving, along with his brother William and his friend James Kirke Paulding, anonymously published the *Salmagundi* papers, a periodical devoted to burlesquing New York society and the "logocracy" of the new nation.[9] According to Irving and his fellow editors, the president of the logocracy (Jefferson), a "man of superlative ventosity," is a "huge bladder of wind" (qtd. in ibid., 200). The vituperative American press also earned Irving's scorn. Journalism in the new republic was hardly virtuous. *Salmagundi* shamelessly ridiculed the rampant less-than-ethical journalistic practices of the Fourth Estate.

His next foray into satire was *A History of New York . . . By Diedrich Knickerbocker* (1809), often considered to be the first American belle lettres. Adopting the persona of the cantankerous Diedrich Knickerbocker, Irving's thinly disguised history of New Amsterdam clearly parallels what he viewed as the shortcomings of post–Revolutionary America. Like the Dutch colony he painstakingly lampoons, the new republic is one that is blinded by the legend of its virtue. Throughout *A History of New York* are not-so-subtle allusions to American leadership at this time (particularly Jefferson, who is burlesqued in the figure of William the Testy).

Another noteworthy picaresque of the period was Royall Tyler's *The Algerine Captive; or, The Life and Adventures of Doctor Updike Underhill* (1797). Tyler's spokesperson, the initially naive Doctor Updike Underhill, undergoes a series of trials and tribulations, most notably his adventures on a slave ship bound for the African continent. Underhill is outraged at the treatment of the African captives by their white captors. He soon, however, finds himself enslaved by Algerine pirates.[10] Like the African slaves, Underhill is treated less than humanely. What ensues is Underhill's account of the various attempts by the Algerian court to convert him to Algerian culture (among these: religion, language, and politics). Not only does Tyler end *The Algerine Captive* with an invective against foreign entanglements (echoing the isolationist federal policy of 1797), but he also firmly establishes the correlation between the piratical culture and the American culture. Barbary cruelty and American inhumanity are explicitly tied.

## REVELATIONS OF NEW REPUBLICAN HYPOCRISY: THE SLAVE NARRATIVE

Tyler was not alone in his efforts to enlighten virtuous republicans to their hypocritical sanctioning of slavery. A heretofore-silenced group of people began to raise their voices and take up their pens. The slave narrative made its appearance in the eighteenth century. Although for the most part, writers in the new nation were White (and often of British ancestry), a small, yet prolific, group of ex-slaves was producing a powerful literature.

The early slave narratives were formulaic in their description of the journey from captivity to deliverance. (The structure is a relatively simple one: a movement from illiteracy to literacy often parallels the movement from captivity to escape to freedom.) Similar in structure to the earlier colonial captivity narratives of the seventeenth century, the slave narratives recount the brutality of slavery, one that was physical and spiritual in nature.

These writers, however, rejected the idea of a new national identity, unlike their White counterparts. In fact, many African American writers considered themselves to be Britons, even after the Revolutionary War when they were subject to the laws of the new nation (Carretta, 1). Many of these writers perceived British laws as being far more favorable to the rights of those of African birth or descent.[11] Thus, loyalty to Britain shaped the tone and subject matter of African American writing. Many asserted their fidelity to British values (if not a British identity) by praising the British government—a marked departure from the subject matter of Euro-American writings at this time. Rather than using fiction to criticize the sociopolitical arena, African American writers used their life stories to illustrate American hypocrisy in regard to the slavery issue.

The most outstanding example of such a narrative in this time period is Olaudah Equiano's *The Interesting Narrative of the Life of Olaudah Equiano, or Gustavus Vassa, the African. Written by Himself.* (1789). Equiano's autobiography reveals the work of an educated writer, the prose refined and knowledgeable (Lowance, 78). It provides a gripping description of his life in Africa, his subsequent capture, and his life in bondage. After he is able to purchase his freedom, Equiano chooses to live in England rather than remain in America (once again emphasizing the more compassionate approach of the British toward the slavery issue than the American approach). At the end of his work, Equiano eloquently pleads for abolishment of slavery (albeit for a British—rather than an American—audience). But the impact of the plea was not lost on audiences on either side of the Atlantic.

## POETRY AND THE REPUBLICAN SPIRIT

Another literary form that American writers used to celebrate the new nation was the poem. Even though by today's standards post-Revolutionary poetry seems stilted in diction and rhythm and didactic in theme, it revealed the direction the poets felt the nation should take. American poets were, as a rule, well educated (predominantly Princeton and Yale graduates) and, understandably, they turned to the poetics of antiquity and eighteenth-century British poetics as their guide for diction and form. Before the war, the major poets of the period (Philip Freneau, Timothy Dwight, Joel Barlow, John Trumbull, and David Humphreys—the last four were a group collectively referred to as "The Connecticut Wits" or "The Hartford Wits"[12]) altered Ciceronian oration poetically in an attempt to convince academia that America's future would be a glorious one (McWilliams, 157). After the ratification of the Constitution, all five had subordinated their poetic writings for significant public careers.[13]

Nonetheless, all of these poets venerated craft. Their intent was to use

Frontispiece from *The Interesting Narrative of the Life of Olaudah Equiano*, 1794. Courtesy of the Library of Congress.

old forms to express new thought, thus subverting English tradition by emulating it (ibid.). Poetic invention became the means of creating a national poetry. To help define America's poetic identity, poets turned to a unique subgenre, that of the "prospect poem."

Based in form on the last two books of John Milton's *Paradise Lost*, the prospect poem used prophecy to propagate republican ideals. These were rather lengthy poetic exercises, running on average from two hundred to six hundred lines. Some, like Barlow's *Vision of Columbus* (1787) and its revised form, *The Columbiad* (1807), were book-length. Prospect poems were noted for their visionary theme. Often the narrative voice spoke, with authority, from a summit. History in the oration shifted from present to near past to future.

The locus of the prospect poem was the Renaissance concept of *translatio studii*, the idea that the progression of civilization follows solar movement—that is, like the heavens, the progress of civilization moves from east to west. For American poets, *translatio studii* validated their belief that the United States would eventually become the global center of culture.

Fine examples of the prospect poem of this period include Humphreys's "A Poem on the Happiness of America" (1786), Dwight's *The Conquest of Canaan* (1785) and "Columbia, Columbia, to Glory Arise" (1783), Freneau's unfinished *The Rising Empire* (1790), and Barlow's *Vision of Columbus*. (*The Columbiad* became an overwrought version of the earlier, superior *Vision of Columbus*.) An example of a variant of the prospect poem is Francis Scott Key's "The Star-Spangled Banner" (1814), a spirited paean, complete with pounding anapestic couplets, grand rhetorical exclamations, and promises of victory and liberty (ibid., 161).

But the patriotic stance of the poets during the early national period was not limited to the prospect poem. One of the most delightful examples of poetic public spirit is Barlow's mock epic *The Hasty-Pudding* (written 1793, published 1796). Although *The Hasty-Pudding* follows epic structure, it veers sharply in tone and subject matter.

Structured in three, four-hundred-line cantos, *The Hasty-Pudding* opens with the homesick narrator gleefully discovering his favorite American dish (cornmeal mush, otherwise known as hasty pudding) in the Alps. After a mock invocation to the Muse, the narrator reflects not on the origins of a people (a standard convention of the epic), but on the origins of the recipe for cornmeal mush. The recipe itself, presented in the most grandiloquent terms, begins, not with the ingredients, but the planting of the corn, the harvesting, and finally the preparing of the mush. The poem ends with sage advice as to what types of bowls and utensils this homey dish should be served in and with and a mock dissertation on table manners. The overall effect is a comic approach to love of country, especially Barlow's New England.

Arguably the finest poet of the early nationalist period was the fiery Philip Freneau. In his poetry, America was transformed into a medley of natural wonder and diversity. Noted for his deistic celebration of nature by incorporating a romantic use of simple nature imagery (such as in "The Wild Honeysuckle" [1786] or "To a Caty-Did" [1815]), Freneau's contribution to the beginnings of the Romantic movement in poetry cannot be overlooked.

His longer poems, too, express his love of nature and country. Many of his later poems—"A Picture of the Times" (1782), "A Warning to America" (1792), "The Millennium: To a Ranting Field Orator" (1797), and "Reflections . . . on the Gradual Progress of Nations from Democratical States to Despotic Empires" (1815)—reveal his growing doubt about the feasibility of freedom (ibid., 164). Meditative in nature, these poems express Freneau's increasing concern over what he saw as the American obsession with the pursuit of happiness. Freneau, the poet of republicanism, does not forsake optimistim entirely. Ultimately, his poetic message is that America will move forward.

All in all, the poetry of the new nation can be characterized as one that was imitative, yet reflective of the promise and hope that imbued the country. The bards of the early republic were resolute in their desire to instill in Americans their vision of what the republic was and what it could be. In early republican poetry, *translatio studii* was exemplified.

## MASON "PARSON" LOCKE WEEMS: MASTER OF THE LITERARY MARKETPLACE

If aspiring novelists and poets during the early nationalist period represented the traditional approach to breaking into the literary marketplace, the entrepreneurial and colorful Mason Locke Weems (1759–1825) exemplifies a more eccentric, yet more effective, approach to garnering public favor. Weems's career, in particular, presents an apt example of the ingenuity and industry of the literary subscription agent and the opportunistic state of the marketplace.

Weems (rhymes with "stems") was an ordained deacon and a consecrated priest with the Church of England. "Parson" Weems, as he is sometimes referred to, was deemed by many of his parishioners and fellow clergy to be rather "tedious in exhortation" (qtd. in Leary, 13). In other words, as well-meaning as his parishioners thought him, they chafed under Weems's monotonous sermons. Perhaps recognizing that his less-than-adequate oratorical skills presaged limited success as a parson, Weems opted to leave the pulpit for a potentially more lucrative career as a subscription agent and author of a plethora of pamphlets and books. For Weems the book-peddling circuit proffered a more effective and wide-ranging pulpit than any country church could provide.

As the rector of St. Margaret in Westminster Parish, Maryland (ca. 1790), Weems had engaged the services of a printer in Wilmington, Delaware, for the purpose of issuing a volume of sermons written by the distinguished English ecclesiastic Robert Russell. Boldly imprinted on the flyleaf were the words "printed for M. L. Weems" (ibid.). Because foreign works were not subject to American copyright laws, Weems (and others like him) could facilely republish and distribute the works of well-known writers (usually British) and keep the profits.

Although Weems's first venture into publishing and book peddling was with sermons, he quickly learned that morally edifying books—and the smaller the better—sold much more quickly and at a greater profit. Initially, Weems would "lift" chapters of previously published adventure stories (albeit, edifying ones). Soon he undertook the self-designated role of editor of the works he appropriated for publication. The market for these emended volumes was much more lucrative than the reprints. His first best-seller, the expanded and edited *Sure Certain Methods of Attaining a Long and Healthy Life* (originally written and published in the fifteenth century by Italian nobleman Luigi Cornaro) appeared in 1793. Weems's version was quite a bargain, selling for half of what the English edition was selling for at the time.

Weems's editorial efforts in *Sure Certain Methods* reveal his true gift: his assessing of and capitalizing on the social temper of the new republic, especially the idea of republican virtue. Many Americans fervently believed that the great political and governmental experiment in which the fledgling nation had embarked was providential. The land itself mandated a different philosophy than the prevalent European view toward life and living. Weems's appendix to *Sure Certain Methods*, entitled "Golden Rules of Health," reflects and panders to this attitude. Added to Cornaro's cautions regarding intemperance are a mixture of classical references (notably, Hippocrates and Plutarch) and his own. Especially of note is his observation that "Americans are under the greatest obligations to live temperately . . . [because] our country abounds in bays, rivers, and creeks, the exhalations of which give the air a dampness unfriendly to the springs of life. To counteract this infelicity of climate, reason teaches us to adopt every measure that may give tone and vigor to the constitution" (see ibid., 15).

Weems augments Cornaro's advice with his own instructions on how a virtuous citizen should maintain his or her health, despite the perils of the lowlands. Overall, Weems admonished his readers to exercise prudence in diet, temperance, and exposure to the elements. Ultimately, Weems's stint as editor of the slender Cornaro volume led to profit and fame. The appended tract, renamed *The Immortal Mentor*, was a strong seller for over 20 years. More important, the great republican icon, George Washington, favorably acknowledged the second edition. (Weems had sent a copy to Washington as a gift.) Ever the self-promoter, Weems immediately had Washington's letter copied and pasted in his remaining stock. The letter would serve as the introduction to subsequent editions.

By 1794, Weems had formed an association with Mathew Carey, one of the most successful printers and publishers of books during the early nationalist period. His alliance with Carey now allowed him to expand his publishing and book-peddling activities. (The latter primarily involved selling subscriptions. The prudent Carey would only print books that he knew would be profitable.) As he traveled the countryside (primarily, southern Pennsylvania, Maryland, Virginia, and North Carolina) hawking subscriptions, Weems also promoted the stock he always had on hand. These were usually romances, plays, or adventures. He urged Carey to publish books about the lives of Revolutionary War heroes. Just as the adventure stories and romances that he sold often had a moral message, the biographies, Weems felt, would serve as positive reminders of Revolutionary valor and patriotism, two qualities he believed all good citizens should possess.

By 1799, Weems began writing his own series of tracts, the subject of which he had deemed not only salable but also enlightening. The first of these, *The Philanthropist; or a Good Twelve Cents Worth of Political Love Powder for the Fair Daughters and Patriotic Sons of Virginia*, was dedicated to George Washington and signed "Your very sincere friend, and Masonic brother, M. L. Weems" (see ibid., 27). *Philanthropist* is a 30-page response to the political debate between the Federalists and the Republicans. Not only was it timely, but, more significant, it was extremely profitable for Weems and Carey.

Thus began Weems's career as an author. In subsequent years, he penned, published, and promoted such instructive missives as *The Devil Done Over, The Beauties and Beatitudes of a Republic, The Drunkard's Looking Glass, The Bad Wife's Looking Glass,* and those that might be flippantly referred to as the "God's Revenge" series: *God's Revenge Against Adultery, God's Revenge Against Cruelty to Husbands, God's Revenge Against Murder,* and *God's Revenge Against Gambling.* But the zealously didactic themes of these volumes did not deter Weems's readership. Indeed, Weems's cautionary tracts were some of the best sellers in his inventory.

None of these exceeded in popularity (or in notoriety) Weems's most famous authorial effort: *A History of the Life and Death, Virtues and Exploits of General George Washington* (1800). Once again Weems demonstrated his astute assessment of the literary marketplace. He knew his audience, its needs, and its predilections.

When Washington died on December 14, 1799, the country came together in its bereavement. Never had an American been mourned so publicly and vocally. Songs, sermons, and essays deified the first president. By 1800 his birthday had been declared a national day of mourning. Although Weems was not personally acquainted with Washington during his lifetime (aside from Washington's short notes of appreciation to Weems on receipt of the latter's gift of *Sure Certain Methods* and *Philanthropist*), he swiftly deemed himself Washington's biographer. In a letter to Carey, Weems proclaimed that the

Washington you know is gone! Millions are gasping to read something about him. I am nearly primed and cocked for 'em. Six months ago I set myself to collecting anecdotes of him. You know I live conveniently for that work. My plan! I give his history. . . . I then show that his unparreled [*sic*] rise and elevation were owing to his Great Virtues. . . .

All this I have lined and enlivened with Anecdotes *apropos, interesting* and *entertaining.* . . . I am thinking that you could vend it admirably; as it will be the first. (see ibid., 82–83; Weems's emphasis)

Weems's biography of Washington is less a record of the historical than it is of the anecdotal. Weems's Washington became the paragon of American citizenry: religious, patriotic, brave, moral, industrious, and benevolent. The *History of George Washington* was and is an exhortation of agrarianism and republican virtue. Indeed, Weems's account is as entertaining as he had promised Carey it would be. It was an instant success. The general public loved it. Those with a more literary bent found it entertaining but, as a reviewer for Charles Brockden Brown's *Monthly Magazine and American Review* asserted, it was filled with material that "can be found in the annals of fanaticism and absurdity" (see ibid., 90).

By the fifth edition, Weems had added such apocrypha as the story that Washington had been found at prayer at Valley Forge (reinforcing the model of the pious patriot), that his many successes had been foretold to his mother in a dream, and, most important, the story of George Washington and the cherry tree.

In Weems's defense, the cherry tree story was not of his invention. Supposedly, one of Washington's distant relatives (at the time of her interview with Weems, she was quite up in years) was the originator of the tale. What has now entered American mythos bears resemblance to the Weems account—but not all.

Young George (age six) does not cut down the cherry tree with the hatchet. He merely strikes at it. The bark, irreparably damaged, withers and dies. Father Washington confronts the young perpetrator, not by the tree (i.e., the scene of the crime), but in the house. But young George forthrightly admits that he did cut the tree with his hatchet because he cannot tell a lie.

Weems added the cherry tree myth to further illustrate Washington's propensity for heroic behavior even at the tender age of six. From his youth, he had been taught the importance of honesty, courage, and benevolence. (The elder Washington embraces the youthful transgressor.) The cherry tree story inculcates republican virtue at its zenith. Weems's inclusion of the story in the fifth edition gives testament to his keen entrepreneurial spirit, his business acumen, and, more important, his devotion to the new government.

As a whole, American writers in the new nation who were perhaps not as picturesque as Parson Weems shared many of his attributes. They were resourceful, versatile, and fiercely dedicated to promulgating and upholding democratic ideals. The novel, more than any other popular form, promoted the propagation of the idea of republican virtue, especially temperance (in all senses of the word), industry, and benevolence. The slave narrative unstintingly critiqued the presence of an institutional evil that shattered the romantic image of a virtuous republic. Poetry gave voice to a vision and a national pride. Literature in America signaled a forging ahead with ideas, of breaking with—yet simultaneously building on—English literary tradition. The American literary marketplace subsequently provided an open forum for ideas, especially for women and ex-slaves who had little or no political access to voicing their concerns. Instructive, entertaining, and uplifting, the literature of the early nationalist period inculcated the desires and vision of the citizenry of a young republic.

# 9

# Music

Americans have always been a music-loving people, dating back to the eras of discovery and colonization. Even the Puritans, who eschewed the rich and intricate arrangements of the sacred and secular music of Europe, were known to indulge in psalmody. By the early nationalist period, Americans had established a time-honored musical tradition. Orchestras had been well supported for decades, singing schools and singing societies had emerged early in the eighteenth century, operas were patronized by those of wealth and culture, and dances were a popular form of republican entertainment.[1] Many people were accomplished musicians, especially in the South where the gentry played the violin, flute, spinet, harpsichord, guitar, and harp (Nye, *Cultural Life*, 274). Native-born Americans, such as Francis Hopkinson (1737–1791) and William Billings (1746–1800), began to compose music that reflected Americans' pride in their country and their honor of God.

Even the political sages of the day engaged in music making. Benjamin Franklin played the guitar, harp, and violin. George Washington, a true patron of the arts, played the flute. Thomas Jefferson was dedicated to playing the violin, although contemporary reviews of his ability are mixed. One account stated that Patrick Henry was second only to Jefferson as the worst violinist in Virginia (ibid.). On the other hand, an unnamed British captain, who during his internment in Charlottesville as a prisoner of war had played duets with Jefferson at Monticello, considered Jefferson to be "the finest unprofessional player" he had ever heard (qtd. in Sablosky, 21).

American music was and is heterogeneous; that is, it is a mixture of varied and sometimes conflicting elements. By the end of the Revolution,

Americans were listening to and performing works that had derivations from such diverse sources as hymnody (including the music of religious dissenters and minority sects such as the Moravians who were renowned for their outstanding choir), African tribal, Anglo-Scottish-Irish folk ballads, and the European standard works found in performance music. Finally, the period produced a rich repertoire of patriotic songs, one of which would become the national anthem in 1931.

## PSALMODY AND HYMNODY

From its colonial beginnings, America was a land that placed great importance on religious music. Even the austere Puritans and Separatists who had rejected the more elaborate rituals and chorale music of the Anglican Church integrated music into their services. (Not until the 1820s did the Anglican Church sanction congregational singing. The Separatist and the Puritan insistence on congregational singing was one more act of rebellion against Anglicanism.) The Separatists were the more severe of the two, having openly rejected Anglicanism entirely. For over one hundred years psalmody (singing of the Old Testament Psalms) was the musical mainstay of the Separatist Church and many other churches as well. New England psalmody basically followed the dictates of the Protestant theologian John Calvin (1509–1564). Calvin believed that the only proper lyrics for a church song were the Psalms and no other, and they should be sung only in the vernacular (that is, not in Latin). Calvin had the Psalms set into French metrical verse. The Psalms were then sung by the congregation rather than by a choir (which was the practice of the Catholic Church and later of the Anglican Church).

By the time of the Plymouth settlement, Protestant psalters included melodies from multiple sources, including tunes from older hymns, popular English melodies, and even altered versions of Catholic chants (Hitchcock, 3). The *Bay Psalm Book* (1640), the first psalter and first book published in the English colonies, did not include tunes, however. Prepared by the Puritan theocracy, the *Bay Psalm Book* included a discussion of the need to sing psalms and a strong suggestion that the Psalms could be sung to the music of Thomas Ravenscroft (1583?–1633?) or those of "our English psalm books."[2]

The Lutheran Church, on the other hand, embraced hymnody immediately. (Martin Luther himself composed some of the greater hymns of the Reformation.) By the eighteenth century hymns had become an integral part of Protestant services, even those aligned with Calvinism. Hymns, because they serve as songs of praise to God or in thanksgiving, were a more immediate reflection of the creative impulse of American religiosity. The first American composer, William Billings, was a noted hymnist. A self-taught musician, Billings had an established reputation as a native composer by the 1780s. He began his career writing psalms, hymns, and fuging tunes or fuges (Anglo-American psalms or hymns that use one or more contrapuntal voice entries), eventually expanding his efforts into the composition of secular works, such as anthems.[3]

Although Billings's works were somewhat rough (he had very limited knowledge of musical rules), they were characterized by vigor, spirit, and individuality. His harmonies and use of counterpoint were flawed, yet his compositions were melodic, rhythmic, and easily memorized, thus appealing to the public (Elson, 19). Even though his career began in New England, Billings's reputation was widespread throughout the infant nation. His "The Rose of Sharon" (a hymn based on the second Song of Solomon) was a particular favorite with the public (Howard, *Our American Music*, 54). By 1790 there were scarcely any American psalters that did not contain his works. His Revolutionary War song "Chester" was popular up through the nineteenth century. Arguably, his works were more popular with his American contemporaries than those of Europe (ibid., 56).

But after 1790 Billings's reputation dwindled, partly because after the war the United States experienced an influx of foreign musicians and composers whose skills and talents far exceeded his. As they became exposed to more proficiently composed musical pieces, Americans were less inclined to include Billings's works on their programs. Not until the twentieth century was there any renewed interest in Billings's hymns and his fuges, and this is largely due to their energy and originality rather than their artistry.

The nineteenth century ushered in a new era of American hymnody. The mid-eighteenth-century evangelical revival led by John Wesley (1703–1791), the founder of Methodism, resulted in the use of the hymnal rather than the psalter in many American churches. Wesley and his brother Charles were instrumental in introducing extraordinary hymns to the laity. John Wesley painstakingly had translated the greatest of German hymns into English, and Charles was a lyricist of talent and innovation. American hymnals began to include the works of the Wesleys among more established works. Moreover, the more poetical hymns of Congregationalist minister Isaac Watts (1674–1748) had supplanted the psalmodies of the early days of Puritanism. Combined with the lively American tunes of Billings and others, the influence of Watts's opus had a profound effect on the American desire for more and better hymns. New hymns (mainly British) began to appear, first as supplements to the Watts collection. Later hymnbooks appeared that included American authors although these were extremely poor in quality (Foote, 187).

But in 1815 the Reverend Samuel Worcester of Salem, Massachusetts, produced a groundbreaking book that was intended to challenge the superiority of traditional hymnbooks, specifically the Watts collection edited by Yale president and poet Timothy Dwight commonly known as *Dwight's Watts* (1801). Worcester's edition had the impressive but wordy title *Christian Psalmody, in four parts; Comprising Dr. Watts' Psalms abridged: Select Hymns from other sources; and select Harmonies.* The fourth part alluded to in the title contained excellent new hymns (ibid., 188). Worcester's edition, as a consequence, signaled the movement in the 1820s toward a wider range of more original hymnody.

Minority sects and dissenters also added a rich contribution to American religious music. This was a time of growing religious discord for Americans. Many dissenting sects now appeared, breaking away from established denominations. For instance, the Baptists had offshoots that determined themselves to be New Lights, Free Willers, and Separatists, whereas the Presbyterians had formed two groups, Old Side and New Side, a group fervently concerned with revivalism (Chase, 44). Other remarkable minority sects were thriving at this time as well, notably the Shakers and the Moravians.

The Shakers, whose formal title was the United Society of Believers in Christ's Second Coming, had broken from a group of radical English Quakers. These Quakers had taken on the French Camisards' ceremonial customs of shaking, singing in tongues, and dancing.[4] The Shakers's leader, "Mother" Ann Lee (1736–1784), brought nine of her followers to America in 1774 in search of "The Promised Land." They settled in New York, where they quickly prospered and grew in number.

The Shakers, a sect that required all members to be celibate, were committed to the idea of a life of perfection and of industry. After Mother Ann's death in 1784, the administration of the Shakers became more systematic, and the sect spread to parts of the Midwest. But the spirit of Mother Ann lived on in the Shaker communities. Shakers fervently adhered to Mother Ann's belief that they were in a duel with the devil. The Shaker rituals that they often employed (Mother Ann had declared that these rituals and holy exercises had been sent to her in visions) eventually made the Shakers an integral influence on American music (ibid., 46). Through music—dancing and singing—the Shakers gave voice and movement to their happiness in their faith. They believed that they had triumphed over the devil and expressed their beliefs in song and dance. Later in the mid-nineteenth century, the Shaker ritual songs and dances would result in a proliferation of Shaker music.

The finest musicians of all of the sects were arguably the Moravians (Unitas Fratrem). Persecuted throughout Europe (their members principally from Moravia, Bohemia, and Poland), the Moravians saw themselves as missionaries and traveled to the New World to carry out their calling among primarily the Native Americans and African Americans. In 1741 they established a major settlement in Pennsylvania—Bethlehem—on the banks of the Lehigh River. Other Moravian settlements soon followed throughout other colonies.

The Moravians emphasized music and produced numerous hymns. Moravian church services included choral music, accompanied by organs, trombones, violins, and other instruments. Their choirs gained almost instant fame. The Moravians also believed in sharing their music with the people to whom they had come to minister. In 1763, the Moravian Church had translated and published hymns in the language of the Delaware tribe. In 1803 David Zeisberger, a Moravian missionary, published *A Collection of Hymns for the Use of the Christian Indians of the Mission of the United Brethren in North America.*

Along with their contributions to religious music, the Moravians developed secular music as well. The most prominent of the Moravian composers and musicians was Johann Friedrich Peter (1746–1813). Peter moved to the Bethlehem settlement in 1770 and brought with him copies of works by significant European composers, such as Johann Christian Friedrich Bach and Franz Joseph Haydn.

In 1786 Peter established and directed the Collegium Musicum in Salem, North Carolina (now Winston-Salem). Under Peter's directorship, the collegium acquired over 500 musical scores, including symphonies, anthems, chamber music, and oratorios (ibid., 51). This impressive collection included religious and secular music, much of it from the early classical period.

Peter's own compositions were as prodigious as his collecting efforts. He was known to have written over one hundred religious anthems and arias. In 1789 he also composed six quintets (for two violins, two violas, and one cello). These are characterized by harmonic freedom, bold modulation, and brilliant execution (ibid.). Peter's compositions were both religious and secular; much of them evince the influence of the works of Haydn.

In particular, the Moravians were dedicated to collecting and preserving their musical heritage, which consisted of the works of Moravian and non-Moravian composers. Many Moravian musicians and composers were more than capable, their musicality famous throughout the United States. To this day, the Moravian Church continues to contribute to American musical culture. The Moravian Music Foundation has, through the years, sponsored concerts, publications, and recordings. In addition, the list of Moravian composers in the annals of American music is exceptional.

There is no question that psalmody and hymnody provided the bedrock for the development of an American musical tradition. American desire for better church music (and the performance of such music) resulted in a flowering of distinctively American hymns and the proliferation of singing schools. This interest in music eventually carried over into more secular forms. One group, excluded from the predominant culture, blended its own singular musical heritage with the American tradition of hymnody to create new and dynamic musical forms. This group, which eventually influenced American music like no other, was that of the African slaves.

## THE AFRICAN INFLUENCE

The institution of slavery, firmly ensconced in American society by the late eighteenth century, had a profound consequence not only on the socioeconomic system, but also on American musical culture. By 1800, people of African descent made up nearly 19 percent of the total population of the United States; 100,000 of these held free status, the rest enslaved (Chase, 55). With such a large portion of the general population having African roots, invariably these cultural ties would permeate the larger, predominant White culture. As the slaves modified African rhythms and songs as a musical response to their American experience, the predominant musical culture was subtly influenced by this infusion of African music. Ultimately, African musical expression would affect all music that is identifiable as American (Sablosky, 41).

Thomas Jefferson, in Query XIV, *Notes on the State of Virginia* (the query deals with "the administration of justice and description of the laws"), proffered the following observation on the slaves' musical proclivity: "In music they are more generally gifted than the whites with accurate ears for tune and time, and they have been found capable of imaging a small catch. Whether they will be equal to the composition of a more extensive run of melody, or of complicated harmony, is yet to be proved" (266).

From the earliest days of their capture and enslavement, African slaves had been compelled to entertain their White captors. Often on the decks of the slave ships, the captives were ordered to dance. With no native instruments of their own, the slaves improvised using the barrels and pots on deck for percussion (Sablosky, 41). Sometimes European instruments on board, such as fiddles, were used as musical accompaniment as well. Other times, they used their voices to sing songs of lamentation (Chase, 59).

After landing in the New World, the enslaved Africans continued to sing, dance, and play musical instruments. Unable to bring their native instruments with them, the Africans quickly transformed indigenous American materials into adaptations of African musical instruments. The most celebrated of these is the banjo. (The word comes from the African variants of *banjar, bangelo, bangoe, banza,* or *banshaw,* six-stringed instruments made from gourds.)

The American banjo was commonly made by scooping out a large gourd, cutting the bowl in half, then covering it with a dried or tanned animal skin (usually coonskin), and strung with four strings that were attached at different points to achieve various pitches (ibid., 60). The banjar-banjo was either strummed or plucked with the fingers, creating a unique sound heretofore not heard on the American continent.

The African drum, however, was largely prohibited on the plantation because slave owners feared that drums could be used to transmit plans of escapes and uprisings. The exception was Louisiana where, because of a large influx of West Indians into a largely French and Spanish population, public dancing by "people of color" was often accompanied by native instruments, including drums, well into the nineteenth century (ibid., 61). Sunday street dances in New Orleans were energetic outpourings of musicality, creativity, and celebration. Dancers often wore native costumes, brightly colored and adorned with animal fur. Many times they were accompanied by bands of drums that provided the intense dance rhythms.

In addition to the banjo and limited geographic use of the drum, those of African heritage also used more traditional native instruments such as the quills (resembling a panpipe), notched gourds with scrapers, dried gourds filled with stones or seeds, and jawbones of horses and asses that were scraped with wires or sticks to make the teeth rattle (ibid., 66). European instruments—violin, oboe, French horn, clarinet, flute—were also mastered (usually by ear rather than training) by talented slaves.

Only highly trusted slaves were permitted to play horns and trumpets for the amusement of the White aristocracy only. (Horns and trumpets were, like drums, considered to be potential means of communication among dissident slaves.) Some slave musicians were hired out by their White masters to perform at balls. The more preeminent slave musicians were outfitted in the height of fashion: powdered wigs, silk stockings, elaborate buckled shoes, and embroidered coats and vests. An early nineteenth-century account of the renowned musician and composer Frank Johnson (1792–1844), a "descendent of Africa" whose services were in demand in both the North and the South, attests to the popularity and influence the slave musician had in White culture: "In fine, he is the leader of the band at all balls, public and private; . . . inventor-general of cotillions; to which add, a remarkable taste in distorting a sentimental, simple, and beautiful song, into a reel, jig, or country dance" (qtd. in ibid., 68).

Although this chronicler had mixed emotions about Johnson's ability to transform song into a source of popular amusement, his comment attests to Johnson's (and other African American musicians') significant contribution to American popular music. It is only conjecture how much of such improvisation was indebted to the musician's African musical heritage. Certainly the rhythm and tonality of African music played some part in the Africans' musical response to established musical forms of White culture in the livelier dances (such as jigs and reels).

African Americans expressed themselves most eloquently in song, which led to a distinctly American phenomenon: the Negro spiritual. The Negro spiritual was fundamentally the result of a unique mixture of forces, circumstances, and influences that could only occur among a specific group of people, the slaves, and a particular American region, the South (Sablosky, 43). An exclusive fusion of West African music, Anglo hymnody, and the emotions of an oppressed people, the Negro spiritual gave voice to the hope and pain of the African slave.

As slaves increasingly became Christianized and were introduced to Anglo hymnody, so did their music begin to meld their own heritage with their new attempts at acculturalization. That is, in their efforts to express themselves spiritually and musically within white society, African slaves appropriated musical practices from two not unlike methods. Both African music and Anglo hymnody use antiphonal song patterns (which are characterized by the leader singing phrases that alternate with those sung by a chorus). In Anglo hymnody this was called "lining out" or "deaconing." The deacon would chant or read a line from a psalm, followed by the congregation's singing of the response. In West African music, the pattern is known as "call-and-response." Differing slightly from other antiphonal song patterns, call-and-response necessitates the leader beginning his or her phrase before the chorus is finished singing its response. The most important element of call-and-response requires that both the leader and the chorus come in at the proper beat of the measure. Many times the leader's part drops out for a time, leaving the chorus to sustain the song. The chorus thus provides the rhythmical structure. The song leader, however, is able to improvise because he or she has a solid rhythmical base provided by the chorus.

The Negro spiritual blends these two patterns of development. The call-and-response allowed the Christian slaves to embellish established hymns that they had been taught by the White church. Furthermore, the outpouring of song also led to the outpouring of emotion, sometimes escalating into ecstasy, which emanated from their African religious roots (ibid., 44). From the 1770s until the turn of the century, both Whites and Blacks in the rural South attended and participated in camp meetings where song was characterized by the release of the emotions.

By 1808 with the abolishment of the slave trade, the African influence on southern church music was somewhat abated. Concurrently, the education of slaves was made illegal. White church leaders now began to preach to the slaves what they viewed as the necessity of subservience. In reaction to this shift in theology, the slaves inventively began to change the words to the old Anglo hymns they had been taught to reflect their frustration and their hope. Because the hymns were no longer sung in the presence of Whites (slaves were now relegated to separate services), the slaves were able to reword the Anglo hymns without reprisal. The old references of Heaven and The Promised Land, which originally developed the hymnal theme of salvation, were now given a more personal, and subversive, meaning: they became metaphors for liberation.

The Negro spiritual quickly moved from church to the field. Although the plantation owners often discouraged their slaves from indulging in their religious songs and dances, the overseers in the fields did not prohibit the singing of the same songs. Songs, because of their rhythmic value, aided in getting the repetitive work done faster and more efficiently. As the spiritual flourished in church and field among the slaves, some White Americans, being struck by the artistry and poignancy of the Negro spiritual, began to appropriate the songs for a White form of entertainment: minstrelsy (ibid., 46).

The minstrel show (White minstrels performing in blackface the song and dance of African American slaves as a form of caricature) reached its peak in popularity later in the nineteenth century (ca. 1850–1870).[5] Elements of minstrelsy did appear in the American colonies as early as 1769 with the appearance of the ballad opera *The Padlock* in New York City. (One of the featured roles, played by the renowned actor Lewis Hallam, was that of the Black character Mungo.) There were other glimmerings of interest in the song and dance of slaves. Around 1801, Benjamin Carr (known as the composer of the 1796 American opera *The Archers*) published "A Negro Song." After the arrival in the 1790s of John Ricketts's circus in Philadelphia, theatrical troupes were forced to broaden their venues to include pantomimes and acrobatics. In the 1820s strolling players eventually ventured into the frontier in search of new audiences. It was out of this movement into the frontier and the effort to pander to the less sophisticated tastes of their audiences that the theatrical troupes turned to novelty numbers such as "plantation songs" and "blackface dances" (ibid., 48).

## FOLK SONGS AND BALLADS

Folk songs or ballads (short narrative songs that originated during the Middle Ages) had always been immensely popular with Americans of all social classes. Indeed, folk music by its very nature has always been considered the music of the people. There was an enormous collection of Anglo-Scottish-Irish folk songs that were already part of the American musical tradition, the so-called pop songs of the time (Hitchcock, 29). During the colonial and early nationalist periods, very few of these were written down; it was not until the mid-nineteenth century that they were compiled. Called the "Child ballads" after Francis James Child (1825–

1896), these songs and ballads that have come down to us exhibit a sprightliness of theme and melody that justify their endurance.

The themes of these popular works did shift from their British origins. Holdover English ballads from the Middle Ages and the Renaissance that glorified courtly love and chivalry did not easily translate into the American experience and were not passed down (ibid., 29). But others that dealt with more universal themes such as sexual rivalry (for example, "Barbara Allen") persevered. Others were transformed to comply with the puritanical strain, such as "The Foggy Dew" that contained the very sexually explicit lyrics "I rolled my love all over the foggy dew." That became the more innocuous "The only thing I did that was wrong/Was to keep her from the foggy dew." Other adaptations of British ballads championed American inventiveness.

Americans also created their own songs and ballads, which entered the national repertoire. The earliest recorded of these was "Springfield Mountain," a song that recounted the death by snakebite of one Timothy Myrick of Springfield Mountain (Wilbraham), Massachusetts, in 1761. The opening lines, "On Springfield Mountain there did dwell / A handsome youth was known full well, / Lieutenant Merrill's only son, / A likely youth, full twenty-one" (from *Folk Songs of North America*, 13), illustrate how Americans used the British ballad to create a ballad with an American theme, immortalizing the hazards and tragedies associated with the American experience. "Springfield Mountain," although it antedates the Revolution, was extremely popular with early republican America, attesting to its appeal.

Some other songs popular with citizens had a long history in England before they were brought to American shores. "The Girl I Left Behind Me" first became popular with the fife and drum corps during the Revolution (Howard, *Music of George Washington's Time*, 7). "O, Dear, What Can the Matter Be" was published in 1795 in *Gentleman's Amusement* and was instantly all the rage. Ben Jonson's (1572–1637) "Drink to Me Only with Thine Eyes" was set to music and sung regularly in the United States (ibid.). Still other British songs sung and performed often were "Greensleeves," "The Vicar of Bray," "Sally in Our Alley," and the children's song "Old King Cole."

Although the folk song was definitely established in American culture by the late eighteenth century, it experienced a renewal because of the great influx of British immigrants to the United States after the Revolutionary War. These immigrants—primarily Scot, Irish, Welsh, and English—saw this new republic as a land where they could build new and better lives for their families. Upon arrival in the Mid-Atlantic states (mainly New York and Pennsylvania), they quickly discovered the land had already been cultivated and settled. They, like other more ambitious and adventurous Americans, moved westward into the new territories.

They settled west of the Alleghenies and lived—most for centuries—in relatively isolated valleys and mountain regions. Generally, their customs, ideas, and traditions changed little from what their forebears had adhered to when they first settled the land (Luther, 43).

Thus, the musical traditions of these post-Revolutionary immigrants virtually remained unchanged. Handed down from generation to generation, these folk songs not only exemplify the immigrants' fierce loyalty to their cultural heritage, but also their experiences in the New World. Some songs honored the rugged individualism of these immigrant people. "My Horses Ain't Hungry," which tells the story of Pretty Polly and her swain, illustrates the pride of the people. Polly's parents do not approve of her impoverished lover. Rather than take hospitality where he is not wanted, he sings, "My horses ain't hungry, / They won't eat your hay. / So fare you well, Polly, I'm going away."

Like other Anglo-derivative ballads, the songs of the Appalachian people deal with the darker forces of human nature. In "Confession," a mountain lad confesses to killing his love, also called "Pretty Polly." He never explains why he had decided to murder her. "Confession," though, is a powerfully dramatic ballad. The fear of the young girl as she is being led to her death and her lover's response is chilling.

"Oh Willie, oh Willie, I'm 'fraid of your way;
Oh Willie, oh Willie, I'm 'fraid of your way;
All nite we've wander'd through the mountains we've strayed."

"Pretty Polly, Pretty Polly, you're guessin' about right;
"Pretty Polly, Pretty Polly, you're guessin' about right;
I dug on your grave 'till twelve-thirty last night."

We went on up a little further and what did we spy?
We went on up a little further and what did we spy?
A new-dug grave, with a spade lying by.

The murderer is apprehended, interrogated by the law (which is the impetus for the song), and confesses to his grisly deed. Not all ballad romances ended so tragically. "Billy Boy," an English tune, tells of a man's quest for the perfect wife. He finds this paragon of female virtue who is "the darling of his life," has "a dimple in her chin," and, most important, "can bake a cherry pie quick as a cat can wink its eye." Billy will, however, have to wait because "she's a young thing and cannot leave her mother."

Sometimes in song, marriage was seen as imprisoning. Such tunes were usually comic. In the popular "I Wish I Was Single Again," the narrator decries ever marrying. His first marriage ("the bane of my life") was to a woman who "beat me, she banged me, / She swore she would hang me." Once divorced, he foolishly marries another whom he describes as the "devil's grandmother."

The western settlers were also known to hold rollicking dances where they sang and danced (usually accompanied by a fiddle) to lively tunes such as "Skip to My Lou." The rhythms and themes of dance music were brisk and saucy. In "Skip to My Lou" the singer has lost his partner but will "get one, prettier than you." Spirited lyrics and melodies were conducive to merrymaking, flirtation, and courtship. Community dances in the isolated West became the social center for most settlers. For them, music became the primary vehicle for expression, both emotional and creative.

## PERFORMANCE MUSIC

Even though ballads and dance tunes were popular throughout American society, there were some who yearned for more "serious" works. Some, like Jefferson and Franklin, were genteel amateurs. Jefferson had an outstanding library of musical works, ranging from operas to sacred music to works by such masters as George Friderich Handel, Antonio Lucio Vivaldi, and Franz Joseph Haydn. Franklin sang, played a variety of instruments, and invented the "glass harmonica," a set of graduated glass bowls that produced tones by turning them with a foot pedal and wetting them intermittently. A contemporary of Jefferson and Franklin, Francis Hopkinson wrote both secular and religious music (words and music) that were well-known. Hopkinson also saw himself as a serious composer. In 1788 when he dedicated his *Seven Songs for the Harpsichord or Forte Piano* to George Washington, Hopkinson declared that he was "the first native of the United States who has produced a musical Composition" (qtd. in Sablosky, 22). The advertisement in the *Philadelphia Packet* announced: "These songs are composed in an easy, familiar style, intended for young Practitioners on the *Harpsichord* or *Forte-Piano*, and is the first Work of this kind attempted in the United States" (qtd. in Chase, 89–90; emphasis in advertisment). Hopkinson's hope was to encourage Americans to become more proficient in music and thus establish a serious musical tradition.

After the Revolutionary War, Philadelphia emerged as the cultural center of the United States. Musical performances that before the war were more or less limited to the South spread quickly throughout the 13 states. Theatrical performances were the order of the day, both the drama and the comedy. Interspersed within these theatricals were musical numbers, such as ballad operas, dances, songs, and pantomimes. With the rise of the theater came a stronger interest in musical performance.

The United States was also becoming a nation of amateur musicians. People from all walks of life took pride in making some sort of music. According to the Philadelphia *Mirror of Taste and Dramatic Censor* (1810), "almost every young lady and gentleman, from the children of the judge, the banker, and the general, down to those of the constable, the huckster and the drummer, can make a noise upon some instrument or other, and charm their neighbors with something courtesy calls music" (qtd. in Hitchcock, 34).

Prior to the war the musical professionals who predominated American concert music were European. This remained the case in post–Revolutionary American as well. After the war foreign musicians flocked to the United States in droves. These musical émigrés saw a great opportunity to teach, compose, and perform their art to a population eager to embrace the works of the European masters. Even if they could not earn a living solely through performing as musicians, they could always supplement their income by teaching or through operating music stores (which they did quite well). But the main reason they migrated to the United States was to perform in concerts and operas.

## Concerts

Concerts had been a part of American culture for decades. From the 1730s onward there were many concerts successfully performed throughout the colonies in such diverse cities as New York, Charleston, and Boston. Americans were not far behind Europeans in their support and patronage of concerts. One explanation for this phenomenon is that in Europe musical patronage was a reflection of the rise of the middle class. The new middle class, eager to show its cultural sophistication, became great concertgoers. Lacking a rigid aristocracy, America was essentially a middle-class culture. Thus, what was happening in Europe, because of the rise of the middle class, was simultaneously occurring in America for the same reason (ibid., 32).

Political and patriotic occasions often called for concerts. A few weeks before the Constitutional Convention was convened, the Urania Academy of Philadelphia offered a concert to mark this soon-to-be-historic milestone. On the program were the overture of Arne's *Artaxerxes*, the "Hallelujah" chorus from Handel's *Messiah*, a flute concerto, and the works of Americans William Billings, James Lyon, William Tuckey, and Philip Phile (Sablosky, 31). Concerts were also held in honor of a visiting dignitary, such as during Washington's inaugural tour.

Generally, American concerts consisted of mixtures of short instrumental pieces or excerpts from larger ones. (The aforementioned Urania concert is an excellent illustration of the type of concert program of the period.) The works performed were usually from the European masters (such as Wolfgang Amadeus Mozart, Handel, Haydn) with an occasional smattering of works by native composers. American performers, although prolific, did not match the artistry of their contemporaries in

Vienna, Paris, or Rome (Hitchcock, 34). The same can be said for American opera, which was also popular at this time.

## Opera

Opera in America was primarily English ballad opera, a comic opera that emphasized preposterous plots. In ballad opera, music was interspersed between spoken dialogues. Ballad opera was usually sung in the vernacular, often in dialect, and consisted of melodic tunes that audiences found engaging. It was popular in the United States for a number of reasons: It was easily staged; it gave Americans a sense of superior well-being (because it was opera) even though the themes and events were not American; and it was fashionable, that is, Americans felt they were taking part in the latest London trend (Sablosky, 25).

Although the English ballad opera predominated American opera, French operas were also performed, albeit sporadically, during this period. (Italian and German operas were rarely staged in the United States at this time.) These, unlike the English ballad operas, were not performed in the vernacular. During the French Revolution, French musicians had begun to immigrate to the United States. They soon found work in theatrical companies, as singers of arias from French and Italian operas. (The latter was performed on a very limited basis.) Some formed their own companies, which allowed them to perform the entire opera, not just excerpts. As a result Americans were now exposed to the great comic works of Pierre Alexander Monsigny (1729–1817) and André Grétry (1741–1813).[6] For a time, Americans enjoyed the novelty of French opera, but it was just that: a novelty (Sonneck, 198).

The language barrier probably prevented Americans from thoroughly appreciating and understanding the nuances of French opera. Soon English and American companies began to take over the French companies as a means of eliminating the competition. French vocalists, now deprived of instrumental support (French orchestral performers chose the economic stability of the English-speaking company over working with diminishing French companies or freelancing), gave up their efforts to propagate French opera and opted to sing in English (ibid.).

## ANTHEMS AND PATRIOTIC SONGS

Like the Revolutionary period, the early nationalist period produced a prodigious amount of anthems and patriotic songs. Anthems (used here to denote songs that express patriotic sentiment) and other patriotic songs are rarely preconceived and often arise from impulse out of the historical moment. Americans, now filled with national pride, were quick to create songs that reflected their patriotism. For the most part, the lyrics to these songs might have been original but their tunes were not. Few American composers wrote the stirring marches and rousing melodies necessary to create national anthems and patriotic songs. Unlike other national songs throughout the world, the American works produced during this period drew on the melodies of other nations (Elson, 140). Many of the melodies "imported" from Europe were British because it was easy for American tunesmiths to set words to music of which the public was already familiar. In addition, the act of supplanting established British songs and anthems with very American words was a continuation of the spirit of the Revolution. For example, there were numerous reworkings of the British national anthem "God Save the King," notably "God Save Great Washington" and "God Save the Thirteen States." ("America" or "My Country 'Tis of Thee," the most famous reworking of "God Save the King," appeared later in the nineteenth century.)

Though there was a proliferation of anthems and patriotic songs, three in particular stand out as representative: "Yankee Doodle," "Hail, Columbia," and "The Star-Spangled Banner." Interestingly, each has a unique history and origin. All exemplify the patriotic impulse of the time. All originated (somewhat) out of a political conflict: the Revolutionary War ("Yankee Doodle"), strained relations with France ("Hail, Columbia"), and the War of 1812 ("The Star-Spangled Banner"). Most important, all have enjoyed a remarkable longevity with the American public.

## "Yankee Doodle"

By the time of the Treaty of Paris (1783), "Yankee Doodle" was fully ensconced in American popular culture. The jaunty tune had been popularized before the Revolutionary War, first by the British who sang it as a derisive act, later by the Americans as a means of self-reflexive humor and as an act of defiance. The exact origins of the song and the term "Yankee Doodle" are still under debate.[7] Nonetheless, "Yankee Doodle" was so popular that the tune and the theme were used in the creation of other patriotic and political songs. During the Constitutional Ratification process, the Massachusetts pro-Federalist party appropriated the tune of "Yankee Doodle" for a song that promoted national unity (S. Murray, 176). This saucy number, entitled "A Yankee Federal Song," glorified New England unity by sketching out the following scenario: At a Bill of Rights ratification meeting, New England Yankees are able to reach "a concil'atory plan" that benefits all citizens. Afterward the happy citizens go out to feast and drink, a true act of conciliation.

The lyrics and/or melody of "Yankee Doodle" served as the theme song for many groups. In the late eighteenth century, the Federalist Party adopted the tune of "Yankee Doodle" as its anthem. One of America's premiere musicians, Benjamin Carr (1768–1831), adapted the tune to create an orchestral interpretation entitled "Federal Overture" (1795). The revolutionaries in France used the tune as a marching song as early as 1789 (ibid., 178). And of course the British were still singing the song as a means of goading and ridiculing Americans.

By 1798, the "New Yankee Doodle" appeared, the product of the tensions between the United States and France. A response to what was perceived as French aggression, the song was a rallying call to arms:

> Yankee Doodle, guard your coast,
> Yankee Doodle Dandy,
> Fear not, then, nor threat nor boast,
> Yankee Doodle Dandy.

The war with France was fortunately averted. But in the nineteenth century, Americans found themselves at war again with Great Britain. Much of the armed conflict during the War of 1812 occurred at sea. Scores of American seamen were captured, many eventually incarcerated in England's Dartmoor Prison. Once again, Americans used "Yankee Doodle" to defy their British opponents. On February 22, 1815, the eighty-third anniversary of Washington's birth, the American inmates gathered to play "Yankee Doodle" with the accompaniment of flutes, bugles, trumpets, fifes, clarinets, and violins (ibid., 184). The British were not amused.

## "Hail, Columbia"

One of the most popular songs of the period was an address to the nation entitled "Hail, Columbia." Written (lyrics) by Joseph Hopkinson (1770–1842), son of Francis Hopkinson, the tune outdistanced in popularity all of the works of the senior Hopkinson (Luther, 54). Like "Yankee Doodle," "Hail, Columbia" originated out of political conflict, in this case, the tension between France and the United States in 1798 (Howard, *Our American Music*, 118). The XYZ Affair (1797–1798) and the passage of the Alien and Sedition Acts (1798) had further strained relations between the two countries. When Hopkinson wrote "Hail, Columbia," he thought that war with France was inevitable.

Hopkinson's composition was the product of a request of a young singer, Gilbert Fox. Fox, in an attempt to draw a full house in Philadelphia, had prevailed upon Hopkinson to write patriotic lyrics to "The President's March." ("The President's March" was an instrumental work that had been in existence for nine years. The march was composed in honor of Washington's becoming president in 1789. It was, however, not published until 1793 or 1794.) In his account of the composing of "Hail,

Columbia," Hopkinson averred that the song's purpose was "to get up an American spirit which should be independent of, and above the interests, passion and policy of both belligerents [pro- and anti-French Americans], and look and feel exclusively for our honor and rights" (qtd. in ibid., 119).

Hopkinson's efforts were an unqualified success. "Hail, Columbia" immediately captured the interest of the public. Upon its first performance, the audience could not hold back its cheers until the song had ended. According to Abigail Adams, "The whole . . . Audience broke forth in the Chorus whilst the thunder from their Hands was incessant, and at the close they rose, gave 3 Huzzas, that you might have heard a mile" (qtd. in Chase, 104). Not all citizens approved. The first publication of the work bore a very partisan inscription: "The favorite new Federal Song, Adapted to the Federal March [President's March]." The Republican newspapers criticized the work harshly, one labeling it "the most ridiculous bombast and the vilest adulation to the Anglo-monarchical party" (qtd. in Elson, 150).

"Hail, Columbia" eventually overcame the criticism of partisan politics, becoming a national song. Even though the first edition reveals the song to be fraught with highly exaggerated metaphors and crude harmonies, the song became more polished (and less politicized) over time (ibid.). It is now one of the most beloved of American patriotic songs.

## "To Anacreon in Heaven": Drinking Tune Turned Anthem

Ironically, one of the most popular tunes for American patriotic songs was an English drinking song, "To Anacreon in Heaven." Written for the Anacreontic Society of London (founded in 1766), "To Anacreon in Heaven" reflected the spirit of the society that commissioned it. The Anacreontic Society was a musical community whose boisterous and good-humored antics were well-known. Named in honor of Anacreon, a lyrical poet of fifth century B.C. Greece, the society was devoted to conviviality, musicality, and drinking. Inspired by their "patron saint," the members created clever and entertaining musical numbers (ibid.).

The lyrics of the song denote a playful approach to music, poetry, and the grape. The primary author was the society's president, Ralph Tomlinson, although the rest of the membership probably assisted him. A court musician and Anacreontic, John Stafford Smith (1750–1836) provided the music for this paean to poetry and drinking.[8] The bold, vigorous style of its progressions and its strong ending cadence made it a fit Bacchanalian anthem (ibid.). It was not, however, particularly conducive to singing.

Regardless of its difficult and challenging range for the human voice, Americans quickly appropriated the music of "To Anacreon in Heaven."

In fact, the first song associated with an American president was set to the tune of the now-popular drinking song. Written in 1789 by Robert Treat Paine (1731–1814), the son of the jurist, signer of the Declaration of Independence, and founder of the American Academy of Arts and Sciences (1780) Thomas Paine, the song ("Washington Presidential Theme Song") was a moving praise of George Washington.

At Washington's first inauguration, his supporters sang this first presidential theme song:

> Should the tempest of war overshadow our land
> Its bolts could ne'er rend Freedom's temple asunder;
> For, unmoved at the portals would Washington stand
> And repulse, with his breast, the assaults of the thunder.
> His sword from the sleep of its scabbard would leap
> And conduct with its every flash to the deep'
> For ne'er shall the sons of Columbia be slaves
> While the earth bears a plant, or the sea rolls a wave.

Paine's rendition was a complete success. Soon "To Anacreon in Heaven" was the musical basis for many songs that exhorted the virtues of political heroes. In 1798, Paine again set another song to the English drinking tune. This time his subject was "Adams and Liberty" in honor of the second president. When Jefferson took office in 1801 still another interpretation appeared. This time, the tone was less laudatory of its subject than celebratory over the triumph of one political party over another. But it still employed the well-known drinking tune:

> The Federalists are down at last,
> The Monarchists completely downcast,
> The Aristocrats are stripped of power
> Storms o'er the enemy faction lower.
> Soon we Republicans shall see
> Columbia's sons from bondage free;
> Lord, how the Federalists will stare
> At Jefferson, in Adams' chair!

At the time of the War of 1812, many Americans easily recognized the tune of "To Anacreon in Heaven." The tune had been used in a variety of songs, from presidential themes, to Masonic hymns, to a celebration of Napoleon's withdrawal from Moscow (1812). It did not, however, become immortalized until a young Baltimore lawyer, Francis Scott Key, set his prospect poem to the tune.

## "The Star-Spangled Banner"

The song that would eventually become the national anthem was written during the British bombardment of Fort McHenry, Maryland, in 1814.[9] The story of Key's writing of "The Star-Spangled Banner" has become an American legend. It certainly is a tale of drama and intrigue, well deserving of its legendary status.

By September 1814, the British had successfully burned the city of Washington during the War of 1812. Part of their stratagem was to blockade the Chesapeake Bay. The British had arrested a prominent Upper Marlborough citizen, Dr. Beanes, as a "collaborationist." Friends had prevailed upon Key, a friend of Beanes and a man who had many Washington connections, to intervene on Beanes's behalf. Key was ultimately successful, but the British detained him aboard ship during the shelling of Fort McHenry on September 13–14.

Key stayed on deck throughout the night, watching the "bombs bursting in air." An emotional man, Key was extremely apprehensive during his watch. When in the dawn he spied the American flag still flying over Fort McHenry, in his elation he wrote the first stanza of "The Star-Spangled Banner" on the back of a letter he was carrying.[10] After his release on the fourteenth, Key went back to a Baltimore hotel, recopied the poem, and added three more verses, adapting the completed poem to the tune of "To Anacreon in Heaven." (Earlier, around 1805, Key had adapted the tune to one of his poems that celebrated the American naval victory over the Barbary pirates: "When the Warrior Returns.") The next day it was published as a broadside. By nightfall Key's song (first titled "Defence of Fort McHenry") was being sung in a tavern (Elson, 123). On September 20, it had been published in a Baltimore newspaper. Its popularity quickly spread, its place in American history secured.

"The Star-Spangled Banner" serves as the quintessential American musical response to external and internal forces. Simultaneously, it evinces the coalescing of a European cultural heritage with the formation of an American one. Ironically, a song whose lyrics (especially in stanzas two and three) are vehemently anti-British uses the melody of a convivial British song to rouse the citizenry. But the effect of "The Star-Spangled Banner" is not a singular one. Americans employed music to express a host of emotions and expressions. They were not above drawing on old forms to establish a new, patriotic voice.

Generally speaking, music in America reflected its citizens' belief in individual expression, whether that expression was manifested in songs that advocated faith in a higher power (psalmody and hymnody), articulated their experiences and heritage that came from diverse racial and ethnic roots, reflected their promotion of serious music, or championed the American cause. American music served as a bridge between the pride in one's cultural heritage and the creation of a new national identity. This period in American history in many ways established a uniquely national musical tradition.

# 10

# Performing Arts

The new nation experienced an increased interest in and a serious awareness of the performing arts. The acrobatic acts, pantomimes, and other
unsophisticated theatrical diversions of the early part of the eighteenth
century gave way to somewhat more refined, aesthetic amusements.
Drama, dance, and opera were gradually becoming a more integral part
of American cultural life. Arguably, this era could be deemed as the
formative period of American performing arts, especially the play. After
the Revolutionary War, Americans were ready to be entertained by
plays, harlequinades (a pantomime or comedy featuring the character
Harlequin, a masked fool in parti-color costume), and ballets, all of
which were largely European in importation and influence. But post-
Revolutionary Americans soon were interested in creating theatrical
pieces that reflected their own unique history and culture.

Early American colonists regarded the performing arts (the theater in
particular) with distrust, yet by the 1740s acting troupes from England
had begun to tour the American colonies. (In fact, the first documented
play performed in America, *The Bear and the Cub*—also known as *Ye Bare
and Ye Cubb*—was performed in Virginia as early as 1665.) The famous
Hallam family acting troupe arrived in Virginia (via Jamaica from England) in 1752. The Hallam troupe was instrumental in introducing the
colonists to not only plays, but to spectacles, incidental dances, and harlequinades (Terry, 25). At the onset of the Revolutionary War, the major
cities—New York, Philadelphia, Charleston, and Williamsburg—had relatively well attended theatrical seasons. By 1800, many other cities had
followed suit—or at least had built theaters to accommodate the public's
growing interest in the theatrical arts. (Even theater-resistant Boston fi-

nally had its first theatrical season in 1794.) Although still held with suspicion by the public at large, the American theater slowly began to play a substantial role in American social life.

There were several reasons why the theatrical arts had not exactly flourished prior to the war. First, the protraction of a vital theatrical culture requires a relatively intellectually sophisticated urban community, which was not present in Colonial America (Nye, *Cultural Life*, 262). The colonies were essentially agricultural and still influenced by religious institutions in regard to the performing arts.

Second, many religions were prejudiced against the drama, notably the Puritans of New England and the Quakers of Pennsylvania. Puritan and Quaker alike found the symbolic (such as the arts in general) anathema. The drama, in their minds, was linked with monarchical politics and religion (Quinn, 2). Also, these two religious communities, known for their emphasis on the utilitarian and on thrift, objected to the expense incurred over mere entertainment.

Third, Americans had traditionally held the view of *theatrum mundi* (the world as a stage), which tied in with their focus on the conquest of the continent (Richards, x). New World explorers and early colonists believed that they were playing a role in the annals of history. There was no need to create a drama that was the product of the imagination when, by virtue of their exploration and transformation of the wilderness, they were a part of a real-life drama.

The fourth and strongest objection to the theater was a moral and civic one. Even in Renaissance England, the theater had tended to draw unsavory types (pickpockets and prostitutes, among others). Actors and other players had a reputation for sexual licentiousness. (Whether the reputation was a deserved one is a matter for conjecture only.) Although religious communities, such as the Anglicans (found predominantly in Virginia and South Carolina) and the Roman Catholics of Maryland, were not averse to the drama (indeed, the drama came out of church ritual), they did come from a culture that was wary of theatrics because of the petty criminal behavior that surrounded the great playhouses of England. Actors and playhouses, they reasoned, would attract criminals and others of low morals. Still another objection was that playacting was believed to be a form of hypocrisy (the pretending to be another person), thereby encouraging the young to imitate immoral or questionable behavior (ibid., xii). The possibility of the rise in the crime rate and the negative influence on the young were more than enough reasons for Americans to oppose the establishment of the theater. Thus, throughout the colonies, citizenry, regardless of denomination, objected to the influx of acting troupes.

Yet, despite the objections of and the resistance by many citizens, during the Revolutionary period the theater began to be accepted. Many times plays were turned into "lectures" to ease concerns about the worthiness of playacting. Key scenes of well established plays were performed as lectures on morals. Commander in chief George Washington (an avowed aficionado of the drama) had Joseph Addison's *Cato*[1] performed for his troops. He thought that perhaps this play, the underlying thesis of which was the idea of liberty, and its stirring speeches would lift the badly sagging morale of the army.

Despite Americans' cautious interest in the theater, in 1778 the Continental Congress banned plays in American-held territories. Only British-occupied cities had theatrical seasons during the Revolutionary period. After the war New York (the only large city occupied by the British for the duration of the war) became the sole location for the debut of theatrical seasons (ibid., xii). Other communities had a more difficult time starting up a theatrical community. Theater, after all, was the entertainment of the enemy, the British. In some patriots' view, for Americans to embrace a British pastime was tantamount to treason.

## DANCE, MUSICAL PERFORMANCES, AND SPECTACLES

The performing arts did, however, win out. The Hallam troupe returned after the Revolution to play for American audiences. The Hallams, like other troupes, did not limit their theatrical performances to acting. Plays were the predominant form, but dance and musical acts were often presented in conjunction with the performance of the play. Sometimes dances and pageants were intermingled on the theatrical bill alongside the play.

The introduction of the dance as a performing art in America was not new. Ballet had been performed in the colonies as early as 1735, primarily for the entertainment of the Charleston, South Carolina, aristocracy (Coe, 17). Like the drama, dance also had its detractors. The most common argument against the dance was its sensuality. The descendants of the Puritans viewed the dance and its sensual component as a holdover of European wantonness (ibid.).

But after the war, the dance in performance became more prevalent and became linked to the theatrical productions of the time. The first American dancer of note, Pennsylvania-born John Durang (1768–1822), was a valued member of the predominantly British Hallam troupe. A natural, gifted dancer rather than a classically trained one, Durang made his debut in 1784 as part of Hallam's lecture and patriotic extravaganza.[2] Later, Durang secured his fame by way of his hornpipe dance (a lively British folk dance) in patriotic dramatic pantomimes.

Durang's career reflects the nature of dance performance in post–Revolutionary America. Not only a dancer, Durang was a skilled acrobat, juggler, and actor. Frequently, his talents even expanded to include that of writer, director, and stage director. To add a note of variety to his famous hornpipe dance, Durang occasionally performed it on a tight-rope—and sometimes even on eggs (Terry, 26). His other dance perform-ances were comprised of ballet pas de deux with popular ballerinas of the period, the minuet, and the Allemande (an eighteenth-century dance performed in 2/4 time).[3]

Women also performed as dancers in the theater during this period but did not share the acclaim and respect afforded to a dancer such as Durang (with the exception of a prima ballerina). A great theatrical un-derclass had emerged: the ballet girls (Richards, xxii). These unfortunate women dancers (as a group) played essential roles in theatrical perform-ance but at low pay and with little or no recognition. Because plays often incorporated pantomimes and incidental dances (designed to lighten the tone of the play), they sometimes required sprites or other fanciful crea-tures to carry out these routines. For these parts, the manager assigned the corps de ballet to the roles.

Unfortunately, the corps de ballet had a precarious existence. Under-paid and regarded as sexually profligate (a bias that harkened back to Renaissance England), the ballet girls risked their lives in these parts. To replicate flight, ropes and wires hoisted the women above the stage; sometimes they were caught in the machinery, other times burned by the gas lamps (ibid.); some were even killed.

Musical stage entertainment was also part of the theatrical scene, albeit on a limited basis. The English ballad opera, a comic opera that featured farcical or extravaganza plots, was sometimes performed. (John Gay's *The Beggar's Opera*, a parody of Italian serious opera and a satire on the morality of politicians, was a particular favorite with American audi-ences.) Soon Americans began to compose ballad operas as well. Francis Hopkinson, a signer of the Declaration of Independence, composed an "oratorical entertainment" entitled *The Temple of Minerva* (1781) that most theatergoing Americans, including George Washington, found pleasing (Kupferberg, 133). Others followed suit, composing and staging ballad operas specifically for American audiences. Worthy of mention is James Hewitt's *Tammany, or The Indian Chief* (1794), which was sponsored by the early Tammany Society of New York (at its inception a social organ-ization, rather than the political one which it would become in the nine-teenth century). *Tammany* was highly praised for its ardent expression of liberty, equality, and, most of all, republicanism (G. Hughes, 68). Also notable is James Nelson Barker's *The Indian Princess; or, The Belle Sauvage* (1808), an adaptation of the legend of Pocahontas and John Smith. In American territories, specifically New Orleans, the French light operas were staged. Italian opera did not, however, appear in the United States until after 1819, probably due to lack of interest.

For the most part, music was primarily used to introduce a character or create a specific mood (Richards, xxvii). In such popular American plays as *The Contrast* (1787) and *The Indian Princess*, key characters sang. Actors were often expected to be accomplished singers as well as dramatic performers. Music was used to heighten mood, underscore the action, or provide additional commentary, making it a crucial component of early American drama.

The spectacle (a combination of pantomime, masque, and pageant) was another popular performance that drew large audiences. In the case of the spectacle (unlike other performances), the authors of skits and dialogues were primarily American, not English. Often the spectacle celebrated an event or an occasion. Some of the more famous spectacles included *The Death of Major André, and Arnold's Treachery; or, West Point Preserved* (1798), *The Apotheosis of Franklin; or, His Reception in the Elysian Fields* (1796), *American True Blue; or, the Naval Processions* (1799), and *The Constellation; or A Wreath for American Tars* (1799), a reenactment of the battle between the frigates *Constellation* and *L'Insurgente*.

Spectacles were immensely popular. During a regular season, a theater would offer at least one spectacle commemorating a seasonal event. Occasionally a spectacle would focus on past history (such as *The Death of Major André*). Many had a pronounced patriotic theme. For example, an updated musical and allegorical masque from the Revolutionary period entitled *Americana; or, A New Tale of the Genii* (published in 1802) incorporates such allegorical figures as Elutheria, the Genius of Liberty; Galiana, the Genius of France; Typhon, the Genius of Tyranny; and Fastidio, the Genius of Pride. Typhon and Fastidio have aligned themselves with Britain in war against Americana. Galiana joins with Americana in battle, defeating Britain who admits that she had been misled by Typhon and Fastidio. The spectacle ends with Americana clipping the wings of the two evil genii. Galiana and Americana then place Elutheria's feet on the necks of Typhon and Fastidio. America is praised by all.

Despite the interminably long speeches and the rudimentary verse, *Americana* was a spectacular pageant designed to foster American patriotism and pride. The somewhat sympathetic treatment of Britain (for Britain does acknowledge her error) appealed to American audiences that, despite the Revolution, harbored warm feelings for the former mother country.

Spectacles were not performed exclusively in the theater; circuses were also a venue for them. By 1793, the United States had its first circus: John Bill Ricketts, a circus rider who had worked in English circuses, opened his circuses in Philadelphia and New York. By 1800, the circus as entertainment had a solid base in the United States. Unlike the posh new theaters of the period, circuses staged performances in poorly con-structed buildings, some permanent, others semipermanent (Meserve, 130). Despite the shoddy construction, lack of creature comforts, and sometimes danger (circus fires were common), attendance was high, par-ticularly for patriotic spectacles. Audiences could be assured that pag-eants, spectacles, and extravaganzas would be continually performed at the circus (alongside the traditional circus acts of acrobatics, horseback riding, and juggling). Pantomimes, dancing, music, and stirring speeches were the order of the day and Americans flocked to see them.

## THEATRICAL COMPANIES AND PLAYHOUSES

But as an American art form, dance, musical entertainments, and spec-tacles were secondary to the emergence of the drama. Post–Revolution-ary America witnessed the steady increase in the number of theatrical companies. The aforementioned New York–based Hallam troupe, which once held a virtual monopoly on the theater up to the Revolution, began to have rivals from up-and-coming theatrical troupes. Thomas Wignell (1753–1803), a talented comedian of the time, left the Hallam troupe, which by this time was known as The Old American Company, and in 1794 formed his own troupe. Wignell's company focused its attention on Philadelphia and its environs. His troupe was immensely popular, partly because of his reputation as the foremost comedian of the day. As a result, Philadelphia surpassed New York as the nation's center of the-atrical entertainment, a distinction it would hold through the first three decades of the nineteenth century.

Theatrical companies and seasons required playhouses, structures America was lacking. Thus, Americans began to build lavish playhouses not seen before on the North American continent. Theater owners hired skilled scene painters and proficient musicians. There was to be nothing second-rate about the appearance of the American theater or its staging. Americans used the finest materials and native talent available in build-ing their new theaters. In Boston, the preeminent late Georgian architect Charles Bulfinch designed the Federal Street Theater (1794). The play-house became a symbol for American artistry, inside and outside.

The most impressive of the new theaters was Philadelphia's Chestnut Street Theater (1794), which became the home of Wignell's company. Its interior replicated the Theater Royal at Bath, England. Seating two thou-sand, the Chestnut Street Theater was similar in design to an Elizabethan theater. Along the sides were tiered boxes and balconies. The seats in the pit (ground floor) were, however, not quite as comfortable as those in a theater box. Rows of backless benches accommodated those who could not afford a box. The stage was imposing; it was extremely large

A typical theater, view of the house from the stage. Courtesy of the
Library of Congress.

for the time, 37 feet in width with a 12- to 15-foot apron that projected
out in front of an elaborate proscenium arch.

But as splendid as the facades, the scenery, and the music might have
been, savvy theatrical managers were always sensitive to the republican
spirit of their patrons. In other words, patrons expected to be treated
equally. For instance, the astute (but tempted) Wignell declined an offer
by a leading society matron to purchase a box "at any price to be fixed
by the manager" because all citizenry should be equal in his theater
(Coad and Mims, 30). Wignell did, however, make an exception in his
treatment of frequent patron President Washington. When Washington
attended Wignell's theater (which he often did), Wignell himself in formal dress greeted the president at the box door and escorted him to his
seat (ibid., 32).

The conduct of theater patrons belied the republic's belief in virtuous
behavior. A military guard always accompanied Washington's visits to
Philadelphia theaters. Four soldiers were assigned to overlook the gallery
(site of the worst behavior), and one was posted at each stage door. The
high constable and other police officers were also on hand to ensure that
order would be maintained. "The gods of the gallery" (that is, those in
the "cheap seats") when displeased, for whatever reason, would throw

bottles, glasses, nuts, vegetables, and apples down on the stage and into the orchestra (Chase, 97). Ladies of the evening often plied their trade in the best boxes of the theater. This practice became so intolerable to the stage managers that on January 21, 1795, the public was duly informed that "no persons of notorious ill fame will be suffered to occupy any seat where places are already taken" (qtd. in Sonneck, 121).

There were other egregious examples of offensiveness as well. Theater patrons were known to bring their own liquid refreshment, and this consistently led to riotous behavior. One account describes the actions of two inebriated sea captains during a performance in New York on November 2, 1796. The two began to heckle the orchestra during an overture of "Yankee Doodle Dandy." The audience hissed at them. The drunken captains retaliated by hurling missiles into the orchestra and at the audience. Eventually, the rioters were ejected from the theater, only to return with a number of sailors who led an attack on the theater entrance (ibid.). Although "No Smoking" signs were prominently displayed throughout the theater, patrons casually smoked throughout performances with impunity (Chase, 97).

American audiences were no less well behaved than European ones (Sonneck, 122). The theater on both sides of the Atlantic served as a meeting place to gossip and debate the political issues of the day. Often the performance itself was ignored entirely. The theater was a place where aspirants to lofty social heights came to be seen. Dramatist Royall Tyler in his play *The Contrast* criticized such behavior through the speech of one of the play's more frivolous characters, Charlotte Manly. Charlotte, a pampered product of New York society, describes for her brother the typical decorum employed by the theatrical set:

Everything is conducted with such decorum. First we bow round to the company in general, then to each other in particular . . . then the curtain rises, then our sensibility is all awake, and then, by the mere force of apprehension, we torture some harmless expression into a double meaning . . . and then we [the women] giggle and they [the men] simper, and they giggle and we simper, and then the curtain drops, and then for nuts and oranges, and then we bow . . . and then the curtain rises again, and then we blush and giggle and simper and bow all over again. Oh! the sentimental charms of a side-box conversation! (ibid., 22–23)

Despite the rowdy and discourteous behavior of the audience, American theater began to flourish. Gifted actors became the rule, not the exception, in early republican theater. Mainly because of the efforts of the Philadelphia directors, extraordinary English actors were lured to the American shore (Coad and Mims, 30). These English imports invigorated the theatrical scene. Some had had impressive careers in England, many had worked with the leading actors of English theater, and most had undergone rigorous training in London and regional theaters. With the exception of the Hallam company, prior to the Revolution, American actors had little or no connection with English theater. Because travel (especially foreign travel) was demanding and sporadic, Americans as a whole were categorically behind in matters of attire and protocol. Thus, American actors suffered in technique and manners. Prior to independence, American actors were decidedly provincial. With the infusion of the gifted English players, American theater was affected. The English player not only established a new standard for performance, but one for culture as well (ibid.).

Along with the extremely popular Wignell, many actors were great favorites of the public. Known as the "Provincial Garrick,"[4] John Hodgkinson (1767–1805) was deemed by many as the most gifted actor to appear on the American stage. He was renowned for his versatility: he could play comic, tragic, and operatic roles with equal ease (ibid., 35). His wife, known on the stage as Mrs. Hodgkinson,[5] was an accomplished singing actress, especially noted for her portrayal of Ophelia in *Hamlet*.

The premiere actress of The Old American Company, Mrs. Owen Morris, captivated audiences in her roles in stylish comedies and dignified dramas (ibid., 32). Lewis Hallam was her male counterpart in The Old American Company. Hallam was especially known for his handling of genteel comedy. His partner in the ownership of The Old American Company, John Henry, was a fine comic actor, although his portrayal of Othello received high reviews as well.

Eliza Kemble Whitlock (1762–1836), the younger sister of the remarkable Sarah Kemble Siddons (1755–1831), was extremely popular with patrons of Boston's Haymarket Theater (1796). Mrs. Whitlock was considered by many one of the finest tragic actresses to grace the American stage. Mrs. Oldmixon, another distinguished actress, became the favorite of Philadelphia (ibid., 37). She was principally renowned for her beautiful singing voice and was often considered the finest vocalist in America during the early nationalist period. The premiere tragedienne of the American stage, Mrs. Merry (Anne Merry [1769–1808]), was deemed as powerful an actress as the world-acclaimed Sarah Siddons.

As beguiling and vital the actors were to the American theater, the manager's function was perhaps more crucial than that of the procession of highly acclaimed players. A manager was essentially a lessee. (Theater owners very rarely became involved in the production of a performance.) American theatrical managers fulfilled the same duties and responsibilities as their English counterparts. In essence, the manager was responsible for casting, directing, negotiating and paying salaries, editing scripts, interviewing, staffing of non-acting personnel, scheduling, hiring, and sometimes acting (Booth, 28–29).[6] To succeed, the manager, fundamentally a businessperson, had to be attuned to the preferences and shifting tastes of a fickle public. This presented quite a dilemma to a manager who saw himself as a purveyor of art and an assessor of the marketplace. Did one pander to the "cheap seats" and stage "low" (or what might be seen as "vulgar") comedies or attempt to edify the audience's sensibilities?

## THE EMERGENCE OF THE AMERICAN DRAMATIST

For the most part, familiarity and popularity willed out. As with the novel, Americans preferred the works of established British writers to be on the theatrical bill (Meserve, 127). The taste of American audiences ran the gamut: from tragedy to farce-comedy, from melodrama to history. Very few plays produced were written by Americans, even though playwriting and production had been popular college activities for years. Early college literary and social societies (Harvard's Hasty Pudding Club, established in 1795, is a notable example) produced dramatic exhibitions.

Along with the amateur playwrights of college productions, a few American dramatists tried their hands at playwriting. The overall quality of plays written by these aspiring playwrights—both amateur and professional—is uneven. A primary example of a college production is Barnabas Bidwell's (1763–1833) *The Mercenary Match*, produced in 1784 at Yale College.[7] *The Mercenary Match*, a tragedy in five acts, centers around the misdeeds of the villainous Major Shapely, a seducer, a cad, and a murderer. Typical of the period, the tragedy ends on a moralistic note. Shapely's paramour, Mrs. Jensen, dies of shock at his evildoing (Shapely murders her husband), and Shapely is sent to the gallows. William Dunlap, in his *History of the American Theatre and Anecdotes of the Principal Actors*, reported *The Mercenary Match* to be unintentionally comic, citing such profound lines as "Night follows day, and day succeeds to night" (136). Bidwell's work was popular with his fellow collegians, even though the audience would burst into raucous laughter throughout the performance.

### Royall Tyler

The first intentional and professional comedy written by an American was Royall Tyler's *The Contrast*, first performed at New York's John Street Theatre on April 16, 1787. Tyler, who would go on to have a distinguished career as a jurist and some success as a novelist (*The Algerine Captive* [1797]), a poet, and an essayist, attended his first play (Sheridan's *The School for Scandal*[8]) in New York early in 1787. Almost immediately Tyler embarked on creating an American play with an American theme, no small task for a writer with no dramatic experience.

Tyler was faced with a unique situation for a playwright. He wished to write a play for a country that historically was hostile to plays in general and one that had a limited dramatic tradition. And it was a country that, as far as the performing arts were concerned, supported Anglo, rather than American, works. His solution was an ingenious one. The play, *The Contrast*, satirizes the affectation of social theatricality and those who know nothing of the theater in general (Richards, 3). Tyler's attack (through the speech of one of the characters) on socialites who go to the theater for myriad reasons—except to watch the play itself—is a contemptuous appraisal of New York high-society manners. Theater patrons in *The Contrast* are described as flirtatious, simpering, and predisposed to immature behavior. (The "patrons" revel in exacting double meanings from innocent lines when they are not indulging in gossip and flirtations while the play is in performance.) Tyler, in a sense, uses the theater as a criticism of itself (ibid.). Fashionable New Yorkers are not portrayed as virtuous but as ridiculous and wayward.

*The Contrast* is unquestionably the most important play in the history of early American drama. In the character of Jonathan (a part he expressly wrote for Thomas Wignell), Tyler established the stock character of the shrewd, comic Yankee that would be a mainstay in American comedies to come. The play's theme of the triumph of American honesty over European affectation and deception also became a favorite theme for American dramas that followed.

The plot of *The Contrast* is relatively simple. Each of the five acts is broken into two scenes that contrast form and content (Meserve, 98). The heroine, Maria Van Rough, is being forced by her father to marry the Anglophile Dimple, a fop and a scoundrel. Maria is taken with Colonel Manly, whose name exemplifies his character. (Manly, unlike Dimple, has served America honorably in the Continental Army.) The servants of Manly and Dimple, Jonathan and Jessamy, provide a contrast in ethics and behavior as do their employers. Jonathan is the epitome of rural honesty, whereas Jessamy has been corrupted by European sophistication. Eventually, Dimple is revealed to be the rogue that he truly is, and Van Rough relents and blesses the union of Manly and Maria.

Tyler was very aware of the prejudices and preferences of his audience—and structured his play accordingly. The text reveals an irony and a sly humor that would not have been lost on republican audiences (although today this would not be as evident without a working knowledge of the theatrical scene). In Act 3, scene 1, Jonathan unintentionally delights Jessamy and Jenny (a friend of Jessamy's) with his account of his visit to a playhouse. The first joke is that the Calvinist Jonathan was unaware that he had attended a play. (He refers to the theater in general as "the devil's drawing-room.") He had naively believed that he had entered something akin to a meeting-house gallery where a "great green cloth" was lifted up, allowing him and the others to "look right into the next neighbor's house."

One of the "family members" in the "next neighbor's house" Jonathan took a liking to in particular was "Darby . . . his other name I forgot. Oh! it was Wig—Wag—Wag-all, Darby Wag-all." The joke here is that Jonathan (portrayed by Thomas Wignell) is watching Wignell play the stock Irish character Darby in *The Poor Soldier*.[9] Thus the good Calvinist who would never intentionally patronize "the devil's drawing-room" feels a kinship with, in his words, "a wicked player." Eventually Jonathan rationalizes that Darby (Wignell) is "the old serpent himself, and had a cloven foot in his pocket."

The true hero of *The Contrast*, of course, is Manly. Manly is very much a hero of the republic in the image of Washington. He is a man of few words, of immense courage, and a patron of the theater. Contrasted with the affected Dimple (who is revealed to be almost as ignorant of the theater as Jonathan), Manly is shown to be the intellectual and cultural superior, despite his less fashionable clothes and straightforward manner. The audience learns that Manly appreciates and comprehends the role of theater in the republic, that is, that laughter is a curative to iniquity and thus an impetus to virtue (Richards, 4).

*The Contrast* was an instant success, the first American play by an American playwright to be so. By 1804, it had been performed in major cities: New York, Philadelphia, Boston, Charleston, Baltimore, Richmond, Alexandria (Virginia), and Spanish Town (Jamaica). As a testament to its reputation, *The Contrast* was also staged in smaller communities. Today, it is one of the few American plays from this period that is consistently included in anthologies of American literature and American drama.

Tyler's keen ear for dialogue (especially the Yankee patter of Jonathan) and his employment and knowledge of dramatic technique are the play's fundamental strengths that are evident today (Meserve, 98). As a comedy of manners, the play holds up well, lampooning the fashions, affectations, and, of course, the theater itself. Most important, *The Contrast* encapsulates the national temper and pride of 1787 (a significant date in itself since the Constitution was drafted in that year). *The Contrast* signals a change in the nation's perception of itself. No longer a loose confederation of individual states, the United States was beginning to develop a national mentality; that is, they saw themselves as a united people, a people of virtue and strength. *The Contrast* echoed that perception.

## William Dunlap

An aspiring young painter was intrigued by the *The Contrast*'s ability to draw audiences. The painter, a student of the renowned Benjamin West, subsequently decided to embark on a playwriting career of his own. Because of that momentous decision, America had her first professional playwright: William Dunlap (1766–1839).

Dunlap was, as were many of the major personalities of the time, a multitalented man. He maintained his portraiture career while becoming the most prolific of all American playwrights (Richards, 58). Dunlap is also known for his literary efforts, such as his biography of the writer Charles Brockden Brown (*The Life of Charles Brockden Brown*, published in 1815); his comprehensive *History of the American Theatre and Anecdotes of the Principal Actors* (1797), a massive tome that provides an uneven history but tantalizing gossip and insight into early American theater; and various translations of European texts. Dunlap was also the manager of two of New York's foremost theaters: the John Street Theater (1767) and the New Park Theater (1798).

One of Dunlap's first dramatic attempts was *Fontainville Abbey* (1797), a play with obvious gothic overtones. Based on popular gothic novelist Ann Radcliffe's *Romance of the Forest*, the play was well received by a public that enjoyed supernatural effects, horrific atmospheres, and stormy nights, even though the plot and dialogue were contrived. To prevent any prejudicial criticism, the author's name was left off the playbill. (Critics were quick to criticize harshly any work by an American writer.) *Fontainville Abbey* does, nonetheless, reveal Dunlap's astute reading of public tastes. Because gothic novels (especially Radcliffe's) were the rage, Dunlap correctly concluded that a gothic play would appeal to the theatergoing public as well as to a novel-reading one.

His most distinguished effort was a historical drama: *André* (1798), first performed at the New Park Theater in New York. *André* was based on the life and execution of the British spy, Major John André (1750–1780).[10] The play was perhaps problematic for audiences since the André affair was still too recent. (Many Americans were outraged at the time that Major André had been hanged rather than shot, an ignoble death for a soldier. The episode was a very sensitive one in American history.) *André* is, by and large, Dunlap's best and most interesting drama.

The play is subtitled "A Tragedy in Five Acts." Although not the first American play to deal with an event of a historic consequence (that honor went to John Daly Burk's *Bunker-Hill*, written in 1794 and produced in 1797), *André* was a bold effort. In its first performance, one scene drew hisses from the audience. A key character, the young American officer Arthur Bland (played by English actor Thomas Abthorpe Cooper) pleads in vain to General Washington for André's life. In anger, Bland pulls the cockade from his hat. The American audience was incensed by such an unpatriotic act. The reaction was so vehement that there was talk of withdrawing the play altogether. Dunlap wisely altered the scene so that Bland picked up the cockade and placed it in his hat. Subsequent audiences found the revision to be acceptable.

The uniqueness of *André* is that its action does not center on the title's hero. The true action in the play is sidetracked to other characters who are trying to save the hapless British spy from a shameful death. In some respects, the play is allegorical. Washington represents the country, and the American General M'Donald presents national and international views that contrast with the isolationalism of the character of Seward (Meserve, 109).

Bland's youthful impulsiveness is the real focus of the first half of the play. But as the play progresses, his character matures, mirroring the fate of the fledgling country. At the execution, Bland tries to understand Washington's unpopular decision and rues his earlier insubordination. (Bland was not alone in his resentment. Britons and Americans alike were angry about Washington's orders to hang André, because André was extremely well liked by New York society. Also, the proper method of execution for an officer of André's rank would be by firing squad.) Dunlap's technique was to shift from Bland's uncontrolled actions to the more controlled, philosophic ones of Washington and M'Donald (ibid.). The play ends with M'Donald's eloquent speech invoking that "the Children of Columbia still / Be taught by every teacher of mankind" (act 5, scene 3). M'Donald (the voice of rationality) praises Washington and, thus, extols the direction that the country has taken.

Dunlap was compelled to rewrite *André*. In 1803, the play was transformed into a patriotic spectacle entitled *The Glory of Columbia—Her Yeomanry*. Performed at the New Park Theatre on the Fourth of July, *The Glory of Columbia* little resembles the five-act tragedy. André's story was now interwoven with song and spectacle. American soldiers provided comic relief along with a captured Irishman. (The Irish were stock comic characters for the American stage at this time.) The tragic Honora (André's fiancée who goes insane in the earlier version) was now supplanted by a feisty young woman from the country—who also provides comic relief.

Unlike *André*, *The Glory of Columbia* was popular with the public for years, indicative of the American preference for glorious spectacle and their love and devotion for Washington as a cultural icon. According to an account listed in a program, the finale of *The Glory of Columbia* consisted of a "transparency descend[ing], and an Eagle is seen suspending a Crown of Laurel over the Head of General Washington with this motto, 'Immortality to Washington' " (qtd. in Odell, 182). Nothing could have pleased a republican audience more.

## Susanna Haswell Rowson

Dunlap was not the only dramatist of note who capitalized on the new nation's interest in past and contemporary historical events. Susanna Haswell Rowson was a woman of multiple talents and of even more public opinions. Known for her best-selling cautionary novel *Charlotte Temple* (1791), Mrs. Rowson (as she was known by her stage name) was an actress, educator, essayist, singer, musician, dancer, novelist, and dramatist. While a member of Wignell's acting company, Rowson penned *Charlotte Temple*. Although an actress of average ability, Rowson was known to have written at least four plays for the American stage: *The Female Patriot* (1795); *The Volunteers* (1795), which dealt with the Whiskey Rebellion; *The Columbian Daughter; or, Americans in England* (1800); and her best play, *Slaves in Algiers; or, A struggle for Freedom. A Play interspersed with Songs* (1794).

The texts for *The Volunteers* (a musical play) and *The Columbian Daughter* are lost. What is known of *The Volunteers* is from the vocal score by Alexander Reinagle (a Philadelphia musician and Thomas Wignell's partner). The songs themselves deal with the joys of the frontier life; however, her primary concern was for the militia (the "volunteers" of the title) whom Washington called out to put down the Whiskey Rebellion (Meserve, 117). In the play, the volunteers are praised as men of truly heroic stature.

*The Columbian Daughter* was originally titled *Americans in England* and was first performed at Boston's Federal Street Theater in 1797. After Rowson gave the rights of production to John Hodgkinson, the play was renamed, most likely to reflect the primary focus of the play. The heroine, Jemima, is a true daughter of Columbia, a woman of strength and resilience. From all accounts it appears that Mrs. Rowson was not only the author of the play, but also its star. *The Columbian Daughter* was most likely a farce that underscored English eccentricities and American virtues (ibid.).

*Slaves in Algiers* was a comic opera, with songs written by Reinagle. It was a work that played well in many cities, notably Philadelphia, Baltimore, and New York. Though the play garnered the ire of the malicious Peter Porcupine (the arch-Federalist and strong proponent of the aristocracy), *Slaves in Algiers* expressed Rowson's anger at the barbarities inflicted on American citizens at the hands of the Barbary pirates—and at the American policy at this time to pay tribute to the Dey (ruler) of Algiers. Rowson adeptly contrasts two nations (Algiers and the United States) that represented the two extremes of freedom and oppression (Kritzer, 6). Government, in this drama, plays a key role in character development. The captors (Algerians) who live under an oppressive regime prove to be cowards when threatened, whereas the captives (Americans), products of a free society, behave courageously (ibid.).

The play is fraught with patriotic and Christian sentiments. It is a highly romanticized drama, replete with self-sacrificing Christian women, an Algerian woman disguising herself as a boy in her quest for liberty, and various villainous infidels engaging in despicable acts. The underlying theme of the play is a criticism of tyranny and personal free-dom and was designed to expound Rowson's views on this highly charged political issue. In addition, *Slaves in Algiers* signifies the emer-gence of the American woman (ibid., 8). The American women are just as defiantly against tyranny as the men, illustrating their equality. More-over, the actions of the American women correlate to the actions of the United States during the Revolutionary War. Just as Americans had de-fied the British, gaining independence, the American women in *Slaves of Algiers* defy the Dey, winning their freedom. In both cases, rebellion be-comes the defining moment.

## Judith Sargent Murray

Rowson was not the only woman dramatist of note during this period. The accomplished and acclaimed Judith Sargent Murray (1751–1820) was known to have written at least two dramas for the Boston stage: *The Medium; or Happy Tea Party* (1795) and *The Traveller Returned* (1796). Mur-ray, unlike Rowson, chose anonymity, perhaps to avoid the stigma attached to the theater or as a reaction to criticism (Meserve, 154).

Murray is chiefly known as an essayist and editor, not necessarily as a dramatist. She published her essays on women's rights and moral, patriotic, and religious issues in the *Gleaner* (her own periodical). A well educated and brilliant essayist, Murray was profoundly influenced by the writings of English feminist Mary Wollstonecraft (1759–1797).[11] Mur-ray's essays expressed her belief that women, especially young women, should be afforded an equal role in the new republic.

By 1793 Murray expanded her literary efforts to include prologues and epilogues for plays, which she published in the *Gleaner*. Her essays on drama reveal a desire that American theater would transcend entertain-ment and that eventually young audiences might "learn to think, speak, and act with propriety ... [that] they will gradually proceed to more important inquiries" (230).

Murray wrote and published both of her plays in the *Gleaner*. The first, *Virtue Triumphant*, was performed at Boston's Federal Street Theater in 1795 under the title *The Medium*. (The "medium" refers to the quality of self-balance.) *Virtue Triumphant* is a domestic drama with touches of so-cial comedy (Quinn, 126). A strong-minded, moral young woman deci-sively refuses the hand of the man she loves until her own financial and social standing are firmly determined. The heroine, Eliza Clairville, in-sists on a marriage of equals, not one of advantage. Thus, *Virtue Tri-umphant* emphasizes sensible attitudes that might only be acquired through education and freedom of choice (Kritzer, 9).

Murray's second play, *The Traveller Returned*, was performed at the Federal Street Theater a year later. Above all, in it Murray extols Washington and the citizenry of the new republic. The setting is the Revolutionary War though the war does not play a significant role in the play itself. Basically, *The Traveller Returned* uses the stock plot of a father who has abandoned his family for 20 years but returns in time to prevent the marriage of an engaged couple who are unaware that they are siblings. (This is, however, a happy ending for all involved because the brother/sister/fianced relations are in love with other people.) *The Traveller Returned* appealed to audiences who loved spectacle, patriotic themes, and stock characters complete with heavy dialects. (The play abounds with Yankee, Irish, and German secondary characters.)

## James Nelson Barker

But the most preeminent of dramas by Americans that expanded on American themes and history was James Nelson Barker's *The Indian Princess; or, The Belle Sauvage*, performed at the New Park Theater in 1809. Barker (1784–1858) originally wrote *The Indian Princess* as a play, but quickly converted it to a light opera and melodrama. The play is unique in that it is the first staged play that featured Native Americans. *The Contrast* may have been the more successful play, but *The Indian Princess* is equally important in the development of American drama—but not for the same reasons. In its favor, *The Indian Princess* holds the distinction of being the first original American play to be performed in London.

Barker's source was John Smith's *Generall Historie of Virginia* (1624), a history from which he veered sharply. Barker flagrantly romanticizes Smith's work, often at the expense of accuracy. Some of his additions are laughable, even by early nineteenth-century standards. Virginia, according to Barker, was heavily populated with White women, Irishmen, and flamingos. Worse, the characters have little in common with their historical counterparts. Smith's Powhatan, the chief and Pocahontas's father, was a skilled and powerful leader. In Barker's version, Powhatan has been reduced to a sentimental father. Pocahontas becomes a romantic young girl who eagerly embraces English acculturation. In Barker's play, the noble savage either must die or withdraw or witness the erotic alteration of his women into European love objects (Richards, 111).

However troublesome we might find Barker's themes and depictions today, for his audience the drama that unfolded was mesmerizing. Because it was a musical, republican audiences flocked to it. Also, it catered to audiences on both sides of the Atlantic intrigued by the figure of the Native American. *The Indian Princess* began a trend in American theater of featuring plays about the Native American. Still, *The Indian Princess* is far from being an accurate portrayal of the indigenous people. Instead, the play is a historical register of the White American view and fear of the native people they were displacing (ibid., 112).

Despite the unevenness of quality and a heavy reliance on the European, the performing arts in America characterized the way Americans regarded themselves and their changing culture. Sometimes inventive, often derivative, the performing arts exemplified the progressive spirit of the new nation. The United States had begun to move away from its puritanical roots, embracing the creative and the imaginative. Americans were moved by not only the dramas of William Shakespeare and the comedies of manners of Joseph Addison and Sir Richard Sheridan, but also by stirring patriotic spectacles and extravaganzas that celebrated their history and heroes. The drama itself was transformed into a vehicle to honor and rejoice in American victories and ideals. Other branches of the performing arts (the dance, musicals, and operas) became instrumental in the expression of the American self. In the early nationalist period, the American theater moved from the provincial to its initial venture onto the world stage.

# 11

# Travel

At the close of the Revolution, the American continent had been transformed from an assemblage of 13 very distinct and separate colonies into
a new nation of 13 "United States." Although the national movement
from a loose confederation of states to a federal republic was not immediate (roughly from 1783 to 1787 with the convening of the Constitutional Convention in Philadelphia), it became the catalyst for the
revolution in transportation resources in the United States. For a nation
to be able to communicate, conduct business, expand westward, and
secure its government, it needed to engineer a necessary network of
roadways and waterways.

Prior to the Revolution, land and waterways and all modes of travel
were, at best, rudimentary. City streets, when paved, were cobblestoned.
Otherwise, narrow dirt streets laid out haphazardly were the norm.
(Only Philadelphia, which used a gridiron pattern, showed any semblance of urban planning.) On the outskirts of cities, only a few roads
were of passable quality. Corduroy roads, which were made of logs laid
side by side then covered with three inches of dirt, were only passable
when new. After a good rain, the dirt covering was often washed away.
The logs then would sporadically sink several inches.

Rural roads were also very primitive. Most were heavily rutted, dusty
in the summer months, and muddy in the winter ones. Frontier roads
were simply old Native American trails widened by wagon traffic. In
rural areas and on the frontier, the most common modes of transportation were by foot or astride a horse, with the occasional wagon or pack
train used as a means of transporting freight.

There was one other form of land travel, but it was considered an oddity. Early in the nineteenth century, a primitive form of the bicycle—known by various names such as a velocipede, an accelerator, a Drais-ena, a Hobby Horse, or a Dandy Carriage—was imported from Europe. Unlike the bicycle, the contrivance was propelled by pushing off from the ground with the feet. (There were no pedals.) A relatively expensive vehicle (around $30), only the more affluent could afford the velocipede. But it did catch on—somewhat. Baltimore became known for its manu-facture of velocipedes; and by 1819, the use of velocipedes had spread as far west as Louisville, Kentucky (Dunbar, vol. 2, 348).

There was little cohesiveness in interstate travel overall because trans-portation (and travel) was expensive and out of the reach of most citi-zens' finances. Yankee ingenuity became the order of the day. In one documented example, a Rhode Island cabinetmaker did not have the means to buy a wagon to transport his goods. He resorted to delivering his wares by carrying them balanced on the ends of a sturdy fence rail (Train, 244). Other citizens either had to walk or ride to their destina-tions. With the exception of Boston, when in 1807 a tramway was con-structed to carry gravel to Beacon Hill as a part of the renovation of the Massachusetts state house, railed pavements and railways were virtually nonexistent during this period.

Travel conditions on the frontier were worse yet. Braddock's Road (named for British General Edward Braddock [1695–1755], whose troops during the French and Indian Wars first used the road) was the primary road used by New England and Mid-Atlantic states travelers to journey through heavily forested central and western Pennsylvania. This was the only established route open to those on the frontier. In the autumn, the frontiers people would trek Braddock's Road by pack train to transport their goods to eastern towns for exchange. (The frontier largely produced whiskey, furs, and skins. These were used as barter for staples they could not produce, such as salt and iron.) Frontier inhabitants did not have money and could only acquire provisions and materials through trade (Dunbar, vol. 1, 198). In order to trade, frontier settlers were forced to travel.

Since it was impractical for the frontiers people to carry large, bulky quantities of goods (such as grains and fruits) to market, they converted produce into whiskey and brandy (which were far more portable). A packhorse could be loaded with two kegs of whiskey (each keg contain-ing eight gallons), netting the distiller $1 per gallon east of the Allegh-enies and 50 cents west. Homemade distillery proved to be an efficient way to move grain products from west to east.

However, the federal excise tax on whiskey in 1791 placed a serious financial burden on the western distillers. Outraged western Pennsyl-vanians rose up in armed rebellion against the tax. Thus the Whiskey Rebellion of 1794 was caused directly by the transportation problem of moving goods from west to east (ibid.). The consequences were calamitous. The rebellion was not easily suppressed.

Aside from wilderness rebellion, the late eighteenth and early nineteenth centuries ushered in the beginning of the movement westward. Congress, under the Confederation, had passed the Northwest Ordinances in 1784, 1785, and 1787, opening up the territory that now is the states of Ohio, Indiana, Illinois, Wisconsin, and Michigan. The three ordinances were enacted to encourage and set up procedures for the settlement of the Northwest Territory. The Northwest Ordinance of 1785 mandated the formal survey of the territory's lands, as well as the basis of American public land policy (until 1862 when it was superceded by the Homestead Act). The price of northwest territorial land was relatively inexpensive, set at a minimum of $1 per acre. For this reason many Americans were lured westward by the promises the Northwest Territory held.

Another impetus to western travel was the purchase of the Louisiana Territory from France in 1803. The United States had now doubled in size. The territory, a landmass of 828,000 square miles, established a strategic American hold on the North American continent—and provided a momentous drive toward westward expansionism. The territory was a land area abundant in grazing land, forests, mineral resources, and rich soil. (The states of Louisiana, Arkansas, Iowa, North Dakota, South Dakota, Missouri, Oklahoma, and Nebraska were carved out of the territory. Sections of what are now Colorado, Wyoming, Kansas, Minnesota, and Montana were also part of the purchase.)

Arranged by President Jefferson before the Louisiana Purchase, the Lewis and Clark Expedition (1804–1806) was conducted to survey the land to and from the Pacific coast. Led by army officers Captain Meriwether Lewis (1774–1809) and Lieutenant William Clark (1770–1838), the expedition was successful in providing the federal government with vital information about the western continental terrain and natural environment. The newly acquired Louisiana Territory, along with the Northwest Territory, attracted the intrepid, the ambitious, and the speculative. Most of all, it harkened to those who wished for a new start. But the travel into these new territories would be treacherous and rigorous. In the case of the Louisiana Territory, Lewis and Clark discovered there was no easy waterway by which to traverse the continent. In fact, Lewis noted in his journal the lack of water: "The great number of large beds of streams perfectly dry which we daily pass indicate a country but badly watered, which I fear is the case with the country through which we have been passing through for the last fifteen to twenty days" (qtd. in Walker, 3). As pioneers headed westward, they would need to blaze new trails and establish safe water routes.

Those who chose to remain in established areas also needed to forge ahead. Because of such limited and rudimentary travel options, in the past many had chosen to stay home unless necessity dictated otherwise. This was no longer feasible. For the nation to grow politically, commercially, and physically, a transportation revolution was now in order.

## COACHES, CARRIAGES, WAGONS, AND STAGECOACHES

Americans were still using the traditional British modes of transportation: coaches, carriages, and wagons in addition to riding horseback and walking. For those of the lower classes, the last two forms were the only alternatives open to them. For those of wealth and property, coaches (carriages with closed tops) and carriages were the preferred mode of travel.

At first, there was a problem with coach design. English coaches were designed for the smooth, evenly graded roads of England, not the rough and rocky roads of North America. The suspension of an English coach lent itself to a very bumpy, uncomfortable ride for passengers. American coach makers altered the suspension of the English style coach so that the ride would be smoother, making it far more comfortable. The Concord, or thoroughbrace, coach used "thoroughbraces," leather straps of various thicknesses attached to the springs, to provide a more substantial suspension that rugged American roads and trail ways required.[1] The thoroughbrace coach offered a more comfortable ride, but one at the expense of significantly added weight. More horsepower was necessary. Four to eight horses were required to pull the heavy thoroughbrace coach (Train, 243).

Coaches were particularly popular among southern gentry. Southern coaches were noted for their lightness and fine-looking facades. The attendant slaves were outfitted in the finest of livery, and the horses were the fleetest money could buy. The coach itself was often hand-painted by foreign artists, inside and out. The inside was heavily draped in "hammar cloth" (embroidered silk). The outside panels were decorated with painted medallions, often quite elaborately rendered. Some sustained a thematic motif. For example, one of George Washington's coaches, imported from England, had four medallions on the outside, each representing one of the four seasons.[2]

But coaches were not the safest of vehicles. They were bulky and difficult to maneuver, except for the most skilled of drivers. President Washington's life was imperiled several times in his trips to the North and to the South. One time the presidential coach plunged into the Occoquan River (Virginia). Another time the Father of the Country almost drowned when his coachman attempted to cross the Severn River a mile from Baltimore. "I was in imminent danger from the unskilfulness [*sic*] of the hands and the dullness of her [the presidential coach's] sailing," the President maintained (qtd. in Johnson, 222).

Carriages had increased significantly in number from colonial days, but they were still the province of the rich. They were highly decorative—and highly impractical. Carriages came in various models, some imported, some domestic.[3] They were opulent vehicles designed to enhance the passenger's prestige, rather than afford him or her an expedient form of travel. The once New England "riding chair," now known by the French name chaise (which Americans pronounced as "shay"), was an open, two-wheeled carriage that incorporated a folding cover over the back seat. The driver had a seat on the dash. The calash (from the French *calèche*) seated two to four passengers (excluding the driver), had two to four wheels, and a calash (collapsible) top. The gig, the favorite of country doctors, had a narrow seat for one person, no springs, high wheels (making it easier to get out of ruts), and heavy shafts.

The working classes resorted to less ostentatious means of transportation. Until the turn of the century, most people walked or rode horses. Many citizens, when needing to place an order for goods, walked or rode to place their orders, had the order shipped (if it was in bulk), and returned to their homes the same way they came. By 1800, farmers began to use wagons as a means of travel. These early wagons were very primitive, without springs, and little more than a box on wheels (Train, 244).

The Conestoga wagon (also known as a covered wagon) made its appearance in the latter part of the eighteenth century. The Conestoga took its name from the Conestoga Creek region of Lancaster County, Pennsylvania, the home of the Pennsylvania Germans who had brought the covered wagon to America. The enterprising Pennsylvania Germans used the covered wagon to carry their goods to the Philadelphia marketplace. Soon it became the standard mode of freight transportation for farmers and pioneers alike.

The Conestoga had a white canvas cover that shielded the contents of the wagon from inclement weather. A heavy wagon (it had a hauling capacity of six tons), the Conestoga had to be pulled by four to six horses. Brightly colored (the underbody was painted bright blue and the upper woodwork and upper gears were trimmed in red), the Conestoga was pulled by specially trained and matched horses (usually the dapple-gray Conestoga breed). Even the harnesses were unique—often brightly colored to complement the body of the wagon.

Conestoga wagons were particularly adapted for the hilly terrain of Pennsylvania (and subsequently other parts of the United States). They had concave beds that were higher at the ends, thus stopping the freight from sliding when going up and down hills. Because of the overhang in front of the wagon, the team could not be handled from the seat of the wagon. Instead, the driver walked behind the nigh-wheeler (left wheel) or rode the nigh-leader horse (Walker, 104). Drivers had to be powerful men to control the large, strong team.

Known as the "ship of inland commerce," the Conestoga had removable large wheels that would allow the teamster to float the wagon across rivers. Thus the wagon proved to be a versatile mode of transportation, something that was much needed in the largely agricultural United States. The Conestoga's wheels were also quite unique. The rear wheels measured six feet in height and a foot in width, the front wheels smaller. The larger back wheels provided more traction over uneven and heavily rutted dirt roads than those of conventional wagons.

At the turn of the century, the prairie schooner made its appearance. The schooner (the name came from the wagon's white canvas top that, from a distance, resembled a ship's sails billowing in the wind) was a smaller version of the Conestoga. It had lower sides and a flatter body than the Conestoga and was significantly lighter. It could only carry about 2,500 pounds in contrast to the Conestoga's freight capacity of six tons. Westward travelers quickly adopted the prairie schooner as their mode of transportation. Because the prairie schooner was lighter than the Conestoga, it was less likely to become stuck in prairie mire. Instead of horses, three or four oxen or six mules pulled the prairie schooner. (Horses did not fare well in the rugged terrain of the West.) Like the Conestoga, the prairie schooner could be floated across rivers. To float the wagon, usually trees were cut down and hastily dug out. Two dugouts were fitted with a cross frame. The schooner's wheels were then placed in the dugouts, thus lifting the wagon above the water for the transportation across.

Stagecoaches became an acceptable mode of public travel at this time. They were the only means many citizens had for traveling long distances (although several changes in coaches were necessary to reach one's destination). These cumbersome vehicles offered little in creature comfort. There was no protection from the elements. Even the backs of the seats were low, offering little or no back support to weary travelers. One improvement over earlier stagecoaches was that the newer versions had "dished wheels" with spokes forming a cone that could throw off mud (Train, 244). At least travelers were not as likely to be stuck in muddy ruts as they had been in the past.

Some stagecoaches had no storage space for luggage. Travelers had to squeeze in their belongings within the coach. These stagecoaches had only one entrance and that was from the driver's seat. Those traveling in the back of the coach thus had to climb over luggage and fellow passengers to get to their benchlike accommodations. On the whole, land travel in America was slow and uncomfortable. The bright spot for most travelers in their journeys was the stop at an inn or tavern.

New York coffee house, circa 1797. Courtesy of the Library of Congress.

## STOPPING BY THE WAYSIDE: INNS AND TAVERNS

Domestic travel in the United States was arduous and even dangerous, regardless of one's station in life or the mode of transportation. Roads were poor. Vehicles were uncomfortable. Terrain was often treacherous. Footpads presented still another peril. Hence, those traveling throughout the new nation and its territories welcomed the appearance of a tavern or an inn on the horizon.

The names for rest stops varied from region to region. Originally, in New England and New York State, "tavern" was used, in Pennsylvania, "inn," and in the South, "ordinary" (Lathrop, viii). Later, tavern came to mean a place where drinks were served, as opposed to an inn where patrons could be served both drinks and meals. After the Revolution, the terms "hotel" and "house" came into use to designate places where one could bed down for the night.

However, one usually would not find various classes under the same roof. Inns or hotels were designed to appeal to a specific class of traveler; that is, there were inns for aristocrats, others for wagoners and teamsters, still others for drovers. There is a documented case of an inn catering to gentry that was obligated to offer lodging to a drover. The drover was only accommodated after he promised to leave before the more affluent guests might see him (ibid., 143).

Of all the states Pennsylvania had more inns than any other, primarily because all travelers had to pass through Pennsylvania to get to the northern and southern states, as well as the western territories (ibid., 142). Travelers of all classes passing through the Keystone State were assured of finding food and lodging that would be to their satisfaction. Some inns, notably the Sun Inn in Bethlehem, became famous nationwide. Built by the Moravians, the Sun Inn was renowned for its cuisine and elegant (for the time) dining facilities. Some of the inn's more illustrious guests included Richard Penn; John Hancock; John Adams; Lyman Hall (a signer of the Declaration of Independence); Generals Schuyler, Greene, and Gage; the Minister Plenipotentiary from France; and George and Martha Washington (ibid., 149).

Philadelphia, in particular, did a brisk inn and tavern business. Besides the usual coach and stage trade, the boat trade—passengers and crew—frequented Philadelphia inns. (A line of boats destined for New Castle, Delaware, used Philadelphia as their point of departure.) Subsequently, the bill of fare in Philadelphia inns was targeted for travelers and seamen with hearty appetites. A typical inn dinner consisted of ham, roast beef, leg of mutton, fowl, and cabbage with port, ale, Madeira, or hot rum with water as a beverage (ibid., 168).

There was a difference between city and rural inns. Sleeping accommodations in the city were almost Spartan, usually a bed in a small, whitewashed room with a bare floor (ibid.). Country inns were more sumptuously furnished, probably because rural inns lodged travelers for more than one night. City inns, on the other hand, were known more for a brief (one night) stopping place for food and drink. Some city inns, such as Philadelphia's City Tavern that included Washington among its more notable dinner clientele, did advertise pleasant dining conditions: "a long room divided into boxes, fitted with tables, and elegantly lighted" (qtd. in ibid., 171).

Inns and taverns were not only places where hungry and tired travelers could sup and sleep. In many cases, they were political gathering places. Thus, the significance of the roadside inn and tavern in American history cannot be emphasized enough. For instance, Jefferson wrote the Declaration of Independence at the Indian Queen Tavern in Philadelphia; the Green Tavern, Boston, was the headquarters for the Whig Party; The Bunch of Grapes, Boston, was the site of the formation of the Ohio Land Company (instrumental in the settlement of Ohio); and western politicos chose Frankfort as the capital of Kentucky at Brent and Love's Tavern, Lexington (ibid., viii–ix). Merchants held regular meetings in taverns and sometimes even courts and legislatures did also (Dunbar, vol. 1, 214). Consequently, the inn and the tavern played significant roles in travel and political intrigue in the new republic.

# LAND ROUTES: ROADWAYS, TURNPIKES, AND BRIDGES

Land routes were in dire need of improvement. The weather and local conditions had deteriorated American roads. Even established routes were fraught with dangerous conditions. *The American Annual Register* in 1797 gave a horrific account of the hazards of travel between two large cities, Philadelphia and Baltimore:

The roads from Philadelphia to Baltimore exhibit, for the greater part of the way, an aspect of savage desolation. Chasms to the depth of six, eight, or ten feet occur at numerous intervals. A stage-coach which left Philadelphia on the 5th of February, 1796, took five days to go to Baltimore [98 miles]. The weather for the first four days was good. The roads are in fearful condition. Coaches are overturned, passengers killed, and horses destroyed by the overwork put upon them. In winter sometimes no stage sets out for two weeks. (See Dunbar, vol. 1, 191)

Obviously, Americans needed more and better roads. Owing to their investment in turnpikes, private chartered corporations became the saviors of the American land route system. Turnpikes were first engineered in these years where safe and efficient roadways were desperately needed. They were a vast improvement over previous roads, their surface being a mixture of crushed gravel and stone and mud. Tolls were instituted to pay for the initial construction and subsequent repairs, assuring that the turnpike would be passable under normally favorable conditions.

The first turnpike in the United States was the Pennsylvania and Lancaster Turnpike (constructed 1793–1795). The Lancaster Turnpike connected Philadelphia with Lancaster, Pennsylvania. (Lancaster served as the capital of Pennsylvania from 1799 to 1812. It had been under consideration for the site of the national capital in 1790.) The Lancaster Turnpike was a successful connecting route between these two important Pennsylvania cities (a distance of 62 miles). In particular, the financial success of the Pennsylvania and Lancaster Turnpike led to a movement toward the conception of similar roads in other parts of the country, all prior to 1800 (Meyer, 63). Other significant turnpikes of the period included the Catskill Turnpike (1804) and the Mohawk and Schenectady Turnpike (chartered 1800). Unfortunately, these soon fell into disrepair.

But the most magnificent of the turnpikes was the Cumberland Road project (also known as the National Pike), which was financed by the federal government. The Cumberland Road was an even more impressive engineering accomplishment than the Pennsylvania and Lancaster Turnpike. Presidents Washington and Jefferson had been enthusiastic supporters of the Cumberland Road project. The project was expressly designed to promote national unity and provide better access to the western territories. In 1806 a congressional act was approved to regulate and plan a road from Cumberland, Maryland, to the State of Ohio. The Commonwealth of Pennsylvania objected to such a construction, fearing that the Cumberland Road was being constructed to serve the interests of Baltimore and that it would deter westward trade through Pennsylvania. The act was modified in 1807 so that the Cumberland Road would pass through Fayette and Washington Counties, Pennsylvania. By 1811 work on the Cumberland Road was underway. Construction was completed between Cumberland and Wheeling (now West Virginia), for a distance of 130 miles. Unfortunately, by the 1820s the road had deteriorated despite the tolls charged to preserve it. The project was eventually abandoned in 1841. Control of the Cumberland Road was then shifted to the states that it passed through.

Poor roads and limited roadway systems were not the only impediments to travel in the new republic. Since colonial times Americans had preferred ferries as a means to cross rivers and streams that could not be forded. By the early nationalist period the lack of bridges also contributed to transportation woes. Large rivers had no bridges; smaller rivers were spanned by insubstantial ones (Train, 245). Jefferson noted that as late as 1801, of the eight rivers that lie between Monticello and Washington, DC, five of them had neither bridges nor ferries (Meyer, 41). By the end of the eighteenth century if rivers had bridges, then they were "floating" bridges. Floating bridges were a precarious means of crossing a river. Large tree trunks were placed side by side and chained together, creating the bridge. As a coach or carriage passed over the floating bridge, the bridge would sink several inches below the surface. Even though floating bridges did not appear to be the most secure way of crossing a river, they were a common means of getting across a river. In fact, by 1789 the Schuylkill River in Philadelphia had three floating bridges (ibid., 39).

Fortunately, floating bridges were not the only types of bridges being constructed. New Englanders adopted the covered bridge. The cover was implemented not to protect the traveler, but to protect the bridge from rain, snow, and ice. Because their floorboards were not nailed (to reduce strain), as a vehicle would cross the bridge, the bridge would rattle noisily.

In the future Americans would excel in bridge design and engineering. One can see evidence of the promise of such mastery in the eighteenth century. In 1786, the longest bridge in the world (at that time) was constructed over the Charles River, thus connecting Boston with Charlestown. An engineering marvel, the bridge was 1,503 feet in length, 43 feet in width, with a passage of six feet for pedestrians. Forty lamps for evening travel, accommodating travelers' needs even further, illuminated this noteworthy bridge.

The first suspension bridge built in the United States (1796) spanned Jacob's Creek (Pennsylvania) between Uniontown and Greensborough (ibid., 42). (Uniontown was to become a key point on the Cumberland Road in the nineteenth century.) James Findley, the engineer of the Jacob's Creek Bridge, received a patent for his design. Subsequently, between 1801 and 1811, eight suspension bridges were built in the United States. Though American bridge engineering was in its formative stage at this time, there was still great need for better and more effective ways to cross inland waterways.

There were also few means of connecting one waterway to another. No federal funds were used for waterways and shipping purposes (Mertins, 5). Not until the 1820s was there any federal interest in expanding a national canal system. By and large, the early republic was a nation of small, limited canals. (Work on the Erie Canal did not begin until 1817; it was completed seven years later and finally opened in 1825.) Some cities, such as New York, did have a system of canals. (New York's canal system was a result of its Dutch colonial heritage. When settling New Amsterdam the Dutch had employed their considerable skills at windmill and canal construction in designing an artificial waterway system.) These were the exception, not the rule.

## FLATBOATS, STEAMBOATS, AND SHIPS

River travel, before the advent of the steamboat, mainly consisted of flatboats (also known as "Ohio boats" or "Kentucky boats") and their counterparts: arks and keelboats.[4] Such watercraft were popular with those migrating into the Northwest Territory. Large numbers of pioneers chose to set out for the rich, fertile lands the new territory promised. But getting there was a problem.

The Northwest Territory was densely forested and hard to reach by wagon. The Ohio River, and its numerous southern tributaries, provided an excellent means of alternate transportation. In later years wilderness roads and pack train trails made the upper region of Ohio more accessible to the migrating populace. But in the 1780s, the Ohio River was the best means of transport.

Once the overland settlers reached the western boundary of Pennsylvania, they bought boats or, more often, built the boats themselves. (The heavily forested western Pennsylvania wilderness provided travelers with ample material for boatbuilding.) Flatboats were the customary mode of travel for families in the Ohio Valley, but they varied in size according to the needs of their passengers. They ranged from 20 feet in length and 10 feet in width to 60 feet in length and 18 to 20 feet in width

(Dunbar, vol. 1, 285). Flatboats were a curious mixture of a floating barn-yard, log cabin, fort, and general store (ibid., 272). The flatboat allowed westward settlers to load all their worldly goods on the boat—and to establish some semblance of a home life on the river. The journey was a long one, at the minimum, weeks, sometimes months.

Flatboat travel was dangerous. Native American tribes, not amenable to this western encroachment by Americans onto their lands, fired upon the flatboats. At nightfall, all family members were pressed into service to ward off attacks from the riverbank. Women would load the rifles of the men, while children would hold the flickering lights to enable the riflemen to see better (ibid.).

Daytime was less hazardous for flatboat travelers. Pioneer families would go about their daily tasks in the daylight hours. Women would clean, do laundry, milk the cow on board, and kill and cook the dinner. To augment the family's diet of poultry, the older sons would fish. Often the travelers would entertain themselves with song and dance. (The roof of the flatboat lent itself to a serviceable dance floor.) Others would engage in long sessions of storytelling. Life on a flatboat was a study in contrasts: menace, amusement, and the mundane.

Even larger than the flatboat was the ark. Arks were extremely popular on the Ohio and the Mississippi Rivers. Because of their vast size, arks were difficult to maneuver. Arks could only be guided by the long side sweeps (oars), were usually buffeted by the current, and could only be navigated downstream. When the family reached its destination, the ark was customarily dismantled and sold for timber (about $10 to $25) or converted into a cabin and furniture (ibid., 284).

Other types of watercraft were used to transport people and goods though the Ohio Valley. Simple boats, such as log canoes and pirogues (large canoes of 40–50 feet in length and 6–8 feet wide), skiffs (wide, flat bottom small boats), and bateaus (large skiffs maneuvered by sweeps) transported people on shorter trips. Keelboats (a precursor of the canal boat) were used on every navigable waterway in the country to transport freight (ibid., 282). The barge was somewhat like the keelboat in design but much larger. Barges also were equipped with masts, sails, and a rudder. Downstream barges were powered by sail or by a crew who used sweeps to propel the vessel. For the time period, barges were quite swift. Some were clocked at four to five miles per hour with the current and two miles per hour against the current.

Businesspeople, government officials, and land speculators, for whom time was at a premium, used barges. To accommodate passengers, most barges offered some sort of enclosure to protect them from the elements. Many barges had small houses located in their centers for this purpose. When shoreline attacks were feared, the entire ark was completely covered by a flat top that had an opening for a cannon.

Unlike western water travel, eastern modes of water travel were undergoing a radical evolution. Commercial water travel, rather than travel for settlement and exploration, was of primary concern in the East. Boats and barges were in use, but these were considered too slow. Steam power was investigated and adapted to the waterway during this period with some success, although a cynical public harshly labeled its innovators and advocates as eccentrics and fools.

The first steamboat in America appeared on the Delaware River on August 22, 1787. In 1785 John Fitch (1743–1798) had exhibited his small brass model of a ship powered by steam. With the financial backing of a Philadelphia watchmaker, he was able to power a skiff based on the brass model. By 1789 Fitch improved and enlarged his steamboat. Later he built a larger steamboat, propelled by paddle wheels, designed to carry freight and passengers. This paddle-wheeled boat made regularly scheduled trips on the Delaware River between Philadelphia and Burlington, New Jersey, at the rate of eight miles per hour.

Although Fitch's steamboat was a mechanical success, it failed to make its inventor money, largely because he overlooked the importance of building and operating costs. As a result, Americans failed to see the monetary value of steam propulsion. Fitch's boat did, however, run as a passenger packet on the Delaware, eventually covering over one thousand miles (Dunbar, vol. 2, 350). Disappointingly, Fitch's invention was at best viewed as an oddity, at worst, as a folly.

In 1805, Oliver Evans (1755–1819) designed and constructed a steam-engine scow, which he christened the *Orukter Amphibolos* (meaning "amphibious digger"). It was able to move on land as well as water. The scow was, in brief, a steam dredge. Its steam-powered system of a chain of buckets was able to raise mud from the bottom of the river, allowing the dredge to navigate efficiently through muddy rivers. Evans transported the *Orukter Amphibolos* under its own power (it was equipped with wheels) to the Schuylkill River. Launched from the Schuylkill, it was propelled by a steam-driven paddle wheel to the Delaware River, arriving in Philadelphia. Because of its brief stint as a land vehicle, the *Orukter Amphibolos* was the first road locomotive in the United States.

The first truly functioning steamboat in America was the *Clermont*. Designed by American engineer Robert Fulton (1765–1815), the *Clermont* resembled a two-masted schooner powered by two side paddle wheels, each having a diameter of 15 feet. The *Clermont* was 133 feet in length and 18 feet wide and had a draft (depth of the keel below the water line) of 7 feet. Her steam engine had a 24-inch cylinder with a 4-foot stroke.

On August 7, 1807, the *Clermont* was ready for her maiden voyage. Scores of detractors lined the banks of the Hudson River to scoff at what was popularly known as "Fulton's Folly." To their wonderment, the *Clermont*, belching black smoke, headed upstream to Albany (a trip of 150 miles) at the astounding speed of five miles per hour. (Barges were capable of the five-miles-per-hour speed, but only with the current.) The *Clermont* successfully completed the trip from New York to Albany in a record 32 hours. (The commonly used sailing sloop took four days to complete the same trip.) Fulton's success soon began the era of steamboat building and navigation in the United States.

The sailing ship still predominated the high seas during this period. The strength of early nineteenth-century American shipping had its basis in the formative years of the early republic (Train, 249). While France and Great Britain were at war in the waning years of the eighteenth century (thus channeling their shipping efforts not into commerce but into warfare), the American shipping industry quickly took advantage of the need for commercial sea transport. American ships began to sail everywhere with great success. From 1787 to 1790, the *Columbia*, captained by Bostonian Robert Gray, circumnavigated the world. One result of this extraordinary voyage was that Gray discovered the river that bears his name on the West Coast, which helped established the U.S. claim to the Oregon Territory.[5]

Independence had radically affected the American shipping industry, with the end result being a flurry of industry. After the Revolution, the British government prohibited the United States all access to British (including British colonial) markets. New England was particularly hit hard by this new regulation. Prior to the Revolution, the port of Boston had been part of a significant shipping trade with Newfoundland. Worse yet, American trade with the West Indies was now completely cut off.

Enterprising New England and Mid-Atlantic shippers subsequently focused their efforts on establishing trade routes and agreements with Atlantic and Mediterranean islands. They looked to Mauritius and China as well. As early as August 1784, an American ship arrived in Canton, China, under the stars and stripes. (Its cargo was ginseng, a rare herb treasured by the Chinese. Ginseng grows in China and North America.) America's ginseng trade with China was so profitable that American traders were able to obtain tea and other products from the Chinese, at considerable additional profits (Boorstin, 8). By 1803, a sizable number of American cargo ships were trading throughout the world (Train, 250). In fact, American merchants were now directly competing against the formidable British East India Company for the world market. New England seafaring enterprises were so successful that in remote parts of the world Boston or New England, not the United States, was the name of the new nation (Boorstin, 9).

American traders now required ships that could be built, manned, and operated efficiently and economically. By the nineteenth century, the American shipbuilding industry seriously began to redesign ships, basing their designs on studies of sail propulsion. Because longer ships with larger sails were faster, Americans began to build longer and larger ships. When shipping perishable cargo, time was of the essence. The faster American ships were able to deliver perishables quicker and in fresher condition than European ships. In the early years of the nineteenth century, an Atlantic ship crossing took roughly three and a half weeks, a considerable waterway speed for the time. Every day that a ship could cut from its total travel time meant fresher cargo, therefore higher profits.

The American whaling industry also began to flourish at the turn of the century mainly because of the demand for sperm oil. The French had recently begun making sperm oil candles. Because the French were generally perceived as the arbiters of taste and style, wealthier classes throughout the world quickly adopted the French penchant for sperm oil candles. New England whalers promptly increased their efforts throughout the world to harvest the prized oil. More ships and crews were needed for the rapidly growing whaling industry. By 1800, Americans predominated the whaling market, hunting along the western South American coast as well as into Alaskan waters.

Likewise, the War of 1812 accelerated the shipbuilding industry's interest in designing and building even fleeter ships. The American navy, was small but it was formidable. Although the naval fleet consisted of seven frigates, a couple of corvettes (small, fast warships armed with a single tier of guns), and an insignificant number of brigs (two-masted sailing ships), the American navy was a match for the British, primarily because American seamen were professionals (Train, 250).

The small American navy was light and fast, which added to its capability. Unlike the heavy oak British frigates, the American frigates were planked with lightweight pine. Each American frigate carried 24–44 guns on a single flush deck and on the forecastle and quarterdecks (ibid.). They were also designed to roll easily, adding to their maneuverability.

The most renowned of the American frigates was (and is) the U.S.S. *Constitution*, better known as "Old Ironsides."[6] Launched in Boston on October 21, 1797, Old Ironsides has an impressive naval history. During the Tripolitan War (1801–1805), it served as the navy's flagship. Because of its flagship status, the peace treaty between the United States and the North African Barbary States was signed aboard the *Constitution*.

Old Ironsides was instrumental in one of the greatest of all American naval victories. On August 19, 1812, the ship and its crew scored a glorious victory over the British frigate *Guerrière*. Naval legend maintains that during this fierce battle, the British guns could not break through the sides of the *Constitution*, hence the new moniker Old Ironsides.

Old Ironsides was then a marvel of ship design. With a length of 204 feet, beam of 43.6 feet, draft of 23 feet aft, displacement of 2,200 tons, and a gun range of 1,200 yards, Old Ironsides proved to be an astounding opponent in war. Although her armament was made in England (originally 44 guns), Old Ironside's sheathing and fittings had a very American origin. Revolutionary War patriot Paul Revere produced the copper sheathing for the ship's bottom and the bolts used to fasten the timbers.

Ships were not used exclusively for commerce and warfare. They were also used for passenger transport. Travel to and from Europe could only be accomplished by the use of sailing ships. (American oceanic steam navigation did not appear until 1818 with the refitting and launching of the oceangoing *Savannah*.) Oceanic travel for passengers was slow, difficult, and often expensive. A transatlantic voyage usually took up to 12 weeks. Steerage passage (used by those of modest to lesser means) was hazardous. Steerage passengers were crammed into very small spaces (frequently less than four cubic feet per passenger). Conditions were filthy, leading to hundreds of passenger deaths due to smallpox, typhoid, and "ship fever" (Nye, *Cultural Life*, 122). Only those with money, position, expressed purpose, or who were immigrating to the new country braved the waters of the Atlantic.

One group of people had no choice in oceanic travel: Africans captured and transported to the New World to be sold as slaves. Lamentably, the new nation that commonly held that "all men are created equal, that they are endowed by their Creator with certain unalienable Rights, that among these are Life, Liberty, and the pursuit of Happiness" was still engaging in the trafficking of human beings. Some states—Connecticut, Delaware, Maryland, North Carolina, South Carolina, and Virginia—had passed laws prior to 1790 outlawing or discouraging the importation of slaves (Morgan, 97). Regrettably, the slave trade was in effect until 1807 when, as stipulated in Article 1, Section 9, of the Constitution, "migration or importation of such Persons [slaves] as any of the States now existing shall think proper to admit" would be prohibited. (There was a possible tax or duty on the importation of slaves at no more than $10 per person.)

Conditions on slave ships were so horrific that a sizable percentage of the human cargo did not live to reach the New World. The cargo hold was extremely crowded. Hygienic conditions were deplorable. Because of overcrowding and the subsequent filth, slave ships were rife with disease. Many African captives were physically abused. As a result, the mortality rate was high, within the 15–20 percent range.

In consequence, American oceanic transportation reflected the best and the worst of American initiative. As traders in the world marketplace, Americans were establishing themselves as astute and enterprising businesspeople. As shipbuilders and designers, they were regarded as innovative and resourceful. During the War of 1812 the American navy proved itself to be one of the powerful naval fleets in the world—while still being small. But as agents in the perpetuation of the slave trade, they contradicted the American ideal of a benevolent and virtuous society.

In its infancy, the United States was a republic that was shackled by a primitive transportation system. Due to its English colonial heritage, America was a country of poor roads, little urban planning, outmoded bridges, and a vast uncharted wilderness. Only after it had undergone a rapid expansion in territory, conducted a famed expedition, and engaged in another war with Great Britain could the United States begin to create what was to become an incomparable system of roads and waterways. The transportation revolution of the early nationalist period provided not only the impetus, but also the basis, for American travel to come.

# 12

# Visual Arts

Independence brought a self-awareness not seen before on the North American continent. Despite their many differences, the former colonies, at best a loose confederation of states that each promoted its own regional and secular interests, began to realize that they were now all Americans. With the emergence of a new nationality came an awareness of the need to establish a national culture, one that could immortalize, whether it would be in stone or on canvas, the events and the promise the Revolution had brought forth. In no other cultural form was this more evident than in the visual arts produced during the early nationalist period.

The production of an American visual art was patronized and encouraged not only by the established pre-Revolutionary aristocracy, but also by the populace at large whose fortunes had risen dramatically. Affluent merchants and businesspeople were no longer content to possess a few family portraits or engravings (O.W. Larkin, 109). Americans now desired to own art that exalted not only their recent glorious victory, but that also would establish an American identity. In painting, artists engaged in portraiture, as well as landscapes and still lifes that would embody Americana. Graphic artists reproduced the more popular paintings, making them accessible to more of the citizenry. Sculptors immortalized statesmen and heroes of the Revolution. Finally, the country's interest in folk (or popular) art grew exponentially during this time.

# PAINTING AND THE ARTISTS OF THE EARLY REPUBLIC

Painters in the early republic faced two crucial obstacles in promoting their craft. First, up until this time the majority of American citizenry had had little or no interest in professional painting, and second, there was very little formal instruction available to aspiring professional painters in the United States (R. Hughes, 70). Many of the more successful painters, such as Benjamin West, John Singleton Copley, Charles Willson Peale, and John Trumbull, were initially self-taught. (Only later, under the tutelage of West in London, did Copley, Peale, and Trumbull receive any formal instruction.) American professional painters were at a disadvantage but produced art of true merit, despite the limitations of instruction.

## Benjamin West

Not surprising, American painting in the early republic was predominated by the influence of an American who spent nearly his entire professional career in England. A native Philadelphian and product of a Quaker home, Benjamin West (1738–1820) became a powerful influence on the development of English and American painting. An intimate of George III (he served as "Painter to the King" from 1772 to 1801), West helped found the Royal Academy of Art (1768), and succeeded Sir Joshua Reynolds as president of the Royal Academy in 1792.

Mainly an expatriate (although throughout his life West declared himself an American), West was the teacher and mentor of a group of American artists whose names read like a "Who's Who" of early American republican painting. Among his students were John Singleton Copley, perhaps the finest American painter of the time; Charles Willson Peale, portraitist, naturalist, and museum curator; Rembrandt Peale, painter, writer, and son of Charles Willson Peale; Gilbert Stuart, the best portraitist on the American continent; John Trumbull, the historical painter; and Washington Allston, author and first American Romantic painter. With students of such merit, it is no wonder that sometimes West is referred to as the "Father of American Painting" (ibid., 81).

A showman of the first order, West was a naturally gifted artist. By the age of 18, West was being hired as a portraitist in his native land. Self-taught with no serious works of art to study as models (West had to resort to learning from limner portraits, engravings, and inn signs), he was eventually noticed by the provost of the College of Philadelphia, Dr. William Smith. Soon he realized that he had no chance to grow as an artist without studying the old masters—and those were in Europe (ibid., 71). He also hoped to perfect his skill in the neoclassicist style, a prevalent late eighteenth-century movement that emphasized austere linear designs and classical themes. (Neoclassicism, unlike the concurrent Romantic movement, favored line over effects of light, color, and atmosphere.) So he saved his money and at age 22 West sailed for Rome.

In Rome, West quickly was able to network with some of the leading neoclassical art theorists and practitioners of the day, Johann Winckelmann and Anton Raphael Mengs. Mengs especially took great interest in the young Quaker. He outlined a rigorous course of study for West: study and sketch the best paintings in Rome; then visit Florence, Venice, Parma, and, Bologna; and finally return to Rome to paint a historical subject because, according to Mengs, history paintings were the true test of the artist (ibid., 73). Eventually, West would be renowned as England's chief historical painter and would pass on his technique to aspiring young American painters.

The *cognoscenti* (leading authorities on art) assessed West's early work as being limited in draftsmanship, but superb in painting. Because he was handicapped by imperfect drawing skills, West compensated by simplifying contours and adhering to the tenets of neoclassical style (ibid.). West revolutionized historical painting by depicting historical heroes in contemporary dress, a departure from the traditional convention of draping heroes in the togas of ancient Greece and Rome. In the late eighteenth century such a different approach shocked the art world. This new narrative style, which greatly dramatized subjects taken from contemporary events, profoundly influenced American painters, especially West's students Charles Willson Peale and John Trumbull.

By 1768 his work had attracted the notice of George III, with whom he would engage in a 30-year friendship. Undeniably, West's loyalties during the Revolution remained with his sovereign—despite his American heritage (and often the American subject matter in his paintings). As a prime example of his Tory leanings, in 1776 West painted George III with redcoated soldiers embattled in the background.

Political issues did not deter West from his pursuit of augmenting his already impressive reputation. After the Treaty of Paris (1783), West, ever the opportunist, planned a series of paintings that would glorify the American Revolution. After falling out of George III's favor in 1800 (in an unrelated matter), West even had the audacity to offer his services to Vice President Jefferson as the creator and designer of a memorial to the late George Washington. (West believed that only he had the talent and vision to complete such a project.) There is no record of Jefferson's response, leaving prominent art historian, Robert Hughes, to conclude that for once "Jefferson was at a loss for words" (80).

West's later work, notably *Death on a Pale Horse* (1796), deviates from the neoclassical style he once promoted and taught. *Death on a Pale Horse* is a prime example of English Romanticism, a style that emphasized the imaginative, emotional, subjective, and spontaneous. A depiction of a verse from Revelations,[1] *Death on a Pale Horse* epitomizes Romanticism with its lack of restraint, brilliant colors, diabolic atmosphere, and dramatic shift of light and dark. West's venture into Romanticism also impacted the painters who followed him. The great French Romanticist Eugène Delacroix many years later would return to West's sketches for inspiration and example. Many of West's American students embraced this later style because the subject and theme of the American Revolution lent itself easily to the Romantic realism interpreted by West.

## John Singleton Copley

Arguably West's greatest American pupil was John Singleton Copley (1738–1815), who some say exceeded the skill and artistry of the master. Copley, like West, in due course left his native America for England never to return. (Copley left for political reasons. His in-laws, the Clarkes of Boston, were well-known Tories. Both Copley and his father-in-law, Richard Clarke, were involved in the Boston Tea Party—on the Tory side. Clarke was the importer of the despised tea that had been thrown into Boston Harbor. Copley ineffectually negotiated with the Sons of Liberty over the tea duty.)

Self-taught, Copley became Boston's premier portraitist prior to the Revolutionary War. His finely wrought realistic portraits of Americans demonstrated his scrupulous attention to detail and his use of *portrait d'apparat* (the portrayal of the subject with objects associated with his or her life). Portrait d'apparat and sharpness of line set his work above all other American painters of the time. Copley's early American portraits show an energy and insight usually not found in eighteenth-century American painting. (Oddly enough, West criticized Copley's work as being too "liney"—which, of course, is its vital element.) Copley painted both Tory and patriot alike—and for substantial fees. He was the first American painter to become a financial and artistic success in his native land.

Once in England, Copley studied with West and became entranced by the grand style of subject matter and style that had swept Europe. Later, he turned to large historical painting—much as West had done—as his subject matter. His depiction of *The Death of Chatham* (1779–1781) was enormously popular with the British public, and incited the jealousy and resentment of English artists. His *Repulse of the Floating Batteries at Gibraltar* (1791) began the American propensity for large canvases (it measured 25' × 25', large even by today's standards).

Copley's work in England grew more academically complex in comparison to his American colonial portraits. The later portraits and grandiose histories produced in England lacked the vitality and realism that marked his Boston portraiture. Even though his physical and mental health declined in his later years, Copley's English career was quite successful until the last several months before his death in 1815.

## Charles Willson Peale

If West was the Father of American Painting and Copley the financial and artistic American success story, then Charles Willson Peale (1741–1827) was the progenitor of not only a dynasty of American painters but of Americans' ascendancy in the arts. Also self-taught, Peale was always a pragmatist. He firmly believed that painting could be learned just as one could learn other crafts. (Peale also taught himself saddle making, watchmaking, and silversmithing. A man of many skills, Peale also ventured into dentistry, making a set of false teeth for his friend George Washington. He also dabbled in archaeology.) After an introduction to Copley, he learned of Benjamin West's London studio. By 1766, Peale had persuaded the Maryland governor and some members of the governor's council to send him to London so that he could learn from the ex-Pennsylvanian master.

Unlike Copley and West, Peale was an ardent patriot and a democrat even at a young age. Legend has it that Peale refused to doff his hat as the coach of George III went by. After his three-year sojourn with West, Peale returned to America and settled in Philadelphia. During the Revolutionary War, Peale served honorably under Washington in the Trenton-Princeton Campaign and at Valley Forge.

The Revolutionary War was the making of Peale's career (R. Hughes, 96). Prior to the war, Peale was a relatively successful portraitist. The war, however, inspired Peale as far as subject matter, theme, and agenda. Unlike other painters, he had been a part of the war and knew its heroes (Washington, Lafayette, and their aides), who would become the icons of the new republic. The battles would be the source of epic dramas. Subsequently, Peale's paintings commemorating the battles were documentary in nature. As splendid and stalwart as he might depict the Revolutionary heroes, Peale saw no reason not to include the carnage of war in the scenes. Thus antiromantic scenes frame the glorious heroes, adding to their courageous stature.

Within his lifetime, Peale painted approximately 1,100 portraits, among these his personal friends: George Washington, John Adams, Benjamin Franklin, and Thomas Jefferson. (Not a small feat since Adams saw painting as having little value, adhering to a puritanical mind-set against the arts.) Peale, through his portraiture, embarked on deifying Washington in oils. Washington himself sat for Peale seven times, all of which were reproduced by Peale many times over. His most famous

Washington portrait, *Washington at the Battle of Princeton, January 3, 1777* (1784), is a full-length depiction of the general with sword unsheathed, heroic and imposing. (And perhaps Peale's decision to depict Washington as a warrior was because Washington in full military regalia sold better than Washington in civilian dress.)

Peale was not content just to immortalize the heroes and statesmen of the Revolution. He also produced a number of public shows in Philadelphia that were enormously popular with Americans. Among some of the more well received features was a float that portrayed the traitor Benedict Arnold (complete with two faces) being paid off by the devil, a statue of Washington rigged with a descending laurel wreath, and illuminated "moving pictures" of war scenes, such as John Paul Jones's naval victory over the Serapis (ibid., 99). The latter, exhibited in his studio in 1785, featured undulating waves, cannon fire, and shimmering moonlight.

In 1782 Peale wished to establish a public gallery to house his portraits of Revolutionary heroes. By 1787 he expanded his gallery to include displays of American fauna. The Peale Museum (as it was known) was intended to foster the study of natural history. His purpose, he asserted, was "to bring into one view a world in miniature" (qtd. in ibid.). The museum was rapidly imitated by other museum curators and, in the nineteenth century, by P.T. Barnum.

But the Peale Museum was more than a mere sideshow. Peale's intent was to inspire public virtue through the study of nature (ibid.). He declared "as this is an age of discovery, every experiment that brings to light the properties of natural substances helps to expand the mind and make men better, more virtuous and liberal; and, what is of infinite importance in our country, creates a fondness for finding the treasure contained in the bowels of the earth that might otherwise be lost" (qtd. in ibid.).

He immortalized in oils his most famous excavation. *The Exhumation of the Mastodon* (1806) documented this extraordinary find. The work celebrates technology (a water-bailing machine) and the historic discovery of the prehistoric beast. In the lower right-hand corner Peale and his children hold a sizable artist's rendering of a mastodon femur. This symbolically depicts Peale's assertion that his family will continue his natural discoveries, perpetuating the American search for integrity and liberality.

Peale's legacy went beyond his creation of a museum, promotion of the natural sciences, and veneration of American heroes and events in oils. The father of ten children—Rembrandt, Rubens, Titian, Raphaelle, Angelica Kaufman, Sophonisba Anguissola, and Titian II[2]—Peale named most of them after famous painters. Eight of his children, his brother James (1749–1831), a nephew, four nieces, and three grandchildren became practicing artists. In his famous trompe l'oeil ("fool the eye") paint-

**Portrait of Thomas Jefferson by Rembrandt Peale. Courtesy of the Library of Congress.**

ing, *The Staircase Group* (1795), Peale visually proclaimed that he was passing along his "business" to his sons.

*The Staircase Group* is a life-size portrait of his sons Raphaelle (1774–1825) and Titian (1799–1881). Raphaelle, holding a palette and maulstick (a long wooden stick used to support the brush hand), looks backward from the lower staircase. Titian looks out from up above. To complete the illusion of reality, Peale originally framed the canvas in a doorjamb and nailed on a wooden step. The fool-the-eye technique was so effective that it was said that when Washington encountered the painting, he tipped his hat to the young Peales.

## Rembrandt Peale

The most accomplished of Peale's sons, Rembrandt (1778–1860), had a long and prosperous career. After studying with his father, he left for London to study with Benjamin West (truly following the family tradition). After his return from Europe, he quickly became in demand as a portraitist in the new republic. Rembrandt Peale's most superb work is his portrait *Thomas Jefferson* (1805). Jefferson at the time of the sitting was 62 and now president. Peale's rendition aptly captures Jefferson's intellect and humanity (O.W. Larkin, 117). No glorified icon is this depiction. Jefferson's eyes gleam with intelligence and sagacity. Many art historians consider Rembrandt Peale's portrait of the third president the finest of its subject in existence.

Rembrandt Peale also engaged in the Washington iconography that his father employed and promoted. Rembrandt churned out 65 portraits of the Father of the Country, the most famous of these being the *Porthole Portrait* (1795), which depicts the great hero of the Republic in a head and shoulders pose, resolutely gazing out of a stone oculus. Peale actively promoted the *Porthole Portrait*, painting 76 replicas of it within his lifetime. His ultimate hope was that the *Porthole Portrait* would be the definitive depiction of the noble hero.

## Gilbert Stuart

Another artist's work would be permanently acknowledged as the recipient of that honor, a portraitist whose career relied almost solely on Washington as his subject matter. Gilbert Stuart (1755–1828) was known to have painted 114 portraits of the great national icon, 111 of these as variations of three sittings (R. Hughes, 127). The most famous of these is the Athenaeum head (1796), the source of Washington's likeness on the one-dollar bill. Eventually, Stuart would reproduce the Athenaeum head 60 times. Unabashedly, he referred to these versions as his "hundred-dollar bills" (qtd. in ibid.).

Like other successful painters of the period, Stuart studied under West in London. A quick study and an enterprising young artist, Stuart was able in the 1780s to set out on his own as a portrait painter with some success. The English found his dignified, graceful portraitures to be highly flattering, thus desirable. Unfortunately, by 1792 Stuart, who was as infamous for his profligacy and immorality as he was famous for his skill and artistry, had to flee his creditors by returning to America.

Stuart was unequivocally the finest American portraitist of the Federal style (ibid., 130). Almost immediately upon his return to America, Stuart assumed the role of America's premier portraitist (since neither West nor Copley ever returned to the United States). His commissions from affluent Americans attest to his skill and technique. Stuart astutely recognized and accommodated the republican desire to be immortalized in delicate flesh tones and elegant and graceful poses. Stuart's technique was a relatively simple one: He eschewed preliminary sketches, preferring to block in large masses with color. The palette he employed had few colors, basically vermilion, white, and lake (for skin tones), a mixture for

Engraving of Gilbert Stuart's portrait of George Washington (Athenaeum head). Courtesy of the Library of Congress.

shadows, and another for reflections (O.W. Larkin, 121). In due course the blocked-in study would evolve into the finished detailed portrait of gentle movement from dark to light.

## John Trumbull

Portraiture was the most popular form of painting in the new nation. Despite some ventures into historical paintings and still life, American painters were primarily portraitists. However, John Trumbull (1756–1843) was one of the few of West's protégés who was not transfixed by portraiture (although he had to resort to it for income while he was composing his monumental historical paintings). Instead, Trumbull truly

Portrait of James Madison by Gilbert Stuart.
Courtesy of the Library of Congress.

became the painter/recorder of the Revolution. A scion of a prestigious Connecticut family, Trumbull was continually beset by doubts as to the legitimacy of his chosen profession. (Within his lifetime, Trumbull had other careers, most particularly as John Jay's secretary during the settling of the Jay Treaty.) Trumbull did, nonetheless, overcome his reservations as to the suitability of painting as a career for a gentleman's son. In 1789 he wrote to Jefferson, stating

The greatest motives I had . . . for continuing my pursuit of painting has [*sic*] been the wish of commemorating the great events of our country's revolution. I am fully sensible that the profession, as it is generally practiced, is frivolous. . . . But, to preserve and diffuse the memory of the noblest of series of actions which have e'er presented themselves to the history of man; . . . [and to preserve] the personal resemblance of those who have been the great actors in those illustrious scenes, were objects which gave a dignity to the profession, peculiar to my situation. (See R. Hughes, 132)

Trumbull's historical paintings are the ones that adorn the rotunda in the Capitol for which he received the commission at age 62. Trumbull had to lobby long and hard for this commission. John Adams had tried to dissuade Trumbull, insisting that there was "no disposition to celebrate or remember, or even Curiosity to enquire into the Characters Actions or Events of the Revolution" (see ibid., 134). Fortunately, Congress did not share Adams's misgivings and Trumbull was awarded the commission in 1817.

Trumbull's best-known painting, *The Declaration of Independence, 4 July 1776* (1787–1820) is an ambitious work. In an effort to record history faithfully, Trumbull spent years tracking down 36 of the 47 signers so that he could chronicle them from life. (Early in the creation of the painting, Trumbull was fortunate enough to have Thomas Jefferson, John Adams, and Benjamin Franklin sit for him. Only after 1790 did he embark on his hunt for the remaining signers.) From Jefferson (a wholehearted supporter of historical painting) he received the floor plan and architectural details of the Assembly Room in the Pennsylvania State House (renamed Independence Hall) in Philadelphia. The result was an accurate but lively, colorful depiction of the great moment in American history.

### Washington Allston

The first American painter to explore the full range of art was Washington Allston (1779–1843), another student of West's. (Not only did Allston's painting demonstrate a versatility of form—portraits, still lifes, histories, landscapes—but he ventured into other arts as well: sculpture, poetry, novel writing, and art theory.) Allston is known for his spectacular subject matter, his dramatic employment of light and dark, and his atmospheric color. (His landscapes, in particular, are Romantic depictions of the powerful and rugged landscape of the new nation.) Most important, Allston's landscapes heavily influenced the work of visionary painters to come. The western expansionistic movement in the subsequent years would lead to the rise of American landscape painting, a form that owes much to the skill and vision of Washington Allston. Romanticism and nationalism would become encapsulated in the rendering of the wild and dramatic landscape.

## GRAPHIC ARTS: WORKS FOR THE MASSES

Graphic arts (reproductions of portraits and landscapes) flourished during the early nationalist period. Reproductions afforded the less affluent the opportunity to own art that immortalized heroes of the new nation and that celebrated the beauty of the land. Engravings could also be found in magazines of the day, not simply as illustrations but as prints

*Franklin* by Charles Willson Peale. Courtesy of the
Library of Congress.

that might be taken out and framed. Now every working household
could own copies of Charles Willson Peale's *Franklin* (1787) and Benjamin
West's *Angel of the Resurrection* (1801).

The first types of graphic art employed in these early years of the
republic were that of line engraving and a similar technique known as
mezzotint. Line engraving consists of reproducing prints from metal
plates onto which a drawing has been scored with a burin, a cutting tool
used especially for the process. In line engraving reproduction is made
only by linear marks. Crosshatching creates light and shadow.

Mezzotint (from the Italian meaning "half tint"), like line engraving,
uses metal plates as its medium. However, in mezzotinting the plate is
methodically perforated with small holes. These holes hold the ink.
When printed, the mezzotint plate produces significant areas of shading.

In 1798 Alois Senefelder of Munich invented lithography (a form
where a drawing is made directly on stone; "lithos" is Greek for
"stone").[3] Soon afterward, a few lithographs appeared in America

**Mezzotint of theatergoers. Courtesy of the
Library of Congress.**

(Green, 172). Eventually, lithography would become the most fashionable form of graphic art in subsequent years.

Woodcutting (the design is engraved on the plane of the grain of
wood) and wood engraving (the design is engraved on the end grain of
wood) were the most popular forms of graphic art in late eighteenth-
and early nineteenth-century America. Both woodcutting and wood engraving rendered a bold, almost primitive, visual style and were often
used in almanacs and broadsides, as they had been in the colonial period
(ibid.). As Americans became more sophisticated in their artistic preferences and tastes, other engraving forms eventually superceded woodcutting and engraving. On the frontier, however, these were still
immensely popular, so much so that woodcuts and wood engravings
became folk art (ibid., 173).

During the Revolution unrefined engravings had lent themselves well to the political satire found in broadsides and magazines. After the Revolution as political tensions mounted and hero worship became the order of the day, the engravings became a medium for cartoon illustration. Illustrators such as James Akin lampooned political figures of the period. Portraitist and miniaturist John Wesley Jarvis (1781–1840) created the first newspaper illustration of congressional repeal of the Embargo Act of 1807. Another illustrator, Elkanah Tisdale, produced the drawings used in the poet John Trumbull's rollicking burlesque of Tory philosophy, *M'Fingal* (1775–1782), a best-seller in its day.[4] (As a testament to its popularity, *M'Fingal* appeared in over 30 pirated editions, often in newspapers, chapbooks, and broadsides. Thus, Tisdale's illustrations were probably seen and enjoyed by a large and varied audience.)

Yet it was in the reproduction of portraits and landscapes in which early graphic artists truly excelled. Reproductions of famous works often revealed skillful renderings of the originals. More important, the engravings of the artists of the original into metal or stone beyond a doubt demonstrate Americans' deft handling of the form. Charles Willson Peale's mezzotints of his earlier portraits of Washington (1780) and Franklin (1787) and the middling painter Edward Savage's engraving of his *The Washington Family* (1798) are highly competent in execution (ibid.). West's lithograph of his *Angel of the Resurrection* (the first by an American) further exhibits his inventiveness and willingness to take new risks.

Landscape and architectural engravings, many times composed by the artist of the original drawing or painting, were frequently more innovative than a mere reproduction (ibid.). Of special note are a series of Philadelphia scenes by William Birch (1755–1844) and his son Thomas (1779–1851), both landscapists of some repute. The Birches' engravings—notably the *Bank of the United States, Philadelphia* (1789) and *Congress Hall and New Theatre* (1800)—exhibit a subtlety of radiance and texture that are unsurpassed by any others of the period (ibid.).

## SCULPTURE

The fine art of sculpture in the new nation was more or less imported or created by foreign artists, instead of being a product of American sculptors (ibid., 174). The only two Americans who could be classified as sculptors—Samuel McIntire of Salem, Massachusetts, and William Rush of Philadelphia—worked primarily in wood, rather than stone. McIntire and Rush, unlike their counterparts who sculpted in marble or stone, were considered by their contemporaries as more artisan than fine artist. (Even native sculptors regarded themselves as artisans.)

There existed a distinct aesthetic bias toward stone sculpture over the more rustic use of wood. As president, Jefferson insisted that building ornamentation and statuary for the new capital be carved in stone, not wood. Because native-born sculptors preferred wood, Americans were in a quandary: Who could immortalize the Republic's noble past in the traditional means of statuary and how would this be accomplished?

On the whole, the statues produced during this time were commissioned—and those commissions were given to foreign artists. Italian and French sculptors swarmed the United States in their desire to take part in creating a grand legacy in marble and stone. Jefferson himself led the call for accomplished sculptors of marble and stone, giving preference to foreign-born sculptors whose work was neoclassical in style and thought.

The first American political statue of distinction was Jean-Antoine Houdon's (1741–1828) life-size *General Washington* (signed, 1788) (R. Hughes, 123). Jefferson, on behalf of the Virginia legislature, had commissioned Houdon to capture the greatness of the general in marble. Accompanied to the United States by Benjamin Franklin, the French sculptor sketched Washington and measured his head in preparation for the final work. The result is a magnificent representation of democracy hewn in stone.

Houdon's *General Washington* is not the typical eighteenth-century interpretation of a statesman. In accordance with Jefferson's instructions, the statue is life-size, not bigger-than-life. Even though he is dressed in military uniform, Washington is not depicted as a triumphant commander, but, rather, as an American Cincinnatus, the legendary Roman hero called from his farm to lead the Republic and deliver the army (ibid., 124). Like Cincinnatus, Washington, too, was called from his farm to lead an army and a new republic. Both, after honorable service, chose to return to their farms rather than bask in the glory that a grateful public offered them.

*General Washington* epitomizes the concept of Roman republican character. Houdon sculpted Washington leaning on the Roman symbol of authority, the fasces (a bundle of rods bound together with an ax)—in this case there are 13 rods, one for each state of the Union. No longer a man of war, now a man of peace, the Washington effigy's sword is enclosed in its scabbard. The plow behind him signifies not only agrarian integrity, but also the sowing of a new political order (ibid., 125).

The decorative carving of the Capitol was entrusted to the chisels of foreigners as well. Italian Giuseppe Franzoni was commissioned to carve the eagle over the Speaker of the House's chair. (Franzoni was also the sculptor of the distinctive corncob columns of the Capitol.) Another Italian, Giovanni Andrei, labored on the 24 Corinthian capitals of the House of Representatives.

Native sculptors did produce works of aesthetic merit, although they were not in keeping with Jefferson's conception of what the appropriate medium for sculpture was. Thus they were precluded in offering their skill and aesthetics in the great movement to create a New Athens out of marble. By the turn of the century, America had, nonetheless, produced sculptors of note—even if their primary medium was wood.

One of the first artisans making the transition to artist was the architect Samuel McIntire (1737–1811). Besides being a fairly competent purveyor of Adamesque architecture, he was an adept carver of decorative relief. Often cited for excellence and refinement are his reliefs in Salem homes: the fluted pilasters, sheaves of wheat, and baskets of fruit and flowers (O.W. Larkin, 100). His contemporaries acknowledged his expertise. On his tombstone was engraved, "He was distinguished for Genius in Architecture, Sculpture, and Musick" (see ibid.).

The first American sculptor whose work was regarded as artistically meritorious was William Rush (1756–1833). Originally trained as a wood-carver of ship figureheads and ornamentation, he became a sculptor of national note. He was a great proponent of neoclassicism, which he incorporated in his vision of a republic symbolized in wood. Many of his carvings demonstrate a grace and vigor never before seen in American sculpture. Indeed, his sculptures demonstrate a keen mastery of the human form. Rush was, foremost, a proponent of artistry over mere craftsmanship. He was known to despair over his apprentices' inattentiveness to the human figure, stating, "When I see my boys bungling in the carving of a hand, I tell them, Look at your own hands, . . . imitate them and you must be right" (see ibid., 103). Such accuracy can be found in his own works. Although his medium was wood, Rush was more artist than artisan. He saw himself as a teacher and promoter of American sculpture. In 1805, as an outgrowth of his desire to advance American art, Rush became one the founders of the Pennsylvania Academy of Fine Arts.

Many of his wood sculptures were allegorical, notably *Water Nymph and Bittern* (replaced by a bronze casting of the original wooden sculpture as the *Nymph of the Schuylkill*), *Comedy and Tragedy* (1808), and *Justice and Wisdom*. His works populated Philadelphia, then considered to be the American Athens. *Water Nymph and Bittern* stood beside Latrobe's Pump House, *Comedy and Tragedy* overlooked the Chestnut Street Theater, and *Justice and Wisdom* adorned the arch that honored Lafayette. Rush's interpretation of the American eagle (perched atop the Hibernia Company's fire engine) contrasted sharply with the more famous one above the seat of the Speaker of the House. Rush's eagle was one of ferocity, whereas the House version appears insipid in comparison (ibid.). His life-size *George Washington* (1814), inspired by Houdon, graces Independence Hall to this day.

Younger American sculptors were venturing into other media than wood. The painter and inventor of the Morse code, Samuel F.B. Morse (1791–1872), sometimes made three-dimensional forms to be used as models for his paintings. His plaster *Dying Hercules* (1812) was awarded the gold medal by the Adelphi Society in London. The Hellenistic *Dying Hercules* displays a decided neoclassical inclination, but one that is dynamic. This early work is notable not only for its promise, but for its influence on the work of commendable sculptors of a later period, Morse's contemporaries: John Frazee (1790–1852), Hezikiah Auger (1791–1858), and John Henri Isaac Browere (1792?–1834).

Frazee, in particular, eventually excelled at sculpting in marble and stone. The sculptor renowned for later superb neoclassical marble busts began his career as a stonecarver. During the War of 1812, Frazee embarked on a career as the carver of tombstones. By 1815 he completed his first stone figure—probably the first native stone figure (ibid.). An allegorical figure of "Grief," Frazee's stone figure tenderly leans on the grave urn of his firstborn son.

The work of sculptors such as Morse, Frazee, Auger, and Browere came to fruition in the years following the early nationalist period. Within this time period, only Rush is considered the first sculptor who was an artist, rather than a craftsman (Green, 175). The works of other sculptors during this period fall under another category: popular or folk art.

## POPULAR AND FOLK ART: AMERICAN ARTISANS AND THE NATURE OF ART

After the Revolution, popular art almost instantly commemorated the Americans' victory over the British. Unmistakable liberty motifs flooded the marketplace, among these the American eagle, the Goddess of Liberty, and the "Cap of Liberty" (a Phygian cap on a pole, beneath which flew the American flag) (R. Hughes, 123). Ironically, English companies that marketed them quickly for an American public hungry for liberty curios produced most of these artifacts.

Although the English monopolized the market for Revolutionary curios, American artisans and amateur artists (that is, the nonacademic artists) produced works that celebrated independence and an American way of life. Sign painters, wood-carvers, and carvers of ship figureheads were diligent and industrious in the creation of their works. Wooden inn and trade signs were carved and then painted by adept craftsmen. Wood carvings varied from household utensils to rude busts and small statuary. Ship figurehead carvings were, however, the hallmark of the craft of the period.

Even though very few are still in existence, ship figureheads were carved with great skill and imagination. In the few extant examples, the carver's knowledge and manipulation of his medium are evidenced.

Carvers took advantage of the intricacies of the wood grain to enhance the modeling of the figure. William Rush's figureheads were so deftly conceived and carved that his contemporaries said, "They seem rather to draw the ship after them than to be impelled by the vessel" (qtd. in Green, 174). Unfortunately, the environment was not conducive to longevity.

Fortunately, one form of carving from this period does exist today. Gravestone cuttings attest to the artistry and skill of cutters of the early republic. The best carvings were produced in New England, an area where the carving tradition was firmly ingrained in the Yankee psyche (ibid., 177). Exquisite gravestone carvings were (and are) not limited to the larger cities such as Boston or New Haven. In fact, some of the most original post-Revolutionary carvings can be found in more isolated, rural New England areas (ibid.). Elaborate lettering and precision characterize these carvings, and many are almost baroque in style. The colonial gravestone cutters used English conventions in creating their monuments— and many post-Revolutionary cutters followed this tradition. But Connecticut cutters, in particular, deviated from the convention. These carvers' works are perhaps the finest examples of folk art, their carvings characterized by bold ornamental forms, graceful lettering, and precision.

Women, in their efforts to become good Republican Mothers, expressed themselves with brush and needle. Although home decorative art is often regarded as amateurish (that is, untrained), this was not necessarily the case during the early years of the republic. Often these mothers and their daughters were highly trained in their respective crafts (Little, 68). Many women underwent formal instruction in needlework and painting. Over 40 years prior to the end of the Revolution, newspapers ran ads for instruction in the domestic crafts. Private schools abounded in the teaching of needlework, particularly in the larger coastal cities (ibid., 69).

American women were proficient in their needlework. Landscapes— either copied from engravings or drawn from actual American scenes— were often delicately shaded in silk floss. (Many of these were "chimney pieces," works that hung over the fireplace.) Others were stitched in "cruells" (the eighteenth-century term for crewel, a loosely twisted worsted yarn). The designs for these were drawn on the fabric from patterns imported from London (ibid.).

By the end of the eighteenth century, painting rather than needlework (although needlework did remain a popular medium for women artists) became women's primary medium for expression (ibid., 70). The rise of the female finishing school or academy was instrumental in this shift of media. In March 1793, an enterprising instructor, Samuel Folwell, advertised in the *Pennsylvania Packet* his drawing school for the young women of Philadelphia. Folwell's 30 students were divided into three classes, with each class meeting three-and-a-half days per week (tuition was $8 per quarter). The young women were offered art instruction in the following subjects: pencil work; painting on satin, paper, or ivory; and work in human hair (ibid., 81). Other communities soon followed suit, providing local drawing schools for interested women. Well-to-do women were given individual home instruction.

Female academies also instructed students in the visual arts. The dramatist and novelist Susanna Haswell Rowson advertised in the November 1797 *Columbian Centinel* (Boston) that she "purposes instructing young ladies in Reading, Writing, Arithmetic, Geography and needlework" (qtd. in ibid., 75). By 1803 Rowson expanded the curriculum to include (at an extra charge) a course entitled "Painting and Drawing, Flowers, Landscapes and Figures."

Beautifully and skillfully wrought paintings and needlework were not the only art forms at which women excelled. Often the very frames that adorned paintings, drawings, and needlework were constructed, gilded, and matted by the artist who created them. (Women from wealthy families usually employed a professional framer to mat and frame the decorative hanging.) Women also used their artistic skills to decorate furniture and domestic accessories (such as fans, sewing boxes, and glove boxes) (ibid., 81). Many of the latter were covered in plain paper, then painted or stenciled with floral borders, shells (a favorite motif of this period), or elaborate landscapes in color. Furniture, while presenting a more ambitious challenge, was also ornamented by the brushes of skillful women artisans (although some were also rendered by professional decorators). Many times the furniture piece had matching boxes for apparel items, such as a glove box (ibid., 84). Painted motifs (often landscapes or shell borders) on the primary furniture piece were painstakingly echoed on the accessory boxes.

These delicate and impressive designs were not, however, original. Young women art students and practitioners, whether by pen, brush, or needle, were expected to focus on the quality of reproduction, not the originality of design. Numerous design books were imported from Britain and published in the United States. The designs were derivative of the work of English instructors, consequently leading to a preponderance of works that featured thatched cottages, castles, ruins, stone bridges, and waterwheels (reflecting English, not American, landscapes) (ibid., 88). "Mourning pictures" (memorials to beloved departed relatives) were also quite popular, relying on European stereotypical motifs, such as weeping willows, tombstones, and bereaved maidens inclining over funeral urns (Green, 176). As beautifully executed as it was, American domestic art was decidedly British in its conception.

In contrast, the folk art of the Pennsylvania Germans was original and inspired. As their fortunes increased because of their work ethic and husbandry skills, this resilient immigrant community began to develop a distinctive art and craft tradition. Just as the Pennsylvania Germans refused to give up their native language, almost oblivious to the American acculturation forces, they also declined to follow the more Anglo art tradition that permeated the former colonies. (Pennsylvania German art did not include sculpture and painting. Rather, their work was decorative in nature.) They adorned their countryside homes and farms with a distinctive body of art whose origins were adapted from their native Rhineland. Furniture, buildings, ceramics, textiles, and even manuscripts were embellished with German motifs of vines, flowers (usually tulips), and hearts. Eventually, the eagle of the republic became a popular motif in Pennsylvania German art and craft as well.

The calligraphy of documents (called "fraktur") was almost medieval in design (McLanathan, 102). Fraktur was evident in all important documents, from certificates of marriage to house blessings. By and large, Pennsylvania German folk art has a straightforward and intentional charm as evidenced by the fraktur. The motifs are highly stylized and are used to express a pleasant domesticity.

Even their outer buildings were decorated with this stylized art. Hex signs, usually a round emblem painted on a barn, still dot the Pennsylvania Delaware Valley today. Hex signs were embellished with colorful, minimal floral and geometric motifs. The Pennsylvania German hex sign served two fundamental purposes: as a talisman to protect the farm animals from the "evil eye" or witchcraft (such as disease) and as a means to brighten the surroundings.

The Pennsylvania Germans were not the only people who expressed their creativity in craft and decoration. Citizens of the republic intricately carved household objects (such as utensils, receptacles for cutlery, farm implements, weathervanes, etc.). Many of these more homey implements demonstrate an attention to detail and skill that raise their worth above that of utility to that of pure craftsmanship (Little, 48). Pewter ware was fashioned by professional artisans, but often wood utensils were carved by ordinary people to supplement their metal utensils.

Although at the turn of the century Americans preferred to import china and ceramics from abroad, Americans did become involved in the making of ceramics, especially in New England. Potters created sundry pieces of red earthenware that were characterized by vivid glazes, whimsical decorations, and cheery sgraffito designs (decoration scratched through a layer of glazing to reveal a different color underneath) (ibid., 161). Both imported and domestic pottery and china, however, were designed to appeal to the public's wish for products that were decorated with a patriotic theme, a theme that predominated both fine and popular art of the period.

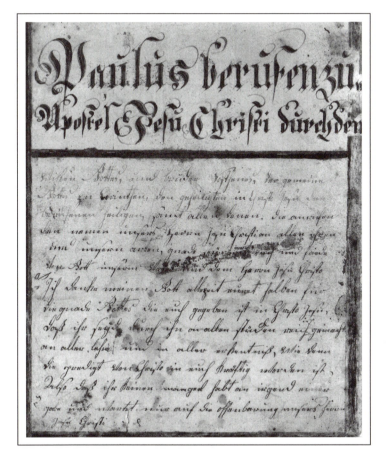

**Fraktur of I Corinthians. Courtesy of the Library of Congress.**

The popular or folk artist had become a significant factor in the evolution of an American art tradition (McLanathan, 104). Domestic art was a reflection of the citizenry's preference and expression of patriotism and an idealized American domesticity. It was also an unequivocal influence on the more academic artists of the time period. Fine artists, such as West, Copley, and Charles Willson Peale, had their beginnings as village artists. (West taught himself by studying signs and engravings. In the case of Copley, graphic art served as his initial model of instruction. His stepfather, Peter Pelham, was a Boston engraver. Peale, by chance, became involved in painting, and then he learned by copying popular art of the day. Until the age of 24, Peale never had been exposed to professional painting.)

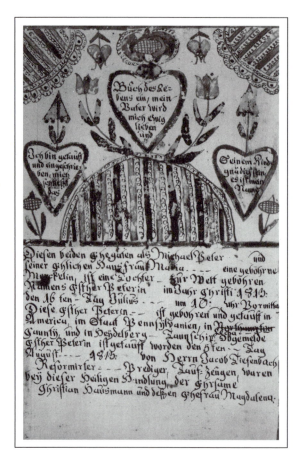

Fraktur of a birth and baptismal
certificate, circa 1797. Courtesy of the
Library of Congress.

On the whole, American visual arts during the early nationalist period reveal the American growing awareness in a cultural identity and a patriotic stance. Artist and artisan alike were committed to fostering a national tradition in the arts. Visual arts were an integral part of self- and national expression in the new republic. Not only did the visual arts help create a national iconography and historical record, but they revealed the talents and imagination of a newly independent people.

# Cost of Products in the New Nation

## ADVERTISING AND NEWSPAPER SUBSCRIPTIONS

One square (12 lines) advertising: 3 shillings first insertion, 2 shillings second
Subscription rate (daily): $6–$10 per year
Subscription rate (weekly and semiweekly): $1.50–$5
Subscription rate (semiweekly and triweekly): $4–$5

## ANIMALS

Thoroughbred race horse: $1,200–$1,500

## BOOKS

Illustrated children's books: 4–20 cents per copy

## ENTERTAINMENT

Week at resort (lodging and meals): $7
Theater tickets: $1 (box), 50 cents (pit), 25 cents (gallery)

## FOOD AND DRINK

Blood pudding (one pound): 3–4 cents
Coffee (one pound): 20 cents
Flour (barrel): $8 (avg.)

Rice (cwt.): $2.30–$4.16

Tea (one pound): 80 cents

Tobacco (cwt.): $6.30–$7.26

Whiskey (one gallon): east, $1; west, 50 cents

Whole pig: 50 cents

## HORSE RACING FEES/PRIZES

Entrance fee (horse race): $20 (nonmembers); free (members)

Jockey club membership: $20+

Racing purse: $300–$500

## POSTAL RATES

Letters per page (during the Jefferson administration): 8–35 cents, depending on distance

Newspapers: 1 cent

Magazines (avg. size 64-page octavo): 4 cents per copy under 50 miles

6 cents per copy 50–100 miles

8 cents per copy over 100 miles

## TRAVEL AND TRANSPORTATION

Stagecoach from Boston to Savannah: $100

Stage wagon fares from (1788, The Philadelphia, Baltimore and Eastern Shore Line of Post-Coach Carriages):

Philadelphia to Chester, Pennsylvania (15 miles): 5s.

Chester to Queen of France, Pennsylvania (7 miles): 2s. 6d.

Queen of France to Wilmington, Delaware (6 miles): 2s. 6d.

Wilmington to Christiana Bridge, Pennsylvania (10 miles): 3s. 4d.

Christiana Bridge to Elk, Pennsylvania (12 miles): 4s. 2d.

Elk to Susquehanna, Pennsylvania (16 miles): 7s. 6d.

Philadelphia to Susquehanna (66 miles): 7s. 6d.

Steerage passage from England or Germany to U.S. (early nineteenth century): £10–£12.

Velocipede (early bicycle): $30

## TUITION

Harvard: $600 per year

Princeton: $171.23 per year

# WAGES

College president: $800–$1,800 per year
Labor (unskilled): 75 cents per day
Labor (skilled): $2 per day
Ship carpenters: $1.06–$2.13 per day

# OTHER

Pair of ice skates: 25 cents

# Notes

## CHAPTER 1

1. White women were considered "free persons" (as were all indentured servants) and thus counted in the determination of congressional representation and taxation. Native Americans were neither considered to be citizens nor countable for purposes of representation or taxation. According to the Constitution "all other Persons" [slaves] counted as three-fifths of a person for representation and taxation purposes (art. 1, sec. 3).

2. George Washington referred to small farmers as "the Grazing Multitude"; John Adams, son of a yeoman farmer himself, labeled them "the common herd of mankind"; and Alexander Hamilton, ever the elitist, regarded them as "the unthinking populace" (qtd. in Johnson, 177).

3. The U.S. Census of 1790 (the first census) lists the total population at 3,929,214; in 1800 at 5,308,483; and in 1810 at 7,239,881.

4. The U.S. Census of 1790 and 1800 list the nation's total area at 891,364 square miles and land area at 864,746. In 1810 the growth was very pronounced: total area, 1,722,685 and land area, 1,681,828.

5. The Louisiana Purchase was arguably the greatest land deal ever negotiated in American history. Purchased from France at approximately three cents per acre (828,000 square miles total), the former French territory doubled the size of the United States, as well as strengthened it strategically on a global scale. The purchase strengthened the country strategically by finally giving the United States control over the Mississippi River and the oft-contested port of New Orleans.

6. The government established by the First Continental Congress under the Articles of Confederation fared poorly. The Articles had created a loose confederation of states. (In a confederation individual units retain their sovereignty. They are united only when dealing with issues that affect the whole.) The Articles

had limited severely the powers of the central government, thus causing many problems rather than resolving them. The U.S. monetary system was in chaos because both the central government and the states could coin money, and the Continental (wartime) and state currencies had greatly depreciated in value. (Not until 1792 with the passage of the Coinage Act, which established a national coinage and a mint, was the national monetary system stabilized.) Congress was also in tremendous need of revenue to pay debts incurred during the war. Ironically, under the Articles, Congress could levy taxes but not collect them. (Tax collection was the province of the states.) The Articles allowed only for a maritime judiciary on the national level. Ex post facto laws (laws that retroactively criminalized a particular conduct, thus permitting those who had committed the act in the past to be tried under the new laws) were in effect. Most important, under the Articles, Congress could only requisition armed forces, but not support them. Because Congress did not have the means to pay the army, it could not be adequately sustained. The military was in shambles. The government without a military to protect it was ineffective and powerless. Accordingly, by 1786 the United States had a broken central government, and the lives of all its citizenry were affected (and often disrupted) in all areas.

7. Slavery was first abolished in the North by the then territory of Vermont in its 1777 constitution, the first region in what was to become the United States to do so. (Vermont was not one of the original thirteen colonies since for many years it had been territory under dispute between New York and New Hampshire. During the Revolutionary War, Vermont declared itself to be an independent republic, first adopting the name New Connecticut, finally Vermont.)

8. The Great Awakening (ca. 1720s–1740s) was an intense religious revivalism movement that had swept through all of the American colonies. Fundamentally, the Great Awakening was a response to what some feared was the increasing secularization of American churches. Ministers preached to zealous audiences the fury of God's wrath for a sinful people. Only through rejection of worldliness (i.e., sin) and conversion to the Christian faith could listeners escape the terrible punishments of God. The result was great numbers of colonists embracing the Christian faith. Members of established churches began to question the authority of the church leadership. Such dissent eventually led to divisions within denominations, sometimes severing with the established church. Church membership in the insurgent denominations grew dramatically, partly because the evangelical styles of worship were now accessible to a wide range and area of the total population. In sum, the Great Awakening was the democratization of the American religious experience.

9. The Embargo Act of 1807, one of the most unpopular legislative acts in American history, was designed by President Jefferson as a means to counteract British and French interference with American shipping. The Embargo Act stipulated that all American ports be closed to export shipping (both foreign and domestic) and that strict trade restrictions be imposed on British imports. The act failed to curb European aggression and harmed the American economy because American goods could no longer be exported. Citizens faced with financial ruin directed their ire toward the president. Extant letters to Jefferson reveal that Americans were not above using threats ("I have agreed to pay four of my friends $400 to shoat you if you don't take off the embargo"), insults ("You are

one of the greatest tyrants in the whole world"), and pathos ("Sir we Humbly your Honur to Grant us destras Seaman Sum relaf for God nos what we do"—from four thousand destitute Philadelphian seamen) (qtd. in Johnson, 257). Under great political pressure, Congress essentially negated the act by passing the Non-Intercourse Act in 1809.

10. *The Federalist* was composed of 85 essays, the bulk of them written by Hamilton, arguing for the ratification of the Constitution. Historians have identified 51 as written by Hamilton, 29 by Madison, and 5 by Jay. The three adopted the name "Publius" in honor of the great Roman politician and emperor Publius Licinius Valerianus who was also known as *"Publicola"* (Latin for "people lover").

## CHAPTER 2

1. Yellow fever (a virus carried by mosquitoes), cholera, and tuberculosis (both caused by bacteria) were particularly virulent and deadly diseases that plagued the world during the eighteenth and nineteenth centuries. Yellow fever, a tropical disease, had been documented as spreading as far north as New England. Cholera reached pandemic proportions in 1817. Tuberculosis was the leading cause of death for all age groups in the United States and Europe. All three were predominant in urban settings, because people lived closer together, which led to the poor sanitation and hygiene conditions that bred the fatal microorganisms.

2. Children born within this time period were, as Joyce Appleby points out in her book *Inheriting the Revolution*, the first Americans born under American, not British, rule. Thus this is the first generation of truly native-born American citizens.

3. Demographics reveal that Euro-American women bore between five and seven live children (out of five to ten pregnancies). Mary Beth Norton, in her discussion of birth rates, uses Abigail Smith Adams as the quintessential example: Out of six pregnancies, Mrs. Adams had four living children, a stillbirth, and one child who died in infancy (72). Most women's experiences were similar to Abigail Adams's.

The statistics for African American births differs somewhat from that of their White counterparts, partly because their patterns were not as uniform. African American women generally began having children earlier (approximately three to four years), but with less regularity, perhaps because of the more rigorous physical conditions that many slave women had to endure on plantations.

4. Southern women, like their northern sisters, were also dedicated to nursing their own children. There is little evidence that late eighteenth-century southern gentility engaged slave women as wet nurses unless there was some physical impediment (Norton, 91).

5. The education available to young girls was based on class and economics. Female illiteracy was still a problem in eighteenth-century America, with 50 percent to 70 percent of American women either barely able to read or not at all (Nye, *Cultural Life*, 168). Lower-class girls were fortunate if they could learn their letters from a parent. Middle- to upper-class girls were educated through either a "dame" school or tutoring. (Female academies were a luxury.) In the New England states (a region that historically had placed more emphasis on educating

the young), girls attended grammar school—in the early hours of the morning before the regular students (males) assembled for class.

6. The first edition of Webster's *An American Dictionary of the English Language* was not published until 1828.

7. These readers were precursors of the famous *McGuffey Reader* that dominated American education in the nineteenth century. Assembled by William McGuffey (1800–1873), the readers (first and second published in 1836, third and fourth in 1837) were a collection of tales and excerpts from accepted works designed to teach American youth moral lessons.

8. A college education was highly prized in the new republic. Despite the chartering of more colleges and universities than ever before, only an extremely small percentage of the population had the opportunity to attend a university. In New England, where higher education had been established longer than in any other area, the ratio of college students to the general state population was 1:513 (Nye, *Cultural Life*, 187).

9. The irony here is father did not know best. Tyler had a long and distinguished career as a jurist (Vermont Supreme Court), as well as artistic success as a dramatist. Adams's choice for a son-in-law and his daughter's eventual deference did not afford Nabby the financial stability Adams had hoped. Colonel Smith (as he was known) would lose great sums of money in land speculation and often leave his family for months at a time. At one point, his in-laws had to raise money to keep him out of debtors' prison.

# CHAPTER 3

1. The rapid growth of the postal system did, however, expand the potential circulation of some newspapers. The Post Office Act of 1792 established the postage rate for newspapers at one cent per copy. This made mailing newspapers economically feasible and legally required delivery of papers by the Post Office. (Prior to the act, some carriers would refuse to carry papers in inclement weather.) Newspapers from one geographical area, in some cases, were expediently delivered to another. Accordingly, many coffeehouses and taverns kept copies on hand of newspapers from diverse parts of the country (Mott, *American Journalism*, 159).

2. Until 1798 paper was made one sheet at a time. Each sheet was made by dipping a screened frame into a mixture of liquid and fibers (that had been presorted) and then drained. The sheet was then pressed and dried.

The first mechanized paper machine was invented in 1798 by Nicolas-Louis Robert of France. Robert's machine consisted of a moving screen belt that produced a continuous sheet of paper that was fed into a set of rollers. The Fourdrinier Brothers of England improved on Robert's design in 1807. The Fourdrinier machine, the brothers' creation, also had a moving screen that produced a continuous sheet. A process that employed suction, pressure, and heat then dried the sheet. Not until later in the nineteenth century were these machines refined enough to be used on a widespread basis.

3. The most grisly symbol appropriated by Americans is the seemingly innocuous candy-cane-striped barber's pole. Barbers, in medieval times, performed

bloodletting in addition to their haircutting duties. The barber would give the patient a pole to grip while he or she was being bled into a basin. The bloody overflow was mopped up with towels. After the surgery the barber would place the pole, wrapped with the blood-soaked towels, outside his shop to dry. Later, the red-and-white-striped pole became the symbol for barbering, a less gruesome vestige of the barber's medieval practice.

4. Ads for runaway slaves were not an American phenomenon—far from it. The oldest known advertisement in existence, discovered on a Babylonian tablet written about three thousand years ago, was a notice about a runaway slave.

5. The Lorillard Company was the oldest tobacco manufacturer in the United States. Established in New York by Pierre Lorillard in 1760, the company started making pipe tobacco, chewing tobacco, snuff, and cigars from cured Virginia tobacco. During the 1890s and up to 1911, the company became part of the American Tobacco Company (maker of Kent cigarettes among others), later known as American Brands. Today, it is again known as Lorillard, a division of Loewes Corporation.

6. The word "patent" did not have the same meaning then as it does today. A "patent medicine" did not necessarily have an ingredient exclusive to the manufacturer. Instead, the term was a holdover from the mid-1700s when small bottles carried the crest of the king, denoting that the king had bestowed a "patent of royal favor" upon the bottled elixir. Merchants began to advertise these patent medicines, thus the name.

# CHAPTER 4

1. Inigo Jones (1573–1652) is generally credited with founding the English tradition of architecture. Furthermore, Jones introduced Palladian architecture to Great Britain. James Gibbs (1682–1754), a Scot, synthesized English (baroque) and Italian (Palladian) styles. His work ultimately influenced both British and American church architecture. William Kent (1685–1748) was considered to be the foremost practitioner of Palladian architecture in England and the premier advocate for the creation of the informal English garden.

2. Ionic columns are distinguished by two volutes (spiral scrolls) in the capital (the top part of the column). Corinthian columns are far more elaborate. A Corinthian column is characterized by two staggered rows of ornate acanthus leaves and four scrolls on its capital.

3. Although the University of Virginia was constructed and established between the years of 1817 and 1825, Jefferson's idea of creating a university (or, in his words, an "academical village") had its genesis during his presidency. In a letter dated January 5, 1805, Jefferson outlined his plans for the university, encapsulating not only his ideas of what and whom the university should serve, but also a brief schema of the building of the university itself. Because the University of Virginia represents the culmination of Jefferson's architectural spirit— and what he had learned in his 40-year building and redesigning of Monticello— it is included in this volume even though the construction begins at the end of the early nationalist period.

4. Deism is classified as a "natural religion"; that is, Deists believe that relig-

ious knowledge is innate and can be attained by reasoning rather than through revelation or church teachings. Deism draws from Newtonian science that conceptualizes God as the Great Watchmaker: God, like a watchmaker creating a timepiece, had created the Universe, provided it with immutable laws that regulated it, and then disengaged Himself from His creation. Divine intervention did not exist in the world. Consequently, supernatural miracles were impossible.

Secular humanism is a philosophy that considers the importance of human achievement, authority, and status to be central to belief. God still exists, but His impact on humanity is less immediate than what organized religion posits.

5. Unfortunately, Latrobe's Bank of Pennsylvania was demolished. All that exists of this beautiful building is a few artists' renderings, notably Latrobe's own detailed watercolors of the exterior and interior.

6. The redesign of the Capitol was an ongoing process not limited to the early nationalist period. In 1857 the House of Representatives wing extension was finally completed and the Senate wing in 1859. The high cast-iron dome (that distinguishes the Capitol from all other Washington buildings) was not completed until 1863. In 1959–1960 the east front was extended 32.5 feet.

7. Baroque architecture accentuated magnitude and vastness, intense spatial and lighting patterns, and movement. Baroque interiors highlighted luxurious materials, striking color, and contrasting texture. The end impression left the observer with a feeling of sensuality.

8. Thornton's designs were so ill conceived that more than one builder had to make much needed corrections—incurring the wrath of Thornton. Latrobe's radical redesigning of the Capitol earned him Thornton's rancor for life.

9. The regional term "Cape Cod" was first used around 1800 by Timothy Dwight, president of Yale College, to describe the hall-and-parlor type of homes prevalent on Cape Cod, Massachusetts.

10. Tile heating stoves had been used in Holland and Germany for years. Benjamin Franklin's invention, the Franklin stove (ca. 1740), was a type of open fireplace. Made of iron, the Franklin stove rested on short legs and had a smoke pipe that connected to the fireplace flue. It had a baffled flue and a cold-air box that heated air in a chamber at the rear of the fireplace. Box stoves were made of cast iron, had legs that were free from the wall, and were equipped with a stovepipe. Many times they functioned as auxiliary stoves for baking.

## CHAPTER 5

1. The eighteenth-century term "jeans" is not interchangeable with the contemporary synonym for denim. Jeans here is a back-formation of the term *jene fustian*, meaning Genoan fustian.

2. These terms were used in relation to a man's wig. Perukes and periwigs were particularly fashionable from the seventeenth century up until the early years of the nineteenth century. Both terms connote a more formal type of wig. (Other wigs were prevalent as well, such as the "bag-wig," a wig that was tied in a leather bag as an expedient way of dressing it.) They were made of long hair (preferably human, although horse's hair and goat's hair were sometimes used), tied back on the nape of the neck. Many times the peruke was curled on the sides as well.

3. The highest-priced wigs were made of gray human hair. The darker the hair, the less expensive the wig. The less human hair in the mix, the lower the price. Those whose social aspirations exceeded their bank accounts often sported shorter wigs called "bob-wigs."

4. Remarkably, the straw-making/braiding trend led to some commercial phenomena among American women. Alice Morse Earle documents that the first American awarded an English patent was Mrs. Sybilla Masters of Philadelphia for straw making (vol. 2, 570). Furthermore, the first patent awarded in the United States was to a woman for an invention to use in straw plaiting. A young Connecticut woman, Sophia Woodhouse, applied for and was granted a patent devising a new straw material for bonnets (ibid.).

5. Umbrellas had been around since ancient times. By the Middle Ages umbrellas were no longer used. The Renaissance, however, ushered in the resurgence of the umbrella. Eighteenth-century Europeans carried umbrellas as protection from the elements. The earliest American umbrellas were made of linen supported by rattan ribs. To make the umbrellas water-resistant, the cloth was oiled. Umbrellas were the only means citizens had to protect their clothes from the rain. Rubber boots and raincoats were not a feasible alternative at this time. Before Charles Goodyear discovered vulcanization (the chemical process by which rubber is strengthened and made more resistant) in 1839, rubber was considered to be too adhesive to be used as a fabric. (It also had a very unpleasant odor.) In the late eighteenth through the nineteenth centuries, the small, delicate parasol (used to protect women from the sun) became a fashion statement as well.

6. The making and the wearing of dentures were sometimes painful—and always uncomfortable—in the eighteenth century. First, impressions were made using plaster. After the plaster was set, it was chipped away (that in itself could be painful) and then pieced together to cast the mold. The denture plate was made from wood, ivory, or tortoiseshell, none of which were pliable (i.e., comfortable) materials. The teeth were usually ivory or porcelain.

## CHAPTER 6

1. The American definition of corn is far more specific than the British definition. Corn, for Americans, refers to maize, an indigenous American cereal grass (sometimes known as "Indian corn"). Corn in British usage means any cereal plant that yields a seed, such as rye, barley, oats, and wheat. For the discussion here, the terms "maize" and "corn" are interchangeable.

2. *The Hasty-Pudding* (1796) parodied the lofty conventions of epic poetry while simultaneously celebrating New England and the cornmeal mush that graced most New England tables. Barlow not only praises his fellow New Englanders and the dish itself, but also the cow that provides the milk for the mush. With highly inflated language, the poet discusses how hasty pudding should be prepared and eaten, right down to what type of spoon should be used to eat a dish "well suited to inspire/The purest frenzy of poetic fire."

3. A common myth (unfortunately perpetuated well into the twentieth century) is that American colonists and early nationals believed the tomato was

poisonous. Recent agricultural and culinary scholarship has proven otherwise. (See Andrew F. Smith, *The Tomato in America: Early History, Culture and Cookery*, 1994.) For instance, South Carolinians grew tomatoes as early as the seventeenth century (and ate them well into the eighteenth century). Although not a popular food, tomatoes were consumed by some citizens in all regions of the new nation.

4. The Church of the New Jerusalem based its theology on the Biblical inter-pretations of Swedish scientist and theologian Emanuel Swedenborg (1688–1772). Church followers, known as Swedenborgians, believed that scripture should be interpreted spiritually. Swedenborg's theological tracts asserted that there was an infinite, indivisible life and power within all God's creatures.

5. The bacillus *Salmonella typhosa* that is found in contaminated food and water causes typhoid, a deadly disease characterized by high fever, rashes, bronchitis, and intestinal bleeding. Cholera, another life-threatening disease, is an acute bac-terial infection of the small intestine caused by the microorganism *Vibrio cholerae*. Often rising to epidemic proportions, cholera's symptoms include severe diar-rhea leading to rapid depletion of body fluids and salts. Like typhoid, the cholera microorganism is found in contaminated food and water.

Yellow fever, a particularly devastating disease, is usually thought to be a tropical problem, although it can occur in temperate climates. Philadelphia dur-ing this time was prone to yearly yellow fever outbreaks. In 1793 when the federal government was still seated there, almost 2,500 Philadelphians suc-cumbed to the deadly fever. Chills, fever, jaundice, and bilious vomiting char-acterize yellow fever. Transmitted from person to person by the mosquito *Aedes aegypti*, the yellow fever virus is able to pass through a fine filter, thus maintain-ing its ability to infect. The virus is found in contaminated water supplies. In short, spoiled food and contaminated water were the primary causes for the high mortality rates due to disease.

6. Volney was a French philosopher and historian. His major work *Les Ruines, ou méditations sur les révolutions des empires* (The Ruins: Or a Survey of the Rev-olutions of Empires), published in 1791, encapsulated eighteenth-century ration-alist philosophical, historical, and political thought. Volney visited the United States from 1795 to 1798.

7. Washington was known to have frequented the Sun Inn, a tavern run by Moravians (people from the region now part of the Czech Republic) in Bethle-hem, Pennsylvania. The Sun Inn (which still stands) did a substantial business with travelers. For most Anglo-Americans, a stop at the Sun Inn was their first encounter with Pennsylvania German cookery.

## CHAPTER 7

1. Central to the obverse side of the Great Seal is an American eagle holding an olive branch in one claw, a bundle of thirteen arrows in the other. Within its beak the eagle holds a ribbon inscribed with "E Pluribus Unum" (out of many, one). Above its head is a cloud of glory encompassing thirteen stars. Over its breast is a striped shield. (The reverse side of the Great Seal, a pyramid with an eye in the triangle suspended above, can also be found on the reverse side of the dollar bill.)

The Great Seal is highly symbolic. Each component was carefully chosen for its imagery. For instance, the eagle represents the nation as a whole. The shield, noticeably lacking any physical support, indicates that the United States should solely rely on its own virtue. The shield's top horizontal bar (known as the "chief") is blue, which symbolizes vigilance, perseverance, and justice. The thirteen vertical bars or stripes (known as "pales") are red (hardiness and valor) and white (purity and innocence).

The purpose of the Great Seal is to serve as the official emblem of the United States. The Great Seal is used to authenticate signatures on treaties and other official government documents, such as international agreements, appointments of ambassadors and foreign service officers, commissions for consular appointments, and letters of credence and recall for ambassadors and diplomatic representatives.

2. Publication information not available. Mentioned in passim in McClintock and McClintock, page 67.

3. The first veterinarian came to American shores in 1810, so in the early years veterinary science was rudimentary at best. Serious dog owners educated themselves through reading and experience.

4. The percussion ignition system is simply the detonation of gunpowder when delivered a blow by a striker mechanism. Alexander John Forsyth of Scotland patented the scent bottle–type of lock mechanism in 1807. Forsyth's scent bottle (filled with powder) released the powder into a hole at the top of a plug. The bottle then was turned back, enabling the striker mechanism (a hammer). When the gunman pulled the trigger, the hammer fell, thereby detonating the powder. Percussion ignition had two key advantages over flintlock: it was waterproof and more dependable.

5. Messenger had an impeccable bloodline. On his sire's side, he was a direct descendent of one of the three Arabian horses that established the thoroughbred breed. On his dam's side, he was a descendent of the other two Arabians. Messenger's modern-day descendants include the legendary Man o' War (foaled in 1917), named by the Associated Press as the greatest racehorse of the first half of the twentieth century; Whirlaway (foaled in 1938), Triple Crown winner; and Secretariat (foaled in 1971), Triple Crown winner.

6. Records show that bets occasionally exceeded $4,000. In the early 1800s, purses at the Harlem Course ranged from $300 to $500. The going price for a racehorse was estimated between $1,200 and $1,500 (Holliman, 110). By late eighteenth- and early nineteenth-century standards, these were extravagant sums.

7. Not until the waning years of the nineteenth century did boxers wear gloves. Although in ancient times boxers would bind their arms and forearms with leather for protection (indeed, the term "pugilism," now synonymous with boxing, was derived from the Latin *pugil*, one who fights with a covered hand), from the sixteenth century onward, boxers pummeled each other with bare fists.

8. Contrary to popular belief, baseball was not invented in 1839 by Civil War General Abner Doubleday. By 1700 the game had appeared in print, evidencing its much earlier origin date (Twombly, 43).

9. In the case of bull baiting, the common belief was that baiting (and the

subsequent torment the animal endured before death) made its meat more appetizing.

## CHAPTER 8

1. Jefferson's more freethinking views alarmed the more fundamentalist portion of the population. Some citizens were so alarmed by the prospect of the country being led by such an "infidel" that they hung their Bibles down their wells for safekeeping. (Rumor had it that when Jefferson would become president, he would order the destruction of all Bibles.)

2. The story of Elizabeth Whitman (1752–1788) was well-known to William Hill Brown's American audience because it had been extensively reported in American newspapers. Whitman was an intelligent, well educated, and accomplished member of society in Hartford and New Haven, Connecticut. After two broken engagements, Whitman engaged in a flirtation with Joel Barlow (the poet and diplomat). In 1788 the unmarried Whitman died of a fever after giving birth to a stillborn baby. (The identity of the father has never been ascertained.) Although she conducted herself with discretion even when dying, Whitman's sad story and end was highly sensationalized within a two-month period. Her life story was redacted as one that would serve as a cautionary tale to young women. The *Massachusetts Centinel* of September 20, 1788, reported that Whitman's untimely demise was because "she was a great reader of novels and romances and having imbibed her ideas of the character of men, from those fallacious sources, became vain and coquettish." In 1797, Whitman's distant relative, Hannah Foster, would fictionalize Whitman's story even more so than Brown's novel did.

3. Radcliffe's five gothic novels are *Castles of Athlin and Dunbayne* (1789), *A Sicilian Romance* (1790), *The Romance of the Forest* (1791), *The Mysteries of Udolpho* (1794), and *The Italian* (1797).

4. Brown's foray into the literary marketplace was relatively brief. After 1799, he turned his efforts to journalism with the establishment of *The Monthly Magazine and American Review*. *The Monthly Magazine* was short-lived. By 1803 he founded *The Literary Magazine and American Register*. Both *The Monthly Magazine* and *The Literary Magazine* were aimed at a well educated audience interested in cultural issues. In 1806, he shut down *The Literary Magazine* in favor of the semiannual *American Register, of General Repository of History, Politics, and Science*. The establishment of *American Register* denotes Brown's shifting interest from the imaginative to the political.

5. Brown's major completed works of fiction include the dialogue *Alcuin* (1798), the gothic novels *Wieland; or, The Transformation. An American Tale* (1798), *Ormond; or, The Secret Witness* (1799), *Arthur Mervyn, First Part* (1799), *Edgar Huntly* (1799), and *Arthur Mervyn, Second Part* (1800), and the sentimental novels *Clara Howard* (1801) and *Jane Talbot* (1801). After 1800, he abandoned novel writing for magazine editing and political pamphleteering.

6. Godwin espoused religious dissent, anarchy, and the freedom of the individual. Central to Godwin's philosophy was the precept that government and social institutions corrupt humanity.

7. Henri Petter misidentifies the river in *Arthur Mervyn* as the Schuylkill.

(Brown never refers to the river by name.) Because Mervyn and Welbeck row to the Jersey shore (where Welbeck makes his suicide attempt), the river would be the Delaware. The Schuylkill flows into the Delaware, but only the Delaware serves as the eastern boundary between Pennsylvania and New Jersey. My paraphrase of Petter's point corrects the geographic misperception.

8. Petter estimates that Brackenridge began writing *Modern Chivalry* in 1788 (161, n. 93). Ever the political animal whose views shifted greatly within this 30-year period, Brackenridge wrote the multivolume work in fits and starts. The subsequent volumes reflect his shifting political views within the period.

9. Logocracy, meaning a "government of words," was a term invented by Sydney Smith. Now considered to be a rather obscure critic, Smith is known for his aforementioned caustic comment, "Who reads an American book?"

10. Tyler uses contemporary events here to sharply criticize the American practice of slavery, from his viewpoint an evil institution. Using an event that preoccupied the American public (the attack of the Barbary pirates on American merchant ships in the Mediterranean), Tyler draws an obvious correlation between the American slave trade and the pirates' continual assaults and offenses.

The conflict between the United States and the pirates of the North African Barbary states of Algiers, Tunis, Morocco, and Tripoli was not easily abated. The ratification by the United States of the Barbary Treaties on January 10, 1800, did not alleviate the tension between the Barbary Coast and the United States. On May 14, 1801, the Pasha of Tripoli declared war on the United States, resulting in the Tripolitan War. A powerful American naval blockade eventually led to a peace treaty (June 4, 1805) that was agreeable to the United States.

11. The Mansfield Decision (King's Bench, 1772) greatly influenced African Americans' perception of how they were treated under the law, in this case the differences between British and American law. Basically, the Mansfield Decision stated that a slaveowner could not force a slave to return to the West Indies; that is, a slave was essentially free once he or she was in Britain (Caretta, 4–5). In 1778, the Scottish government outlawed slavery altogether. In contrast to American law—especially to a Constitution that excluded them from any participation in the government and that counted them as three-fifths of a person (art. 1, sec. 2)—British law afforded those of African descent more opportunity for economic and social freedom.

12. The term "Wits" for this diverse group came from their collaborative work on a mock epic entitled *The Anarchiad* (October 26, 1786–September 13, 1787). Published in 13 installments, *The Anarchiad* was, in part, a Federalist rejoinder to Shays's Rebellion (which was not suppressed until February 1787).

13. Freneau had a turbulent career as a journalist, publisher, and essayist. As for the "Wits," each had a distinguished career: Dwight as the president of Yale, Barlow as a highly respected diplomat in the Jefferson administration, Trumbull as a state legislator and jurist, and Humphreys as a respected lawyer.

# CHAPTER 9

1. The singing school developed from the desire of Puritan ministers to improve the singing during worship. In 1722 the Boston Society for Promoting

Regular Singing had a student body of 90, all of whom could read music (Hitch-cock, 7). Soon singing schools included secular music as part of their curriculum in addition to the singing of hymns and psalms. The singing school, which was created to improve church music, evolved into singing societies or clubs, which emphasized the improvement of leisure time (Sablosky, 67). Dances were held at all levels of society, from the stately minuets and ballroom dances of the aristocracy to the more informal, more spontaneous reels and jigs on the frontier.

2. Ravenscroft was an English composer known for his musical compositions that appealed to the general public rather than the intelligentsia. His *Whole Booke of Psalmes* (1621) contained more than 100 metrical psalm tunes. Ravenscroft's psalter was exceptionally popular, and some of his works are still sung today.

3. The term "fuging tune" or its spelling variant "fuguing" comes from the English phrase "fuging psalm tune." The English version, which was prevalent during the seventeenth and early eighteenth centuries, was characterized by di-atonic harmony and simple, yet precise, rhythmic structure. British fuging tunes placed the fuging section at the last lines of the work, whereas American fuging composers moved the fuging section to the second-to-last line.

4. The Camisards were an early eighteenth-century militant Protestant sect that was organized to resist Louis XIV's imposition of Roman Catholicism on the French people.

5. The first true minstrel show was not performed until 1843 by the first minstrel troupe, the Virginia Minstrels. Christy Minstrels, the most famous of the minstrel shows (founded by Edwin P. Christy), performed on Broadway for nearly ten years, attesting to the popularity of the White appropriation of slave culture (even though it was used for comic, rather than celebratory, reasons). Songwriter Stephen Foster (1826–1864) wrote some of his best works, notably "Old Folks at Home" (also known as "Swanee River") for the Christy Minstrel shows.

6. Monsigny was renowned for his vibrant melodies. His works are charac-terized by his manipulation of timbre for dramatic effect. Grétry, a Belgian, was a master composer of comic operas.

7. There have been countless theories of how the lyrics and melody of "Yan-kee Doodle" came into existence, as well as conjectures on the origin of the word "Yankee" itself. The most plausible theory is that Yankee comes from the Dutch *jonker* (pronounced yonker) meaning a country squire and doodle from the Dutch *doedel* meaning a simpleton (S. Murray, 7). As early as 1664, immigrant Dutch farmers would sing the following song as they harvested their grain on Long Island:

> Jonker, didle, doedel, down
> Didel, doedel, handler,
> Jonker, viver, voover, vown,
> Botermelk en tanther.

All in the New Netherland colony knew the song, and the harvesters were known to improvise (ibid., 6). Soon, there were various versions of this nonsen-sical tune.

Another theory is that when the English began to encroach on the Dutch settlement, the Dutch began to call these new settlers "English Johnnies" or, in Dutch, *Engelse Jankes* (pronounced Yahn-kes). Perhaps that name stuck as well. When the British used the song to ridicule the American troops during the Revolutionary War, Yankee was synonymous with American.

8. Smith is also the composer of the British national anthem, "God Save the Queen (King)," the music of which is used in the 1831 patriotic song "America" ("My Country 'Tis of Thee").

9. Despite its popularity as a patriotic song for over a century, "The Star-Spangled Banner" was not officially adopted as the national anthem until 1931. The armed forces had adopted "The Star-Spangled Banner" as their national anthem much earlier. However, it took an act of the 71st Congress to designate the song as the official anthem of the United States. President Herbert Hoover signed the act into law on March 3, 1931, the day before he left office.

10. Legend incorrectly claims that Key wrote "The Star-Spangled Banner" on the back of an envelope. This is definitely a false perception because envelopes had not been invented yet.

## CHAPTER 10

1. *Cato* was first performed at Drury Lane on April 14, 1713. A dramatization of the career of the great Roman general and statesman Marcus Porcius Cato (234–149 B.C.), the play had decided political overtones. Addison's Cato is the epitome of the defender of liberty and his Caesar a domineering general whose victories posed a threat to liberty. Cato chooses suicide rather than submit to the tyrant Caesar. Washington's choice was thus an inspired one.

2. Because plays and dances were still outlawed in many parts of the country at this time, theatrical manager Lewis Hallam (1740–1808) shrewdly advertised the troupe's performances as "lectures," a term that held a more edifying connotation than "play" or "dance."

3. The eighteenth-century Allemande (the name means German) was a figure dance performed by four couples. It originated in the sixteenth century as a stately dance in 2/2 time. The participants performed intricate dance steps, such as *enchaînements* and *passés*, while elaborately interlacing the arms.

4. The reference is to the great English actor David Garrick (1717–1779). Garrick, also a versatile actor, was particularly known for his depiction of King Lear.

5. Actresses were known by their married names or by the appellation "Miss." Since the Renaissance, actresses had to expend a concerted effort to project an air of respectability. (Actresses, like the ballet girls, were stereotyped as wanton and impure.) By associating the actress with her husband (that is, the use of the "Mrs." and the husband's name), her reputation then became above reproach. For the unmarried, the "Miss" was designed to suggest that the woman was more child than woman, dispelling any idea of sexual suggestiveness. But despite their fame and their appearance of respectability, no actress would have been received by the upper level of society (Woodward, 153–154).

6. Although Booth's description of the theatrical manager's duties is part of his study of the theater in the nineteenth century, the description holds true for the earlier period, discussed here on both sides of the Atlantic.

7. Bidwell had a rocky post-collegiate career. He was elected to the Massachusetts State Senate in 1805 and later became the state attorney general. Subsequently, he embezzled $10,000 and escaped to Canada where he resumed his political career.

8. Sir Richard Sheridan (1751–1816), Irish-born playwright, was the master of wit and satire. *The School for Scandal* (1777), a comedy of manners, was universally acclaimed as a brilliant artistic and financial success.

9. *The Poor Soldier*, a comic opera by John O'Keeffe, had been performed 18 times the previous theatrical season to enthusiastic audiences. Darby Wag-all, although a buffoon-like character, is essentially a kind and decent man. The partiality Jonathan feels for Darby could be construed as identifying with a man who is like himself. (And, of course, in reality they are the same man: Wignell.)

10. André was the confederate of the American general and traitor Benedict Arnold (1741–1801). In the spring of 1779, André (a chief intelligence officer in the British army) began secretly corresponding with Arnold. Arnold was appointed commandant of West Point (New York) in 1780. After meeting with André on September 21, 1780, Arnold agreed to surrender West Point to the British for £20,000. Unfortunately for André, the American militia apprehended him on his way back to New York. After searching him, the Americans found the West Point papers in his boots. He was found guilty of spying and sentenced to death. When British general Sir Henry Clinton refused to exchange André for the traitorous Arnold, André was hanged.

11. Wollstonecraft published the first great work of feminism, *Vindication of the Rights of Woman* (1792). A controversial figure in her lifetime, she married the radical English philosopher William Godwin in 1797. Their daughter, Mary Godwin Shelley (1797–1851), was the author of the gothic novel *Frankenstein* (1818).

## CHAPTER 11

1. The name Concord coach came from its place of manufacture. Concord or "thoroughbrace" coaches were made by the Abbot-Downing Company of Concord, New Hampshire.

2. The most famous of Washington's coaches was the white coach that he used when he was president. A secondhand coach rebuilt by Clarke Brothers of Philadelphia, the coach sported not only a white exterior, but also a leopard-skin-covered coachman's seat. Washington's traveling entourage included his coachman, his aide-de-camp, his valet, two footmen, a mounted postilion, a baggage wagon, and five saddle horses, creating quite a stir in the towns and villages the president passed through (Johnson, 222).

3. English coach and carriage makers had immigrated to the American colonies much earlier in the eighteenth century. An advertisement in the *Virginia Gazette* from March 30 to April 12, 1739, announced that "Samuel Bowler, *Coachmaker from London, is lately come to settle at Williamsburg, and undertakes to serve Gentlemen in Making and Repairing Coaches, Chariots, Chaises, and Chairs, and their Harness for them*" (qtd. in Train, 216).

4. Although flatboats, arks, and keelboats were used to transport people and freight on inland waterways, such as rivers and canals, there are some fundamental differences in design among them. A flatboat had squared ends and a flat bottom. An ark was a very large vessel, around 75 to 100 feet in length, 15 to 20 feet in width, and 3 to 5 feet deep (Dunbar, vol. 1, 284). A keelboat resembled a small ship without sails. Like a ship a keelboat had a curved bottom from which the frame was attached to the keel, thus the name.

5. Grays River is a tributary of the Columbia River in what is now southwestern Washington State.

6. Old Ironsides is still afloat. Rebuilt in 1833, it was removed from active service in 1882. The ship was restored from 1927 to 1931 and based at the Charlestown Navy Shipyard of Boston's National Historic Park. Upon reaching its bicentennial, Old Ironsides was renovated and set sail once more in 1997.

## CHAPTER 12

1. Revelations 6:8: "And behold a pale horse: and his name that sat on him was Death, and Hell followed with him. And power was given unto them over the fourth part of the earth, to kill with sword, and with hunger, and with death, and with the beasts of the earth."

2. Rembrandt Harmensz van Rijn (1606–1669), Dutch painter and etcher, master of brushwork and chiaroscuro; Peter Paul Rubens (1577–1640), Flemish painter known for religious and mythological compositions; Titian (ca. 1488–1576), greatest Italian painter of the Venetian School; Raphael (1483–1520), master painter of the Italian High Renaissance; Angelica Kauffmann (1741–1807), early neoclassical painter known for her decorative wall paintings; and Sofonisba Anguissola (1532–1625), first important woman artist of the Renaissance and first to have an international reputation.

3. Not until 19 years later did a native-born American use this new process. Bass Otis's lithograph published in the *Analectic Magazine* was the first.

4. John Trumbull, the poet, came from a distinguished American family. Among his relatives were his uncle, Connecticut Governor Jonathan Trumbull, the Reverend Benjamin Trumbull; the Connecticut historian; and a cousin, the painter John Trumbull.

# Further Reading

Adams, Charles Francis, ed. *The Works of John Adams*. 10 vols. Boston: Little, Brown, 1850–1856.

Adelio [pseud.]. *A Journey to Philadelphia; or, Memoirs of Charles Coleman Saunders*. Hartford, CT: n.p., 1804.

Appleby, Joyce. *Inheriting the Revolution: The First Generation of Americans*. Cambridge: Belknap–Harvard University Press, 2000.

Axelrod, Alan. *Charles Brockden Brown: An American Tale*. Austin: University of Texas Press, 1983.

Bailyn, Bernard, ed. *The Debate on the Constitution*. 2 vols. New York: Library of America, 1993.

Bauer, Raymond Augustine, and Stephen A. Greyser. *Advertising in America: The Consumer View*. Boston: Division of Research, Graduate School of Business Administration, Harvard University, 1968.

Bleecker, Ann Eliza. *The Posthumous Works of Ann Eliza Bleecker, in Prose and Verse*. New York: n.p., 1793. ["The History of Maria Kittle" can be found on pp. 19–87.]

Blumenson, John J.G. *Identifying American Architecture: A Pictorial Guide to Styles and Terms, 1600–1945*. Nashville, TN: American Association for State and Local History, 1977.

Boorstin, Daniel J. *The Americans; The National Experience*. New York: Vintage, 1965.

Booth, Michael R. *Theatre in the Victorian Age*. Cambridge: Cambridge University Press, 1991.

Bowen, Catherine Drinker. *Miracle at Philadelphia: The Story of the Constitutional Convention May to September 1787*. 1966. Reprint, New York: Little, 1986.

Brackenridge, Hugh Henry. *Modern Chivalry*. Ed. Lewis Leary. 1792–1815. Reprint, New Haven: College and University Press, 1965.

Bronner, Simon J. "Outbuildings." In *Encyclopedia of Vernacular Architecture of the*

*World*, Vol. 3, edited by Paul Oliver, 1845–1846. Cambridge: Cambridge University Press, 1997.

———. "Pennsylvania Dutch." In *Encyclopedia of Vernacular Architecture of the World*, Vol. 3, edited by Paul Oliver, 1846–1847. Cambridge: Cambridge University Press, 1997.

Brown, Charles Brockden. *The Novels and Related Works of Charles Brockden Brown Bicentennial Edition*. Ed. Sydney J. Krause, S.W. Reid, and Norman Grabo. 6 vols. Kent, OH: Kent State University Press, 1977–1987.

Brown, William Hill. *The Power of Sympathy: or, The Triumph of Nature. Founded in Truth*. 1789. Reprint, Columbus: Ohio State University Press, 1969.

Calhoun, Arthur W. *A Social History of the American Family: From Colonial Times to the Present*. 3 vols. 1917. Reprint, New York: Arno, 1973.

Carretta, Vincent, ed. "Introduction." *Unchained Voices: An Anthology of Black Authors in the English Speaking World of the 18th Century*. Lexington: University of Kentucky Press, 1996, 1–16.

Chase, Gilbert. *America's Music: From the Pilgrims to the Present*. Rev. 3rd ed. Urbana: University of Illinois Press, 1987.

Chielens, Edward E., ed. *American Literary Magazines: The Eighteenth and Nineteenth Centuries*. Westport, CT: Greenwood, 1986.

Coad, Oral Sumner, and Edwin Mims, Jr. *The American Stage. The Pageant of America: A Pictorial History of the United States*, Vol. 14. Ed. Ralph Henry Gabriel et al. New Haven, CT: Yale University Press, 1929.

Coe, Robert. *Dance in America*. New York: Dutton, 1985.

Cook, Jeffrey. "Cape Cod." In *Encyclopedia of Vernacular Architecture of the World*, Vol. 3, edited by Paul Oliver, 1835–1836. Cambridge: Cambridge University Press, 1997.

Cott, Nancy F. *The Bonds of Womanhood: "Woman's Sphere" in New England, 1780–1835*. 2nd ed. New Haven: Yale University Press, 1997.

Cowie, Alexander. *The Rise of the American Novel*. New York: American Book, 1948.

Crane, Elaine Forman. *Ebb Tide in New England: Women, Seaports, and Social Change, 1630–1800*. Boston: Northeastern University Press, 1998.

Cummings, Richard Osborn. *The American and His Food*. Rev. ed. Chicago: University of Chicago Press, 1940.

Davidson, Cathy N. *Revolution and the Word: The Rise of the Novel in America*. New York: Oxford University Press, 1986.

Dulles, Foster Rhea. *America Learns to Play: A History of Popular Recreation, 1607–1940*. Gloucester, MA: Peter Smith, 1963.

Dunbar, Seymour. *A History of Travel in America*. 5 vols. 1915. Reprint, New York: Greenwood, 1968.

Dunlap, William. *History of the American Theatre and Anecdotes of the Principal Actors*. 2nd ed. 1797. Reprint, New York: Burt Franklin, 1963.

Earle, Alice Morse. *Two Centuries of Costume in America*. 2 vols. 1903. Reprint, Williamstown, MA: Corner House, 1974.

Elkins, Stanley, and Eric McKitrick. *The Age of Federalism: The Early American Republic, 1788–1800*. New York: Oxford University Press, 1993.

Elliot, Emery, ed. *Columbia Literary History of the United States*. New York: Columbia University Press, 1988.

Ellis, Joseph J. *After the Revolution: Profiles of Early American Culture*. New York: Norton, 1979.

———. "The First Democrats." *U.S. News & World Report* 21 (August 2000): 34–39.

———. *Founding Brothers: The Revolutionary Generation*. New York: Knopf, 2001.

Ellis, Kate Ferguson. *The Contested Castle: Gothic Novels and the Subversion of Domestic Ideology*. Urbana: University of Illinois Press, 1989.

Elson, Louis C. *The History of American Music*. New York: Macmillan, 1925.

Ferguson, Robert A. *The American Enlightenment, 1750–1820*. Cambridge: Harvard University Press, 1997.

*Folk Songs of North America*. Coll. Alan Lomax. New York: Doubleday, 1960.

Foote, Henry Wilder. *Three Centuries of American Hymnody*. New York: Archon, 1968.

Foster, Hannah Webster. *The Coquette; or, The History of Eliza Wharton*. 1797. Reprint, New York: Oxford University Press, 1987.

Fowler, Nathaniel Clark, Jr. *Fowler's Publicity*. New York: Publicity Publishing, 1897.

Franklin, Benjamin. "The Education of Youth," "The Morals of Chess," and "On a Proposed Act to Prevent Immigration." *Benjamin Franklin: Writings*. Ed. J.A. Leo Lemay. New York: Library of America, 1987, 323–344, 927–931, 704–710.

Glassie, Henry. "South." In *Encyclopedia of Vernacular Architecture of the World*, Vol. 3, edited by Paul Oliver, 1896–1901. Cambridge: Cambridge University Press, 1997.

Goodrum, Charles, and Helen Dalyrymple. *Advertising in America: The First 200 Years*. New York: Abrams, 1990.

Goodsell, Willystine. *A History of Marriage and the Family*. Rev. ed. New York: Macmillan, 1974.

Green, Samuel M. *American Art: A Historical Survey*. New York: Ronald Press, 1966.

Hedges, William. "Toward a New National Literature." In *Columbia Literary History of the United States*, edited by Emery Elliot, 187–202. New York: Columbia University Press, 1988.

Hitchcock, H. Wiley. *Music in the United States: A Historical Introduction*. 2nd ed. Englewood Cliffs, NJ: Prentice-Hall, 1974.

Holliman, Jennie. *American Sports (1785–1835)*. Durham, NC: Seeman Press, 1932.

Howard, John Tasker, ed. *Our American Music: Three Hundred Years of It*. 3rd ed. New York: Crowell, 1965.

———. *The Music of George Washington's Time*. 1931. Reprint, New York: AMS Press, 1976.

Hudson, Frederic. *Journalism in the United States from 1690 to 1872*. 1873. Reprint, New York: Harper, 1968.

Hughes, Glenn. *A History of the American Theatre, 1700–1950*. London: Samuel French, 1951.

Hughes, Robert. *American Visions: The Epic History of Art in America*. New York: Knopf, 1997.

Hunt, William Dudley, Jr. *Encyclopedia of American Architecture*. New York: McGraw-Hill, 1980.

Hutchins, Catherine E., ed. *Shaping a National Culture: The Philadelphia Experience, 1750–1800.* Winterthur, DE: Henry Francis du Pont Winterthur Museum, 1994.

Inge, M. Thomas, ed. *Handbook of Popular Culture.* Vol. 2. Westport, CT: Greenwood, 1980.

Irving, Washington. *A History of New York . . . By Diedrich Knickerbocker.* 2 vols. 1809. Reprint, New York: Twayne, 1964.

Jefferson, Thomas. "Letters" and "A Memorandum (Rules of Etiquette)," *Notes on the State of Virginia. Thomas Jefferson: Writings.* Ed. Merrill D. Peterson. New York: Library of America, 1984, 709–1517, 705, 123–325. [This refers to *Notes on the State of Virginia* which is found in *Thomas Jefferson's Writings.*]

Johnson, Paul. *A History of the American People.* New York: HarperCollins, 1997.

Jones, Evan. *American Food: The Gastronomic Story.* 3rd ed. Woodstock, NY: Overlook, 1990.

Kephart, Horace. *Our Southern Highlander: A Narrative of Adventure in the Southern Appalachians and a Study of the Life among the Mountaineers.* Rev. ed. 1922. Reprint, New York: Macmillan, 1929.

Kerber, Linda K. *Federalist in Dissent: Imagery and Ideology in Jeffersonian America.* 1970. Reprint, Ithaca, NY: Cornell University Press, 1980.

———. *Women of the Republic: Intellect & Ideology in Revolutionary America.* Chapel Hill: University of North Carolina Press, 1980.

Kimball, Fiske. *Domestic Architecture of the American Colonies and of the Early Republic.* 1922. Reprint, New York: Dover, 1966.

Kritzer, Amelia Howe. "Comedies by Early American Women." In *The Cambridge Companion to American Women Playwrights,* edited by Brenda Murphy, 3–18. Cambridge: Cambridge University Press, 1999.

Kupferberg. Herbert. *Opera.* New York: Newsweek Books, 1975.

[A Lady of Philadelphia.] *Laura.* Philadelphia: n.p., 1809.

Langdon, William Chauncy. *Everyday Things in American Life.* 1937. Reprint, New York: Scribner's, 1965.

Larkin, Jack. "The Secret Life of a Developing Country (Ours)." *American Heritage* September/October (1988). Reprinted in *Forging the American Character.* Vol. 1. Ed. John R.M. Wilson. Englewood Cliffs, NJ: Prentice-Hall, 1999, 124–140.

Larkin, Oliver W. *Art and Life in America.* Rev. ed. New York: Holt, Rinehart and Winston, 1960.

Lathrop, Elise. *Early American Inns and Taverns.* 1926. Reprinted, New York: Arno, 1977.

Leary, Lewis. *The Book-Peddling Parson: An Account of the Life and Works of Mason Locke Weems, Patriot, Pitchman, Author and Purveyor of Morality to the Citizenry of the Early United States of America.* Chapel Hill, NC: Algonquin Books, 1984.

Little, Nina Fletcher. *Country Arts in American Homes.* New York: Dutton, 1975.

Locke, John. *The Second Treatise on Civil Government. On Politics and Education.* Roslyn, NY: Walter J. Black, 1947, 71–202.

Lowance, Mason I., Jr. "Biography and Autobiography." In *Columbia Literary His-*

*tory of the United States,* edited by Emery Elliot, 67–82. New York: Columbia University Press, 1988.

Luther, Frank. *Americans and Their Songs.* New York: Harper, 1942.

Main, Jackson Turner. *The Anti-Federalists: Critics of the Constitution, 1781–1788.* 1961. Reprint, New York: Norton, 1974.

McClelland, Nancy. *Furnishing the Colonial and Federal House.* 1936. Reprint, New York: Lippincott, 1947.

McClintock, Inez, and Marshall McClintock. *Toys in America.* Washington, DC: Public Affairs Press, 1961.

McCullough, David. *John Adams.* New York: Simon & Schuster, 2001.

McLanathan, Richard. *Art in America: A Brief History.* New York: Harcourt, Brace, Jovanovich, 1973.

McWilliams, John. "Poetry in the Early Republic." In *Columbia Literary History of the United States,* edited by Emery Elliot, 156–167. New York: Columbia University Press, 1988.

Mergen, Bernard. "Games and Toys." In *Hardbook of Popular Culture,* Vol. 2, edited by M. Thomas Inge, 163–190. Westport, CT: Greenwood, 1980.

Melish, John. *Travels in the United States in the Years 1806 and 1807 and 1809, 1810, and 1811.* Philadelphia: n.p., 1812.

Mertins, Herman, Jr. *National Transportation Policy in Transition.* Lexington, MA: Lexington-Heath, 1972.

Meserve, Walter J. *An Emerging Entertainment: The Drama of the American People to 1828.* Bloomington: Indiana University Press, 1977.

Meyer, Balthasar Henry. *History of Transportation in the United States before 1860.* New York: Peter Smith, 1948.

Miller, John C. *The Federalist Era, 1789–1801.* New York: Harper-Torchbooks, 1960.

Mitchell, Isaac. *The Asylum; or, Alonzo and Melissa.* 2 vols. Poughkeepsie, NY: n.p., 1811.

Morgan, Edmund S. *The Birth of the Republic, 1763–1789.* 3rd ed. Chicago: University of Chicago Press, 1992.

Morrison, Hugh. *Early American Architecture: From the First Colonial Settlements to the National Period.* New York: Oxford University Press, 1952.

Mott, Frank Luther. *A History of American Magazines: 1741–1850.* New York: Appleton, 1930.

———. *American Journalism, A History: 1690–1960.* New York: Macmillan, 1962.

Murray, Judith Sargent. *The Gleaner, A Miscellaneous Production in Three Volumes.* Vol. 1. Boston: Thomas & Andrews, 1798.

Murray, Stuart. *America's Song: The Story of "Yankee Doodle."* Bennington, VT: Images from the Past, 1999.

Newell, William Wells. *Games and Songs of American Children.* 1884. Reprint, Baltimore: Clearfield, 1992.

Newman, Simon P. *Parades and Politics of the Street: Festive Culture in the Early American Republic.* Philadelphia: University of Pennsylvania Press, 1997.

Norton, Mary Beth. *Liberty's Daughters: The Revolutionary Experience of American Women, 1750–1800.* Ithaca, NY: Cornell University Press, 1996.

Nye, Russel Blaine. *The Cultural Life of the New Nation: 1776–1830.* New York: Harper, 1960.

———. *The Unembarrassed Muse: The Popular Arts in America.* New York: Dial, 1970.

Odell, George C.D. *Annals of the New York Stage.* Vol. 2. New York: Columbia University Press, 1927.

Olasky, Marvin. *Fighting for Liberty and Virtue: Political and Cultural Wars in Eighteenth-Century America.* Wheaton, IL: Crossway Books, 1995.

Oliver, Paul, ed. *Encyclopedia of Vernacular Architecture of the World.* Vol. 3. Cambridge: Cambridge University Press, 1997.

Petter, Henri. *The American Novel.* Columbus: Ohio State University Press, 1971.

Pistolese, Rosana, and Ruth Horsting. *History of Fashions.* New York: Wiley, 1970.

Pollock, Linda A. *Forgotten Children: Parent-Child Relations from 1500 to 1900.* Cambridge: Cambridge University Press, 1983.

Quinn, Arthur Hobson. *A History of the American Drama from the Beginning to the Civil War.* 2nd ed. New York: Appleton-Century-Crofts, 1943.

Rader, Benjamin G. *American Sports: From the Age of Folk Games to the Age of Televised Sports.* 4th ed. Englewood Cliffs, NJ: Prentice-Hall, 1999.

Redden, Mary Mauritia. *The Gothic Fiction in the American Magazines (1765–1800).* Washington, DC: Catholic University of America Press, 1939.

Richards, Jeffrey H., ed. "Introduction." *Early American Drama.* New York: Penguin, 1997.

Ryan, Thomas. "Hudson Valley." In *Encyclopedia of Vernacular Architecture of the World,* Vol. 3, edited by Paul Oliver, 1840–1841. Cambridge: Cambridge University Press, 1997.

Sablosky, Irving L. *American Music.* Chicago: University of Chicago Press, 1969.

Seelye, John. "Brown and Early American Fiction." In *Columbia Literary History of the United States,* edited by Emery Elliot, 168–186, New York: Columbia University Press, 1988.

Slaughter, Thomas P. *The Whiskey Rebellion: Frontier Epilogue to the American Revolution.* New York: Oxford University Press, 1986.

Smith, Adam. *The Wealth of Nations.* Ed. Edwin Cannan. New York: Modern Library, 2000.

Smith, Andrew F. *The Tomato in America: Early History, Culture and Cookery.* Columbia: University of South Carolina Press, 1994.

Smith, Barbara Clark. *After the Revolution: The Smithsonian History of Everyday Life in the Eighteenth Century.* New York: Pantheon, 1985.

Sonneck, Oscar G. *Early Opera in America.* 1915. Reprint, New York: Benjamin Blom, 1963.

St. George, Robert Blair. "East and Northeast." In *Encyclopedia of Vernacular Architecture of the World,* Vol. 3, edited by Paul Oliver, 1827–1828. Cambridge: Cambridge University Press, 1997.

Sweet, William Warren. *Religion in the Development of American Culture, 1765–1840.* Gloucester, MA: Peter Smith, 1963.

Szatmary, David P. *Shays' Rebellion: The Making of an Agrarian Insurrection.* Amherst: University of Massachusetts Press, 1980.

Tebbel, John. *The Compact History of the American Newspaper.* Rev. ed. New York: Hawthorn, 1969.

Tenney, Tabitha Gilman. *Female Quixotism: Exhibited in the Romantic Opinions and*

*Extravagant Adventures of Dorcasina Sheldon.* Ed. Jean Nienkamp and Andrea Collins. 1801. Reprint, New York: Oxford University Press, 1992.

Terry, Walter. *The Dance in America.* New York: DaCapo, 1971.

Train, Arthur, Jr. *The Story of Everyday Things.* New York: Harper, 1941.

Twombly, Wells. *200 Years of Sport in America: A Pageant of a Nation at Play.* New York: McGraw-Hill, 1976.

Tyler, Royall. *The Algerine Captive; or, The Life and Adventures of Doctor Updike Underhill.* 2 vols. Gainesville, FL: Scholars' Facsimiles and Reprints, 1967.

———. *The Contrast. Early American Drama.* Ed. Jeffrey H. Richards. New York: Penguin, 1997, 6–57.

Walker, Henry Pickering. *The Wagonmasters: High Plains Freighting from the Earliest Days of the Santa Fe Trail to 1880.* Norman: University of Oklahoma Press, 1966.

Washington, George. "The Farewell Address to the People of the United States (September 17, 1796)." *Early American Writing.* Ed. Giles Gunn. New York: Penguin, 1994, 418–429.

Watterson, George. *Glencarn; or, The Disappointments of Youth.* 2 vols. Alexandria, PA: n.p., 1810.

Watts, Steven. *The Republic Reborn: War and the Making of Liberal America, 1790–1820.* Baltimore: Johns Hopkins University Press, 1987.

Weaver, William Woys. *Pennsylvania Dutch Country Cooking.* New York: Abbeville, 1993.

Wharton, Anne Hollingsworth. *Social Life in the Early Republic.* Williamstown, MA: Corner House, 1970.

Williamson, Elizabeth. "Advertising." In *Handbook of Popular Culture*, Vol. 2, edited by M. Thomas Inge, 3–29. Westport, CT: Greenwood, 1980.

Wolf, Stephanie Grauman. *As Various as Their Land: The Everyday Lives of Eighteenth-Century Americans.* 1993. Reprint, Fayetteville: University of Arkansas Press, 2000.

Woloch, Nancy. *Women and the American Experience: A Concise History.* New York: McGraw-Hill, 1996.

Wood, Gordon S. *The Creation of the American Republic, 1776–1787.* 2nd ed. Chapel Hill: University of North Carolina Press, 1998.

———. *The Radicalism of the American Revolution.* New York: Vintage–Random, 1993.

Wood, James Playsted. *The Story of Advertising.* New York: Ronald Press, 1958.

Wood, S[arah] K[eating]. *Julia, and the Illuminated Baron.* Portsmouth, NH: n.p., 1800.

Woodward, William E. *The Way Our People Lived: An Intimate American History.* New York: Washington Square–Pocket, 1965.

# Index

**About the Author**

ANITA VICKERS is an Associate Professor of Humanities and English at Penn State University where she teaches courses in American literature, American Studies, Women's Studies, and humanities. She has published articles on Charles Brockden Brown, Zora Neale Hurston, and popular culture topics.